*Applied Econometrics Association Series*

General Editors: **Jean H. P. Paelinck**, Emeritus Professor, Erasmus University, Rotterdam; and **Henri Serbat**, University of Paris 2

The vital importance of econometrics for understanding economic phenomena is increasingly recognized in every field of economics.

The discipline is based on 'scientific processes which aim to identify, explain and forecast economic phenomena using formalised tools to produce, measure, structure and model the information' (Gérard Duru and Henri Serbat, 1991).

The Applied Econometrics Association, established in 1974, seeks to develop the use of econometric tools by producing regular updates on the state of the art and the progress made in each specific field, and so to further the transformation of unconnected facts into pertinent information for the use in analysis and decision-making.

The series was conceived to form a set of working references for advanced students and researchers in each specific field, as well as a guide to development across the discipline more broadly.

This exchange of knowledge will be continued permanently by the opening of a debate site on the Internet [http://www.aea.fed-eco.org].

*Titles include*:

Françoise Bourdon and Jean Bourdon (*editors*)
WAGE ECONOMETRICS AND MODELLING

Fabrizio Carlevaro and Jean-Baptiste Lesourt (*editors*)
MEASURING AND ACCOUNTING ENVIRONMENTAL NUISANCES AND SERVICES

Arthur Getis, Jesús Mur and Henry G. Zoller (*editors*)
SPATIAL ECONOMETRICS AND SPATIAL STATISTICS

Siv S. Gustafsson and Danièle E. Meulders (*editors*)
GENDER AND THE LABOUR MARKET
Econometric Evidence of Obstacles to Achieving Gender Equality

Hans Heijke and Joan Muysken (*editors*)
EDUCATION AND TRAINING IN A KNOWLEDGE-BASED ECONOMY

Pavlos Karadeloglou (*editor*)
EXCHANGE-RATE POLICY IN EUROPE

Sandrine Lardic and Valérie Mignon (*editors*)
RECENT DEVELOPMENTS ON EXCHANGE RATES

Benoît Mahy, Robert Plasman and François Rycx (*editors*)
GENDER PAY DIFFERENTIALS
Cross-National Evidence from Micro-Data

Danièle Meulders, Robert Plasman and François Rycx (*editors*)
MINIMUM WAGES, LOW PAY AND UNEMPLOYMENT

Carine Peeters and Bruno van Pottelsberghe de la Potterie (*editors*)
ECONOMIC AND MANAGEMENT PERSPECTIVES ON INTELLECTUAL PROPERTY RIGHTS

Emile Quinet and Roger Vickerman (*editors*)
THE ECONOMETRICS OF MAJOR TRANSPORT INFRASTRUCTURES

Philippe Thalmann and Milad Zarin-Nejadan (*editors*)
CONSTRUCTION AND REAL ESTATE DYNAMICS


**Applied Econometrics Association**
**Series Standing Order ISBN 0–333–71460–1**
(*outside North America only*)

You can receive future titles in this series as they are published by placing a standing order. Please contact your bookseller or, in case of difficulty, write to us at the address below with your name and address, the title of the series and the ISBN quoted above.

Customer Services Department, Macmillan Distribution Ltd, Houndmills, Basingstoke, Hampshire RG21 6XS, England

# Gender Pay Differentials

## Cross-National Evidence from Micro-Data

Edited by

Benoît Mahy

Robert Plasman

and

François Rycx

palgrave
macmillan

First published 2006 by
PALGRAVE MACMILLAN
Houndmills, Basingstoke, Hampshire RG21 6XS and
175 Fifth Avenue, New York, N.Y. 10010
Companies and representatives throughout the world.

PALGRAVE MACMILLAN is the global academic imprint of the Palgrave Macmillan division of St. Martin's Press, LLC and of Palgrave Macmillan Ltd. Macmillan® is a registered trademark in the United States, United Kingdom and other countries. Palgrave is a registered trademark in the European Union and other countries.

ISBN-13: 978–0–230–00471–9
ISBN-10: 0–230–00471–7

This book is printed on paper suitable for recycling and made from fully managed and sustained forest sources.

A catalogue record for this book is available from the British Library.

Library of Congress Cataloging-in-Publication Data

Applied Econometrics Association. International Conference (88th)
Gender pay differentials: cross-national evidence from micro-data / edited by Benoît Mahy, Robert Plasman, and François Rycx.
p. cm. – (Applied Econometrics Association series)
A collection of papers originally presented at the 88th Applied Economics Association Conference to stimulate discussion on the "Economics of Labour Demand."
Includes bibliographical references and index.
ISBN 0–230–00471–7 (cloth)
1. Wages – European Union countries – Sex differences – Congresses. 2. Wage differentials – European Union countries – Congresses. 3. Wages – Women – European Union countries – Congresses. 4. Pay equity – European Union countries – Congresses. 5. Sex discrimination in employment – European Union countries – Congresses. I. Mahy, Benoît, 1961 – II. Plasman, Robert. III. Rycx, François, 1974–IV. Title. V. Series.
HD5014.A77 2006
331.2'15082094—dc22 2005058612

10 9 8 7 6 5 4 3 2 1
15 14 13 12 11 10 09 08 07 06

Printed and bound in Great Britain by
Antony Rowe Ltd, Chippenham and Eastbourne

# Contents

# List of Tables, Figures and Boxes

## Tables

## Figures

## Boxes

# Notes on the Contributors

**W. Robert J. Alexander** is Senior Lecturer in Economics at the University of Otago, Dunedin, New Zealand. His research interests include labour market discrimination and the economics of ageing.

**Nabanita Datta Gupta** is Research Professor at the Danish National Institute of Social Research, Copenhagen. Her research areas include wage differentials, occupational choice, discrimination, health, retirement, pension systems and microeconomic analyses of economic development. She is currently serving on the Executive Committee of the European Association of Labour Economists.

**Tor Eriksson** is Professor of Economics and Research Director at the Center for Corporate Performance at the Aarhus School of Business. He is also a research associate at Frisch Centre of Economic Research, Oslo.

**Amynah Gangji** is a researcher at the Department of Applied Economics at the Free University of Brussels (ULB). She has a degree in economics at the Free University of Brussels (ULB) and a Master (DEA) in political economics. Her fields of competence are gender wage inequality, labour economics, unemployment (unemployment persistence and state dependence) as well as poverty measures.

**Dolores García-Crespo** is Associate Professor in the Department of Applied Economics, University of Málaga.

**Hermann Gartner** is research assistant at the Institute for Employment Research in Nurenberg, Germany. His main topic of research is the analysis of wages with employer–employee data.

**Murat Genç** is Lecturer in the Department of Economics, University of Otago, New Zealand.

**Mohammad Jaforullah** is Senior Lecturer in Economics at the University of Otago, New Zealand. He received his master degree from the University of New England, Australia, in 1985 and a PhD from the University of Adelaide, Australia, in 1989. Previously, he taught at the University of Rajshahi, Bangladesh, and was a Postdoctoral Fellow at the Australian National University.

**Olivier Joseph** is researcher in the Entries into Working Life Department of Céreq (French Research Centre for the Analysis of Occupations, Vocational Education and Training).

**Séverine Lemière** is Lecturer in Human Resources Management and Economics at MATISSE Laboratory (University Paris I) and at the Technical College of Paris (University Paris V).

**Benoît Mahy** is Professor of Economics at the University of Mons-Hainaut (UMH), Belgium. He is also Head of the Department of Economic Analysis and Affiliated to the Warocqué Research Centre (CRW) of the UMH.

**Kristian Orsini** is research assistant and PhD candidate at the Centre for Economic Studies, KU, Leuven.

**Robert Plasman** is Professor of Economics at the Free University of Brussels (ULB) and co-director of the Department of Applied Economics of ULB (DULBEA), Belgium. His current research interests are in the fields of gender economics, working time and industrial relations.

**François Rycx** is Associate Professor of Economics at the Free University of Brussels (ULB), Belgium. He is affiliated to the Department of Applied Economics of ULB (DULBEA) and Research Fellow of the Institute for the Study of Labour (IZA, Bonn). His current research interests include applied econometrics, personal economics, wage determination and pay differentials.

**Salimata Sissoko** is Research Fellow in the Department of Applied Economics of the Université Libre de Bruxelles (DULBEA, ULB) and research affiliate of the Institute for the Study of Labour (IZA, Bonn). She is completing a PhD thesis, dealing with the analysis of interaction of gendered social policies and evolution of the pay gap in the European Union countries.

**Ilan Tojerow** is Research Fellow in the Department for Applied Economics of the Free University of Brussels and a PhD student at the DULBEA doctoral school.

**Philippe Van Kerm** is Researcher at the Centre d'Études de Populations, de Pauvreté et de Politiques Socio-Économiques (Differdange, Luxembourg), where he head the Integrated Research Infrastructure in the Socio-Economic Sciences (IRISS-C/I) programme. His research focuses on applied micro-econometrics with particular reference to income-distribution issues.

# Introduction and Overview

*Benoît Mahy, Robert Plasman and François Rycx*

Gender pay discrimination has been outlawed in all member states of the European Union (EU) for many years. Article 119 of the Treaty of Rome, establishing the European Communities in 1957, already introduced the principle that women and men should receive equal pay for equal work. Since 1975, this basic principle has been refined and extended through a number of European Directives. The latter extend the principle of equal pay to work of equal value, guarantee the right to equal treatment in the workplace (that is, access to employment, vocational training, promotion and working conditions), and provide for equal treatment of women and men with respect to both statutory social security and occupational social security (Rice, 1999). Another important development towards the reduction of gender pay inequalities was the adoption in December 1997 of a European Directive on the burden of proof in cases of discrimination based on sex. This Directive implies that:

> when persons consider themselves wronged because the principle of equal treatment has not been applied to them establish, before a court or other competent authority, facts from which it may be presumed that there has been direct or indirect discrimination, it shall be for the respondent to prove that there has been no breach of the principle of equal treatment. (*Official Journal of the European Communities*, 1998, p. 8)

Also noteworthy is the establishment in recent years of gender equality as a central part of the European employment strategy (Rubery *et al.*, 2000). Since the Luxembourg summit of 1997, strengthening equal opportunities between women and men has, indeed, become the fourth pillar of the employment guidelines, next to the pillars of employability, adaptability and entrepreneurship. What is more, since 1999, EU member states are required to adopt a gender-mainstreaming policy throughout their National Action Plans.[1]

During the last decades, a large number of studies have focused on the magnitude and sources of the gender wage gap in Europe. These studies indicate that, while EU countries have brought their laws into line with European Directives, significant gender wage gaps persist in all member states (Blau and Kahn, 2000; Gannon *et al.*, 2005; Plasman and Sissoko, 2004; Maruani, 2000; Meurs and Ponthieux, 2000; and Rice, 1999). Findings also show that gender wage gaps have been decreasing in most EU countries during the 1990s but only slowly (Eurostat, 2001). Therefore, some authors argue that, in spite of EU legislation, there is still no 'natural' trend towards pay equality (Maruani, 2001).

To tackle the gender pay differential, it is crucial to acquire a broad understanding of its structural characteristics and of its evolution so as to be able to assess the impact of labour market policies. Many factors influencing the gender pay ratio have been identified, including, *inter alia*: (i) differences in human capital; (ii) sectoral and occupational segregation and/or concentration, (iii) working time, (iv) the overall pay structure, (iv) the existence and level of minimum wages, (v) the access to internal and public training schemes, the organization of training time, (vi) the industrial organization, and (vii) women's representation in trade unions, employers' organizations and in bargaining or representative bodies (Blau and Kahn, 1992; Joshi and Paci, 1998; and Silvera, 1996). The impact of these factors on the gender wage gap may be affected by labour market or family policies (Concialdi and Ponthieux, 1999). Social security and fiscal regulations are also important for they may lead to changes in the continuity or discontinuity of the career, in the type of jobs taken on by women and in the returns to these jobs (Ruspini and Saraceno, 1999). What is more, results show that policies encouraging low wages or restraining wage progression have a negative effect on the gender wage gap (Concialdi and Ponthieux, 1999). Therefore, 'there is a considerable scope for political choice. Changing the gender pay ratio requires actions on a wide side set of policy agendas, involving the mainstreaming of pay equality across different levels of policy-making' (Grimshaw and Rubery, 2000, p. 2).

Be that as it may, the persistence of significant gender pay differentials in EU member states obviously indicates that EU legislation has still not achieved the necessary impact (European Commission, 2001). This can at least partly be attributed to the fact that: (i) the 1975 European

Directive on equal pay to work of equal value did not specify how equal value had to be established,[2] (ii) the European guidelines lack the force of a Directive, and (iii) the equality guidelines lack specific targets (Barrett *et al.*, 2000). Nevertheless, continuing pay inequalities between women and men also derive from the fact that there is no good understanding of the phenomenon itself (Maruani, 2001).

Assessing the *exact* size and evolution of the *overall* gender wage gap in EU countries is still problematic. There are two main harmonized databases for comparing gender pay differentials throughout Europe: the European Structure of Earnings Survey (ESES) and the European Community Household Panel (ECHP). Unfortunately, neither of these data-sets is fully adequate. The main weakness of the ESES is that it does not cover the public sector or common services. This is a significant limitation since the number of women working in these sectors is considerably higher than the number of men. Moreover, ESES data at EU level are only available for 1995 on an aggregated basis. The main shortcoming of the ECHP is that the information on wages is not fully reliable.[3]

Many uncertainties also remain as to the factors leading to pay inequalities. This is not very surprising since many EU countries have long been reluctant to make individual statistics on wages available to researchers. Nevertheless, data availability is not the whole story. To gain a better understanding of the causes of wage inequalities, the statistics on wages should be completed and improved in various ways (European Commission, 2001). Firstly, there is a need to enlarge the coverage of the EU harmonized statistics. It is essential to collect data for all groups of the working-age population (whether employed full-time or part-time, unemployed or inactive), for all branches of industry (independently of the type of economic and financial control) and for several years (ideally panel data). Secondly, there is a need to gather information on a larger number of variables, including the level and structure of gross wages (for example basic pay, premia, bonuses), the household situation (for example marital status, number and age of the children), individual and establishment characteristics (for example experience, tenure, working time, career breaks, training programmes, occupation, size and profit of the establishment, type of collective agreement). To put it differently, it would be very useful to have a single data-set including (at least) all variables currently available in the ESES and ECHP. Finally, for a number of variables – in particular the occupation – information is required at a much more disaggregated level than is available at present. This is essential if one wants to compare wages of women and men who perform equal work and work of equal value (European Commission, 2001).

Bayard *et al.* (2003) recently reexamined the question of the relative contributions to the overall gender wage gap of: (i) sex segregation and (ii) wage differences by sex within occupation, industry, establishment, and occupation–establishment cells. To do this, they assembled a unique matched employer–employee data-set covering all industries and occupations across all regions of the USA. In contrast to previous research (in particular Groshen, 1991), they found that a substantial part of the sex wage gap takes the form of wage differences between women and men within narrowly-defined occupations within establishments. The authors therefore conclude that 'further research into the sources of within-establishment, within-occupation sex wage differences is apparently much more important than previously thought' (Bayard *et al.*, 2003, pp. 918–9). Unfortunately, to carry out a similar analysis for the EU, it is clear that more disaggregated Community-wide statistics on occupations (preferably at the four-digit level) should be collected.

The 88th Applied Econometrics Association Conference of 6 to 8 September 2004 was organized with the specific aim of stimulating discussion on the 'Econometrics of Labour Demand', and various sessions have in particular focused on Gender Wage Gaps. The collection of papers in this book, originally presented at the Conference, provides new insight into the magnitude and sources of the gender wage gap in European countries and New Zealand on the basis of micro-data. In what follows a short summary of these papers is presented.

## Job access and workplace practices

In the opening chapter, Olivier Joseph (Céreq DEVA) and Séverine Lemière (University Paris I and V) propose some measures of discrimination between young men and women in their entry path into the French labour market. These gender discrimination measures are tested on native and foreign-origin populations. The authors identify two different youth paths. The first one focuses on young people having the same job after their studies and three years after. The second path deals with young people having a first job after the end of their studies and another one three years later. Econometric measures of gender discrimination are computed for both youth paths. These measures distinguish between job access discrimination, wage discrimination and a model of wage discrimination including job structure. Empirical findings, based on the survey Génération 98 developed by Céreq, show that job access is widely discriminating for the first job and the job three years later. They also indicate that wage discrimination increases in the two types of integration processes, although the wage gaps have not the same trend for the two paths. Further findings suggest that wage discrimination is due to wage inequalities in the same kind of jobs.

In Chapter 2, Nabanita Datta Gupta and Tor Eriksson (Aarhus School of Business) investigate the effect of high-performance practices, incentive pay schemes and formal worker performance evaluation procedures on the wages of full-time male and female private-sector employees in Denmark by matching a unique 1999 survey on work and compensation practices of Danish private-sector firms to a large employer–employee database. Their results show that the gains and losses from new work and pay schemes are in many cases the same for men and women, so that we may not expect that they would change substantially the gender wage gap. However, considering differences between skill groups, the picture turns out to be different. Findings suggest indeed that high-performance practices reduce wage differentials between salaried males and other groups, while incentive pay schemes benefit salaried workers (particularly males) more than those on hourly pay. They also indicate that performance evaluation systems (particularly those in which evaluation is based on objective criteria) tend to narrow the wage gap between male and female salaried workers in the private sector.

## Promotions and wage growth

In the next chapter, Dolores García-Crespo (University of Málaga) examines the importance of promotions in the male and female wage process and the contribution of the internal mobility differences into the gender wage gap in Spain. By using data from a nationally representative survey (the Encuesta de Estructura, Conciencia y Biografía de Clase, 1991), the author estimates the usual Mincer equations including the number of promotions received at the current employer taking into account the sample selection according to Heckman's approach. Her main findings are the following: (i) internal mobility at the firm is a very important factor that increases a worker's wage, (ii) there is no evidence showing that intra-firm mobility is rewarded in different ways by gender; (iii) women are held to higher promotion standards than comparable men; and (iv) if the female promotion rate was equal to the male one, the gender wage gap would be lower.

In Chapter 4, Philippe Van Kerm (CEPS/INSTEAD) examines gender differentials in promotion and wage growth using nationally representative panel-survey data for Luxembourg. Empirical results suggest that women lag behind men as far as promotion is concerned, even after controlling for human-capital attributes and the type of jobs held. The gap appears to be especially large for low-earnings women. Despite this disadvantage, the author shows that the expected annual percentage wage growth of women is higher than that of men. However, this advantage largely disappears when controlling for human capital and job characteristics. Finally, when looking at estimates conditional on the base-period wage level, the author finds no evidence of a 'glass ceiling' above high-earnings women, neither in terms of promotion nor of wage growth.

## Sectors, profits and rent-sharing

François Rycx and Ilan Tojerow (Free University of Brussels) examine the interaction between inter-industry wage differentials and the gender wage gap in the Belgian private sector. On the basis of the 1995 Structure of Earnings Survey, the authors report the existence of significant inter-industry wage differentials for both male and female workers, even when controlling for working conditions, individual and firm characteristics. These differentials are highly correlated but statistically different. On average, women have an inter-industry wage differential of 11 per cent below that of men. Further results show that the overall gender wage gap is equal to 0.20 and that industry effects do not very much account for this gap.

In Chapter 6, Hermann Gartner (IAB) investigates gender differences in rent-sharing with the German linked employer–employee data (LIAB) of the Institute of Employment Research (IAB) in the year 2001. Empirical findings show that workers' wages are significantly and positively related to firm profits-per-employee, even when controlling for group effects in the residuals, individual and firm characteristics, industry wage differentials, and endogeneity of profits. The instrumented wage–profit elasticity is equal to 0.108 for males and 0.085 for females. Differences in rent-sharing are found to explain about 20 per cent (4.64 per cent points) of the overall gender wage gap. 0.17 per cent points can be attributed to gender-specific sorting across high and low-profit firms and 4.47 per cent points to differences in the wage–profit elasticities. According to Hermann Gartner, one possible reason for differences in rent-sharing are different positions of male and female workers within the firm. The point is that male workers, more frequently in higher positions in the firm, may have more opportunities to extract rents.

## Dynamics and unobserved heterogeneity

In Chapter 7, Amynah Gangji (Free University of Brussels), Kristian Orsini (University of Leuven) and Salimata Sissoko (Free University of Brussels) provide evidence on the effect of controlling for unobserved individual heterogeneity in estimating gender pay differentials. Using the European Community Household Panel (ECHP), they present a cross-country comparison of the (un)adjusted gender pay gap over time based on cross-section and panel-data estimation techniques. The analysed countries differ greatly with respect to labour legislation, bargaining practices, overall social-legal framework and structure of earnings. Once controlling for unobserved heterogeneity, the authors find a narrowed male–female pay differential, as well as significantly different rates of return on individual characteristics. In particular, the adjusted wage differential decreases by 7 per cent in Belgium, 14 per cent in Ireland, between 20 and 30 per cent in Germany, Italy, the Netherlands and Spain, and by more than 40 per cent in the UK and Denmark.

In the final chapter, W. Robert J. Alexander, Murat Genç and Mohammad Jaforullah (University of Otago) examine the gender wage ratio in New Zealand with data from the first annual New Zealand Income Survey in 1997 and the latest available survey from 2003. To do so, they estimate wage regressions by OLS and two methods, Heckit and Maximum Likelihood, which take account of sample selection bias arising from the exclusion of individuals with no market income. The authors pay particular attention to the sensitivity of the results to exclusion restrictions. Regardless of estimation method or specification, they find evidence of a statistically and economically significant female/male differential. On the other dimension by which individuals are potentially observationally distinct, namely ethnicity, the evidence is less clear-cut.

### Notes

1 For a description of the EU legislation and strategy on gender equality, see European Commission (1994, 2000, 2002).

2 It should be noted, however, that a valuable code of practice on the implementation of equal pay for work of equal value, giving concrete advice to employers and contracting parties at corporate and sectoral level, has been published by the European Commission (1996).

3 For a comparison of the advantages and disadvantages of the ESES and ECHP, see Plasman *et al.* (2001).

## References


Bayard, K., Hellerstein, J., Neumark, D. and Troske, K. (2003) 'New Evidence on Sex Segregation and Sex Difference in Wages from Matched Employer–Employee Data', *Journal of Labor Economics*, 21(4), pp. 887–922.

Barrett, A., Callan, T., Doris, A., O'Neill, D., Russell, H., Sweetman, O. and McBride, J. (2000) *How Unequal? Men and Women in the Irish Labour Market*. Dublin: Oak Tree Press.

Blau, F. and Kahn, L. (1992) 'The Gender Earnings Gap: Learning from International Comparisons', *American Economic Review*, 82(2), pp. 533–9.

Blau, F. and Kahn, L. (2000) 'Gender Differences in Pay', *Journal of Economic Perspectives*, 14(4), pp. 75–99.

Concialdi, P. and Ponthieux, S. (1999) 'L'emploi à bas salaire: les femmes d'abord', *Travail, Genre et Sociétés*, 1.

European Commission (1994) 'Memorandum on Equal Pay for Work of Equal Value'. Luxembourg: Office for Official Publications of the European Communities.

European Commission (1996) 'A Code of Practice on the Implementation of Equal Pay for Work of Equal Value'. Brussels: Communication from the Commission.

European Commission (2000) 'Towards a Community Framework on Gender Equality (2001–2005)'. Brussels: Communication from the Commission.

European Commission (2001) 'Highlighting Pay Differentials between Women and Men'. Brussels: Swedish Presidency Report.

European Commission (2002) 'Equal Opportunities for Women and Men in the European Union 2001'. Brussels: Annual Report from the Commission.

Eurostat (2001) 'Earnings of Men and Women in the EU: The Gap Narrowing but only Slowly', *Statistics in Focus*, Theme 3, Luxembourg.

Gannon, B., Plasman, R., Rycx, F. and Tojerow, I. (2005), 'Inter-Industry Wage Differentials and the Gender Wage Gap: Evidence from European Countries', IZA (Institute for the Study of Labor) Discussion Paper no. 1563.

Grimshaw, D. and Rubery, J. (2000) 'The Gender Pay Gap: A Research Review', Report prepared for the Equal Opportunities Commission of the European Union.

Groshen, E. (1991), 'The Structure of the Female/Male Wage Differential: Is it Who You Are, What You Do, or Where You Work?', *Journal of Human Resources*, 26(3), pp. 457–72.

Joshi, H. and Paci, P. (1998), *Unequal Pay for Women and Men*. Cambridge, Mass.: MIT Press.

Maruani, M. (2000) 'Women's Employment in a Society of Rampant Unemployment', in S. Gustafsson and D. Meulders (eds), *Gender and the Labour Market. Econometric Evidence of Obstacles to Achieving Gender Equality*. London: Palgrave Macmillan.

Meurs, D. and Ponthieux, S. (2000) 'Components of the Gender Wage Gap in 12 EU Countries', Paper presented at the EALE/SOLE 2000 Conference, Milan.

Official Journal of the European Communities (1998) *Council Directive 97/80/EC of December 1997 on the Burden of Proof in the Cases of Discrimination Based on Sex*, L 14, 20 January 1998. Luxembourg: Office for Official Publications of the European Communities.

Plasman, A., Plasman, R., Rusinek, M. and Rycx, F. (2001) 'Indicators on Gender Pay Equality. The Belgian Presidency's Report', Belgian Federal Ministry of Labour and Employment.

Plasman, R. and Sissoko, S. (2004) 'Comparing Apples and Oranges: Revisiting the Gender Wage Gap in an International Perspective', IZA Discussion Paper no. 1449.

Rice, P. (1999) 'Gender Earnings Differentials: The European Experience', Policy Research Report on Gender and Development, Working Paper Series, no. 8, World Bank.

Ruspini, E. and Saraceno, C. (1999) 'Précarité des revenues, pauvreté des salaires: le cas des femmes en Italie', *Travail, Genre et Sociétés*, 1.

Rubery, J., Grimshaw, D. and Smith, M. (2000) 'Gender Equality and the European Employment Strategy: An Evaluation of the National Action Plans for Employment 2000', Report prepared for the Equal Opportunities Commission of the European Union.

Silvera, R. (1996) 'Le salaire des femmes, toutes choses inégales', La Documentation française, Service des Droits des Femmes.

# Part I

# Job Access and Workplace Practices

# 1
# Assessing Gender Discrimination amongst Young People on their Arrival into the Labour Market: Analysis of Young Populations of French and Foreign Origins

*Olivier Joseph and Séverine Lemière*

The subject of this chapter is a topical question in France. There are a great number of measures and laws concerning questions of discrimination and equality between men and women for example:

1. The law of 16 November 2001 concerns the fight against all kinds of discrimination.
2. The High Authority for the Struggle against Discrimination and for Equality (HALDE) will be set up on 1 January 2005.
3. The 'Genisson' Law of 9 May 2001 makes collective bargaining obligatory for professional equality between men and women.
4. In 2004 an 'equality label' will be created, to be awarded to firms that develop actions in favour of equality between men and women, and so on.

The aim of this chapter is to improve understanding of discrimination phenomena against young women (of French and foreign origins), and the evolution of these phenomena, when these young women come on to the labour market. We have used the French database Génération 98 (Box 1.1) realized by Céreq and research carried out by a Céreq work-group called 'Differentiation and Insertion'. And it is also in line with the researches carried out by Dupray and Moullet (2003) and Frickey and Primon (2003), but using an original methodology.

*Box 1.1* The Generation 98 database

The database used is the French 'Generation 98' survey developed by Céreq (French Centre of Research on Education, Training and Employment). In 2001, Céreq questioned about 55,000 young people who had finished their studies in 1998. The survey covered persons with every level of education and who had done all types of studies.

The aim of the database was to analyse the path followed by young persons coming on to the labour market between the time they finished their study in 1998 and three years later, when the survey was made. The database provides a great deal of explanatory data: socio-demographic data, unemployment, times taken to come on to the labour market, mobility, professional situation, wages, types of job, etc.

We are not going to analyse 'double discrimination' here and nor do we compare gender discrimination and origin discrimination between young women of foreign origin. Our analysis is centred on gender discrimination, but we measure it for populations from different origins to reveal any possible differences.

Our analyses have been carried out on young persons who had jobs when the survey was carried out, in 2001. To analyse gender discrimination when entering the labour market, two types of entry path have been identified. The first path concerns young persons who find employment at the end of their studies and hold the same job three years later. The second path deals with young people who find an initial job at the end of their studies and a different one three years later. Gender discrimination is measured in job access and in wages (with job categories). Using two kinds of entry path enables us to carry out an analysis on the two kinds of discrimination liable to be found when young women come onto the job market: job market effects and human-resource management effect.

## Distinction between two types of entry path for young people

As noted above, the first entry path concerns young people who find a job at the end of their studies and still hold it three years later. In this case, we can analyse the degree of integration in a firm and any evolution in discrimination can be studied for a single job and a single firm. Evolution in discrimination is assessed between the situation of the beginning of employment and at the time of the survey.

*Box 1.2* Population sample

Our initial population sample covers all the young people on whom we possess information as far as their origins are concerned (54,880 young people). Among this population, we have only studied people who held jobs when the survey was carried out (48,609) and two situations can be distinguished:

- Young people who have had the same employment when they first began work and when the survey was carried out(20,378).
- Young people who have held several jobs and who were employed when the survey was carried out (25,533).

The population of young people who have had no work during the three years following their studies (2,698), has been used to measure job access discrimination and to correct the selectivity bias in the wage discrimination analysis.

The population of young people who have had jobs during the three years, but who were not employed when the survey was carried out (6,279) is not included in our research analysis.

Our population sample is composed of 47.7 per cent women and of 15.2 per cent young people of foreign origin (6 per cent North African origin and 5 per cent southern Europe origin).

Figure 1.1 gives a simplified presentation of the methodology used to analyse different aspects of gender discrimination during integration into the labour market.

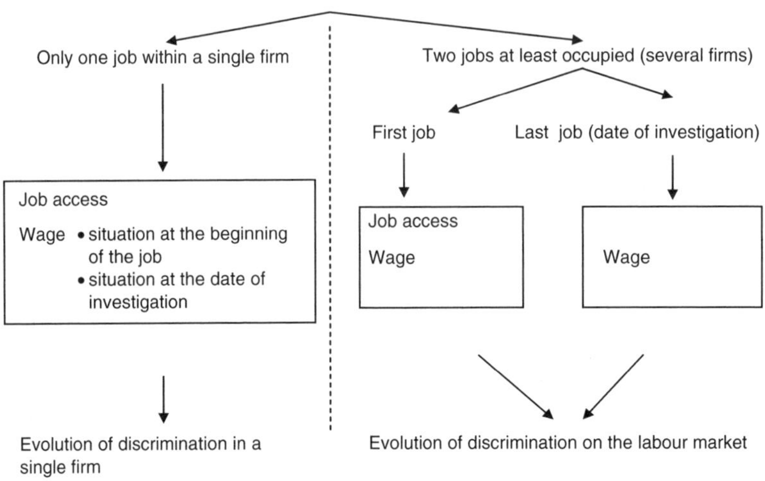


*Figure 1.1* Discrimination analysis of the entry path of youth into the labour market

The second entry path deals with young people who find an initial job at the end of their studies but who have a different job three years later. Two job periods have been analysed: the first job and the job held when the survey was carried out. In this case, we can show any evolution in discrimination on the labour market by using several jobs and firms.

Our sample has been taken from young people who were employed at the time the survey was made. This choice has two advantages. On the one hand, we have a better evaluation of the situation at the end of integration and on the other hand, this population reveals all information concerning the path taken by young people when they come on to the labour market (Box 1.2).

## Details concerning young people interviewed at the time of the survey

Among young people employed at the time of the survey, 55 per cent have held several jobs and 45 per cent only one job. Women are slightly underrepresented in the population who have had several jobs. The ratio of people with foreign origins is similar in both situations (14.5 per cent of young people) but it is lower than the percentage they represent in the total population (15.2 per cent) because they are more represented amongst young people who have never been employed (24.6 per cent have a foreign origin).

Amongst persons who have only held one job throughout the period, there are more with high educational levels (levels I and II) but there are also persons without any educational diplomas (level V bis and VI). Proportionally, there are more young people with III, IV and V educational levels who have changed jobs. On average, young women are more qualified than young men, 53.9 per cent at education levels I-II for young women and only 41.1 per cent of the persons holding poor qualifications (level Vbis and VI) (young women constitute 47.7 per cent of our sample). This observation is even more accentuated for young people of foreign origin; in their case, the gap between men and women is higher; 56.2 per cent of all qualified persons (level I-II) of foreign origin are young women.

Access time to the first job, when the same employment was held throughout the three-year period, is on average 5 months with a median at 2 months; there is very little difference between men and women, but a considerable difference for young people with North African origins, for whom access times are higher. Access times are lower when the first employment is not the same as the one held at the time of the survey (3 months on average and 1 month in median).

Length of service in a job, when the same job has been held throughout the period, is on average 28 months for men (with a median at 32 months) and 29 months for women (a median of 31 months). We see that when young people have only held one job they are employed for long-term positions. Decomposition by sex and by origin in the path taken by people who have only had only one job is the same as for the population employed when the survey was carried out (48 per cent are women and about 15 per cent are of foreign origin).

When the job at the time of the survey is different from the first job, length of service is on average 10 months (8 in median) without any difference in sex or origins. For information, the first job can be called a long-term job because its duration is on average 13 months (12 in median), with very few differences between men and women and between different origins.

The average monthly wage for women at the beginning of the unique job is 1,006 euros (930 in median). This wage is lower for women of foreign origin (904 and 934 respectively for young women from North Africa and southern Europe). Whatever their origin, the average wage for women is always lower than for men (average wage for men is 1,149 euros). When the survey was carried out, 28 months later, wage had increased by 14 per cent if the total population is taken into account. The rate of increase is slightly lower for women (12.6 per cent) than for men (14.7 per cent), and lower for young people from North Africa (9.6 per cent). For women of North African origin, the rate of increase is 8.2 per cent.

For young people who have changed jobs during the three-year period, on average, wages for the first job are lower than those paid to young people who have stayed in the same employment (with the same inequalities of sex and origin). Despite a big wage increase (24.6 per cent on average) between the first job and the job when the survey was carried out, the wages of people who have changed jobs are lower on average than those paid to people who have only held one job at the time of the survey.

Working conditions are different depending on the path taken to enter the labour market (only one job or several jobs) in particular those concerning employment contracts. Seventy per cent of initial jobs are obtained with a form of fixed-term contract (when the first job is not the same as when the survey was carried out), women are slightly less concerned by this practice, but young people of foreign origin are more affected. After initial employment, there are less fixed-term contracts; these only concern 34.5 per cent of young people, but are more prevalent for women (contrary to the situation concerning the first job).

The same trend can be observed for persons' integration the labour market through one job only (when the job held at the time of the survey was the only job held). At the beginning of the job, on average 50 per cent of persons are recruited with a fixed-term contract, 24 per cent continued to hold the same kind of contract when the survey was carried out. Once again, women are more concerned by this phenomenon.

When young people have had only one employment, their job categories are on average better than those of young people who have changed jobs. When the survey was carried out, 15.7 per cent of young people held, executive management jobs, where this job was the only one they have held whereas only 12.2 per cent of young people hold this kind of position after doing several others jobs. Furthermore, 14.4 per cent were executive managers at the beginning of their job, whereas only 8 per cent of persons held this type of position in their first job, when this job was different from the one they had when the survey was carried out. There are fewer women holding executive managerial positions for their first job than men, but the situation is different for young people of foreign origin. Whatever the origin and the path followed, women are more often to be found in intermediary jobs. See Table 1.1.

## Discrimination measures: the methodology

Discrimination is defined by the fact that 'certain people with a common characteristic seem to be specially penalised because of this characteristic, regardless of any productive characteristics they may possess' (Plassard, 1987). Sex or origin is a kind of non-economic characteristic of a group (women, people of foreign origin), a characteristic that takes no account of productivity, but on which discrimination can be based.

The methodology to measure discrimination is based on the decomposition technique. Here is an example of wage discrimination to explain this method.

The average wage gap between men and women measures inequality in wages between the different sexes. This finding reveals all the inequalities between men and women, for example different working hours, different certificates, different sectors of activity, etc. and it is not a precise way of measuring wage discrimination.

To measure wage discrimination, the wage gap is broken down into two parts: an 'explained' part, justified by differences in men's and women's economic characteristics, and an 'unexplained' part. This 'unexplained' part cannot be justified by differences in productive characteristics, but it is the differential of return of individual productive

*Table 1.1* Descriptive statistics according to the origins of young people

| | *Men* | | *Women* | | | |
|---|---|---|---|---|---|---|
| | *French* | *Foreign* | *French* | *Foreign* | *Maghreb* | *South European* |
| Population (%) | 44.3 | 8 | 40.6 | 7.1 | 40.3 | 32 |
| Type of pathway (%) | | | | | | |
| Single firm | 43.6 | 41.4 | 44.1 | 47 | 48.1 | 46.2 |
| Several firms | 56.4 | 58.6 | 55.9 | 53 | 51.9 | 53.8 |
| Without job[a] (%) | 3.5 | 7.4 | 8.2 | 13.9 | 18.4 | 7.8 |
| School level (%) | | | | | | |
| Secondary level | 52.3 | 65.4 | 40.3 | 54.7 | 58.8 | 48.7 |
| Higher level | 47.7 | 34.6 | 59.7 | 45.3 | 41.2 | 51.3 |
| Access time to the first job (mean) | 3 | 4 | 4 | 6 | 6 | 5 |
| According to type of path | | | | | | |
| Single firm | 5 | 6 | 6 | 8 | 9 | 7 |
| Several firms | 2 | 3 | 3 | 4 | 4 | 3 |
| Job characteristics[b] | | | | | | |
| % Open-ended contract | | | | | | |
| Single firm | 77 | 70 | 71 | 65 | 58 | 69 |
| Several firms | 66 | 57 | 59 | 57 | 50 | 63 |
| % Executive occupation | | | | | | |
| Single firm | 18 | 15 | 14 | 9 | 5 | 10 |
| Several firms | 14 | 9 | 11 | 10 | 8 | 10 |
| Average earnings (euros) | | | | | | |
| Single firm | 1.150 | 1.140 | 1.050 | 945 | 900 | 970 |
| Several firms | 1.140 | 1.140 | 1.020 | 990 | 945 | 1.000 |
| % Full time | | | | | | |
| Single firm | 89 | 88 | 78 | 73 | 73 | 73 |
| Several firms | 92 | 91 | 81 | 80 | 80 | 78 |

[a] At the enquiry date; [b] current job characteristics according to the pathway.

characteristics and of the firm, which is then assimilated with wage discrimination.

The technique we have used is based on Oaxaca and Ransom (1994). This method provides for decomposing the 'unexplained' part, assimilated with discrimination, into two elements: the disadvantage suffered by victims of discrimination, women, and the advantage in favour of dominant people, men.

In this approach, discrimination is not only negative discrimination against women but also positive behaviour to men's advantage.

The decomposition technique needs to make a choice of a nondiscriminatory wage structure. The question is what wage structure can exist without discrimination? We will develop this idea below.

In this chapter, we use this decomposition technique for the different aspects of integration into the labour market, and in the two kinds of path already identified. Discrimination is measured in job access, in wage and in wage-inserting occupational segregation.

Our approach to wage discrimination is evaluated on the basis of figures for monthly earnings provided by the different person questioned. Monthly earnings include premiums and/or bonuses.

## Measurement of discrimination in job access

In this section, we measure discrimination in job access, and to do so we use the technique of probit and decomposition of the average job access probability.

To estimate job access, the variables used are: educational levels, specialized training, parents' activities (whether in job or not), professional experience during schooling (training courses, regular jobs, student jobs).

To measure job access, the reference population is composed of young people who have never been employed.

Job access probability is estimated:

$$E_{ij} = \gamma_j Z_{ij} + \eta_{ij}$$

where $i$ is the indicator of individuals and $j$ is the indicator of group of populations studied, the variable $E$ is equal to 1 if the young person has work, 0 if he or she is unemployed.

The probability of having a job is calculated:

$$P_{ij} = Prob\left(E_{ij} = 1\right) = \Phi\left(\gamma_j Z_{ij}\right)$$

Decomposition of the job access probability gap:

$$\tilde{P}_1 - \tilde{P}_2 = \underbrace{\hat{p}^*(\overline{X}_1 - \overline{X}_2)}_{A} + \underbrace{\overline{X}_1(\hat{p}_1 - \hat{p}^*)}_{B} + \underbrace{\overline{X}_2(\hat{p}^* - \hat{p}_2)}_{C}$$

where $\hat{p}^*$ is the estimated non-discriminatory job access probability, $\overline{X}_1(\hat{p}_1 - \hat{p}^*)$, labelled (B), is the estimated advantage in job access probability for young men, $\overline{X}_2(\hat{p}^* - \hat{p}_2)$, labelled (C), is the estimated disadvantage in job access probability for young women, $(\overline{X}_1 - \overline{X}_2)\hat{p}^*$, labelled (A), is the estimated differential of productivity between men and women, this is the explained part.

**Measurement of wage discrimination**

Decomposition of the wage differentials revealed above, according to Oaxaca and Ransom (1994), is as follows (with the correction of selectivity bias):

$$Log(\tilde{W}^1) - Log(\tilde{W}^2) = \underbrace{\hat{\beta}^*(\overline{X}_1 - \overline{X}_2)}_{A} + \underbrace{\overline{X}_1(\hat{\beta}_1 - \hat{\beta}^*)}_{B} + \underbrace{\overline{X}_2(\hat{\beta}^* - \hat{\beta}_2)}_{C} + \underbrace{(\hat{\vartheta}_1\hat{\lambda}_1 - \hat{\vartheta}_2\hat{\lambda}_2)}_{D}$$

where $\hat{\beta}^*$ represents the wage structure considered non-discriminatory, $\overline{X}_1(\hat{\beta}_1 - \hat{\beta}^*)$, labelled (B), is the estimated wage advantage for young men, $\overline{X}_2(\hat{\beta}^* - \hat{\beta}_2)$, labelled (C), is the estimated wage disadvantage for young women, $(\overline{X}_1 - \overline{X}_2)\hat{\beta}^*$, labelled (A), is the estimated differential of productivity between both populations, i.e. the explained portion of the wage differential, $(\hat{\vartheta}_1\hat{\lambda}_1 - \hat{\vartheta}_2\hat{\lambda}_2)$, labelled (D), is the estimated differential in the selectivity term.

Explanatory variables are as follows: educational ladder, the speciality of training, type of contract at present, the grades of employment, the experience in the labour market and its square, the experience in a company and its square, job responsibilities, sectors of activity, sizes of companies, types of employer (private or public), geographic locations of employment, working hours.

For current earnings and for taking account of the evolution between the two dates, professional experience in current employment and professional experience on the labour market before current employment were integrated according to the courses followed. Where only one job has been held, the variables dealing with adult training (except for initial training given for holding the job) and increases in wages were introduced into the earnings equation in order to take certain aspects of human resource management into account.

*The problem of selectivity bias*

As this research programme concerns wage discrimination, it focuses on young people who were employed when the survey was carried out. There is, therefore, a selectivity bias in our sample. Indeed, we cannot guarantee that this population of employed young people corresponds to a population drawn at random from the total population of young people. As a result, any possible selectivity bias has been corrected in the earnings equations estimate by using the Heckman selectivity bias two-stage correction method. This method retains the selectivity equation estimate (the probability being employed) by using a probit model to determine a correct term (the inverse of the Mills ratio) which is then integrated in the earnings equation.

The probit model used to explain the probability of being in employment contains the following variables: levels of education, specialized training, the fact that the father is employed, the fact that the mother is employed, an index giving information about a former occupation and index about the feelings of discrimination concerning young persons.

*Determination and decomposition of wage differentials*

Decomposition of the wage differential cannot be operational without making a choice on non-discriminatory wage structures ($\beta^*$): what would the wage structure be, in the absence of discrimination on the labour market concerning origins? Here, we will not go into detail on the many developments for characterizing wage structures in the absence of discrimination, but only indicate the various assumptions suggested by different authors. In its first formulation of discrimination in 1973, Oaxaca proposed an alternative – either to regard the non-discriminatory structure as being that of the not discriminated population or, on the contrary, as being that of the discriminated population. The choice of one or the other of these two structures leads to considerably different results. Rare are the objective reasons that justify this choice, especially if we simultaneously regard discrimination as real negative discrimination towards a group and a form of nepotistic behaviour towards another group. In the method used by Oaxaca and Ransom (1994), coefficients for the non-discriminatory situation are calculated by estimating an earnings equation on the pooled sample of the two demographic groups. Here the choice of the non-discriminatory population is the whole population (men and women) of the same origin.

## Incorporation of occupational categories access to wage discrimination measurements

The type of job held is another significant phenomenon, which differentiates populations on the labour market and therefore attribution of wages. The introduction of job category variables into wage estimates made in initial models neutralizes this observation but does not give any account of their specific effects. Inequality of access to certain categories of employment was not taken into account in the first models, where the structure of the socio-professional categories of each population was considered as given. The methodology used at the time included these inequalities of access in the explained part of wage differentials, which prevented anything attributed to discrimination in job allocation from being isolated. However, wage differentials may also exist between different categories of job, due to different employment structures (inter-category differential) but also within the same categories of employment (intra-category differential). As a result, the decomposition model of wage differential developed by Brown, Moon and Zoloth (1980) can be used. This model incorporates differences in jobs held in its analysis of wage differentials. It processes differences in employment directly and then makes a more accurate measurement of the wage differences attributable to different employment structures and within some employment categories. These two types of wage differentials are then broken down to distinguish the explained part and the part attributable to discrimination.

Starting from a unit of individual characteristics, this model uses a logit multinomial function to predict categories of probability of access to employment for young men. It then simulates job distribution for women as if they had the same structure of access to employment as men. Wages can then be estimated for both populations in each category of employment. The wage difference between populations is then broken down into different sections:

- the share attributable to the difference between the young men and women in the individual characteristics outputs for considered employments (wage discrimination, itself broken down into advantages and disadvantages),
- the share of the differential attributable to differences in individual characteristics of employment (explained wage differential),
- the share that can be allocated to the difference in employment structure related to differences in individual characteristics
- and, finally, the share ascribable to the fact that the both populations are treated differently in the access to various employments (Meurs and Ponthieux, 1999).

Decomposition of differentials in wages integrating differences in occupations, the Brown, Moon, Zoloth (BMZ) (1980) methodology applied to Oaxaca and Ramson (1994):

$$Log(\tilde{W}^1) - Log(\tilde{W}^2) = \underbrace{\sum_j p_j^2 \hat{\beta}_j^* (\overline{X}_j^1 - \overline{X}_j^2)}_{A} + \underbrace{\sum_j p_j^2 \overline{X}_j^1 (\hat{\beta}_j^1 - \hat{\beta}_j^*)}_{B}$$
$$+ \underbrace{\sum_j p_j^2 \overline{X}_j^2 (\hat{\beta}_j^* - \hat{\beta}_j^2)}_{C} + \underbrace{\sum_j \overline{W}_j^1 (p_j^1 - \hat{p}_j^2)}_{D}$$
$$+ \underbrace{\sum_j \overline{W}_j^1 (\hat{p}_j^2 - p_j^2)}_{E}$$

where (D) and (E) represent the inter-category differential part, (D) being the part attributable to differences in occupation structures in terms of professional position and (E) the part attributable to differences of treatment between male and female populations, (A), (B) and (C) represent the intra-category differential part, which breaks down into an explained part (A), in favour of the male population (B) and a disadvantage for the female population (C).

All these quantities are weighted by the probabilities observed, or estimated to belong to the *j* category (the professional position), for both populations. Therefore, this model needs to give a correct prediction of the probability of access to various categories of employment. The explanation of the distribution of the occupational categories is carried out using the following variables: diplomas obtained (a detailed breakdown), specialized training, the father's situation (employed or not), the mother's situation (employed or not), types of company, sectors of activity, the experience in the company, geographical and economic locations (indicator of urbanization) at the time of the studies, job responsibilities. The same explanatory factors as for wage discrimination are used once again but with a very strong aggregation of information.

These variables try to explain the individuals' preferences concerning their career (present and future). As in other studies (Brown, Moon and Zoloth, 1980), the parents' professional situation is integrated as an explanatory variable of the social context in which the young person handles his schooling and his route for finding work. We assume that this context has an effect on the type of employment held. The wage estimates for each population and occupational category (grade) use the following variables: an indicatrix of high or low diplomas, specialized training, the type of employment contract, the experience in the company and in the job, the responsibility contained in the job, an index on whether the company belongs to the industrial sector or not, the size of the company, working hours, an index on whether the company belongs to the private sector or not, and an index of activity in urban zones.

## Analysis and evolution of the phenomena of discrimination in the 'single employment' insertion path

### Access to employment is largely discriminatory

Overall, the gap in probability of access to employment between young women and young men is 6.4 per cent. This differential is higher for young people of foreign origin (8.8 per cent). It is among young people from Southern Europe that it is the lowest at 4.4 per cent. These various differentials are partially explained by differences in characteristics between men and women, but a part remains unexplained and can be attributed to discrimination. Gender discrimination in access to employment is lowest for young people from South Europe (57 per cent) and highest for young people of North African origin, the only population for whom differentials can solely be attributed to discrimination. Without any distinction in origin, differentials of access to employment are 75 per cent explained by differences in output for identical production characteristics between women and men on the labour market. For every population, this discrimination can be broken down in similar ratios, into an advantage given by the labour market to men's productive characteristics and a disadvantage given to those of women.

### Wage discrimination on the increase: discriminatory wage practices?

A general tendency has been observed for all the populations studied: the wage gap between men and women has increased between wages paid at the beginning of employment and wages paid at the time of the survey. At the same time, discrimination also increases. Indeed, the unexplained part of the wage gap between women and men has increased. Only young women from South Europe, in spite of a wage differential clearly on the increase, do not suffer from increased discrimination; the wage gap in logarithmic terms is 0.1042 at the beginning and 0.1579 at the end of the period and the unexplained part represents

29.7 per cent and 28.3 per cent of the gap. On the contrary, young women of North African origin are not severe victims of wage discrimination at the beginning of employment (10.8 per cent of the gap are unexplained). Then their situation deteriorates (28.7 per cent unexplained). However, they are less concerned by discrimination than other young women.

To understand the way human resources are managed in a company, we must remember that continuous training variables (except initial training given for holding the job) and increasing wage variables have been integrated in the earnings equation.

Wage practices in companies seem to be sources of wage discrimination: promotions, rises in wages for the job, premiums, and so on.

### Incorporation of occupational categories access into wage discrimination: professional segregation in the centre of wage discrimination inside companies

The model for decomposing wage differentials developed by Brown, Moon and Zoloth (1980) incorporates differences in employment in the wage differentials analysis and then measures wage differences more accurately because of different structures of employment and also within same categories of employment.

As analyses of wage discrimination show, the average wage gaps between men and women increase between the time they were first employed and the situation when the survey was carried out, that is on average 28 months later. Incorporation of professional categories in the analysis enables us to understand that practically all the differential can be explained by differences of treatment in intra-category, that is wage differences within the same categories (executives, intermediate occupations, workforces and employees). This intra-category differential evolves in the same proportion as the average deviation. Within the intra-category wage differential, 59 per cent can be explained by differences in characteristics between men and women, a part that has dropped by three points at the time the survey was carried out. This result concerns young women of both French and foreign origins. Therefore, remaining in the same company does not lead to a reduction in wage differentials and wage discrimination, but, on the contrary, to a slight increase. Globally, this does not come from a situation that is related to an employment structure effect but from a situation born from each category of employment, due, for example, to practices concerning access to premiums or individual wage increases.

## Analysis and evolution of discrimination phenomena in the path taken by young people having changed employment

### Access to first employment equally discriminatory for all, but there are some differences in relation to access to a single employment

The differentials in access to initial employment between young women and young men (of all origins) are 79 per cent unexplained by differences in characteristics between the two sexes. The same result as for access to a single employment: young women of North African origin are more concerned than those from Southern Europe (the unexplained part is 84.3 per cent of the gap for young women of North African origin and 55 per cent for those from Southern Europe). Nevertheless, some differences are of interest. Even if young women of French origin obtain an initial job more easily than single employment, they suffer from discrimination slightly more. The situation for young women of North African origin testifies to a more important differential in access to a first job; 84.3 per cent of this gap remains unexplained by differences in characteristics between men and women. The situation of young women with Southern European origins is very different: only a slight differential of which only a small proportion is unexplained. Their situation is less unequal than the situation of the other young women, even those of French origin.

### Reduced differentials in wages and rising wage discrimination: an increase in under-evaluation of female characteristics by the market?

For all origins, except for young women of Southern European origin, the wage differential between men and women decrease slightly between the first job and the job held three years after leaving the educational system. In this respect, Professional mobility seems to reduce inequalities. In all cases, we note that this average gap differential takes place with a strong increase of the unexplained part; 29.9 per cent of the wage gap is unexplained for the first job and 47.7 per cent for the current job. Similar characteristics amongst men and women are valued differently by the labour market, which disadvantages those of women and, in slightly smaller proportions, favours those of men. Young men and women of North African and Southern European origins suffer from more important differentials in wages than young men and women of French origin, but these differentials seem largely explained by differences in characteristics.

### Incorporation of occupational categories access into wage discrimination: wage discrimination explained by differences inside occupational categories

Incorporation of access to different occupational categories in the wage discrimination analysis shows that differentials in wages are totally explained by differences in wages within the same occupational categories. And it is within these occupational categories, that female characteristics are under-valued compared with identical male characteristics (16 per cent of the gap are to the disadvantage of female characteristics) and that male characteristics are over-valued compared with identical female characteristics (13.8 per cent of the gap are to the advantage of male characteristics). This discrimination increases between the first job and the current job three years after finishing education (the unexplained part of the intra-category gap is 30 per cent for the first job and almost 45 per cent for the current one). This wage discrimination in the same occupational categories is linked by the market, in virtually the same proportions, to an over-evaluation of male productive characteristics (21.1 per cent of the gap) and to under-evaluation female characteristics (23.4 per cent of the gap). For the whole population of young people of foreign origin, individual characteristics are more to the disadvantage of women than to the advantage of men.

## Limits to and thoughts on discrimination measurements

This aim of this section is to reflect on the results and measurements carried out in this research operation. The section highlights certain limits and makes a number of non-conclusive comments, which are nevertheless useful for measuring such a complex and significant phenomenon.

A first series of limits is based on the techniques used for measuring discrimination. These methods are based on wage estimates, on access to occupation categories or to employment. These estimates are used as a basis for measuring and decomposing differentials. As a result, discrimination may be detected or not. However, depending on the population under study, the various estimates done (wage estimates, probit for being in employment or multinomial logit for accessing occupational categories) show significant differences in adequacy to the data. Therefore, the relevance of some human capital assumptions or earnings functions could be questioned to explain phenomena that do not concern exclusively young men from populations of French origin. Other populations (women and people from foreign origin) could be influenced by particular logics of insertion on the labour market and where some variables would have different impacts.

We must also deal with the question of selectivity bias correction. As a result, the introduction of selectivity bias can strongly modify observations made on discrimination phenomena. However, there is no consensus on this method, as Johnston and DiNardo (1997) (in Meurs and Ponthieux, 1999) point out, because of the central role played by the specification adopted for the model used for estimating access of employment. The corresponding probit model must be well specified to predict a relevant correct term whatever the population is. Moreover, the bias introduction gives an account of a specific measurement (access to the labour market) and appears in another measurement (wage discrimination); therefore, two distinct measurements, which is what we have taken here, may be more relevant.

A second series of limits concerns the decomposition methods used, which must be considered with care. Indeed, the part attributable to discrimination is the residue unexplained by differences in characteristics between populations. This unexplained share is therefore conditioned by the explanatory variables used in estimates. As a result, some non-available, omitted or wrongly estimated variables can distort measurement of discrimination. Moreover, some variables not usually taken into account (the social network, for example) could appear significant for some populations. Therefore, the measurement method, as a residue method, can at the same time over-estimate discrimination by omitting certain variables and under-estimate the global phenomenon of discrimination, because discrimination is only considered on the labour market and does not integrate discrimination phenomena that occur before coming on to the labour market (pre-discrimination).

Results from first estimates on wage discrimination also show the impact of the reference population in the measurements; there is an interest here to show results from two types of reference populations and from several analysed populations.

In the same way, reflections can be made when the explained part of the gap is higher than the gap (this is the case for some results we present here) that means that the differences in characteristics between both populations give more differentials than the estimated gap. This would mean that the unexplained portion of gap would compensate and would even favour average characteristics of the lower discriminated population.

A last series of limits relates to the data of the survey. The data received through declarations can generate consequent effects on matters like wages or the employment categories concerned. In this case, descriptive statistics would produce structural effects. We can speculate on any consequences in the earnings estimates.

Therefore, all these limits and initial thoughts mean that the question of discrimination and its measurement methods must be dealt with carefully. As a result, the multiplicity of measurements is justified here (different reference populations, taking into account or not selectivity bias and measurements of the various types of discrimination possible on the labour market, and so on).

## Conclusion

This study testifies to the various phenomena of gender discrimination on the route from school to work for young women, with all the limits the analysis contains. By distinguishing two types of route three years after leaving school or university – insertion by means of a single job and experiment into at least two different types of employment – discrimination phenomena can be visualized when accessing a job, in wages, both on the labour market and within the company. Discrimination in access to employment is largely observed on access to a first job as well as on the job held when the survey was carried out when this job is different. In case of discrimination in access to employment and particularly when the first employment is won on the path from school to work, the under-evaluation of characterisics amongst young women is accentuated for young people of North African origin. Amongst populations from Southern Europe, young women appear to be less penalized than the general female population.

The analysis in evolution of wage discrimination in the same job or between the first job and the subsequent job held when the survey was carried out shows an increase in discrimination phenomenon, whereas the average differentials evolve differently depending on the routes taken. We note that penalization in wages for women appears to be less for populations of North African and Southern European origins than for young people of French origin.

Wage practices within a company and the labour market reinforce wage discrimination both against young women, and so for all populations, even populations of foreign origin. This wage discrimination seems to be formed by differences in wages within occupational categories. The differences of treatment and evaluation within the main categories of employment can indicate human resources management or work evaluation on a finer level (hierarchical coefficients, workstations, etc.). This is discriminating for women, whether they have only held one job and thereby an amount of seniority in the company or whether they have tried several solutions on the labour market.

Young women, whatever their origin may be, and whatever their school to work path may be, remain victims of discrimination. This phenomenon tends to increase during the route from school to work.

# Appendix

*Table 1A.1* Discrimination measures in the entry path for young people having only one job during integration: summary table

| | *Total population men–women* | | *French-origin population men–women* | | *Foreign-origin population men–women* | | *Maghreb origin population men–women* | | *South Europe origin population men–women* | |
|---|---|---|---|---|---|---|---|---|---|---|
| | *beginning* | *end* | *beginning* | *end* | *beginning* | *end* | *beginning* | *end* | *beginning* | *end* |
| *Job access gap* | | | | | | | | | | |
| gap | 0.064 | – | 0.06 | – | 0.088 | – | 0.089 | – | 0.044 | – |
| explained | 23.1 | – | 27.2 | – | 20.8 | – | −6.54 | – | 43.2 | – |
| unexplained | 74.9 | – | 72.8 | – | 79.2 | – | 106.54 | – | 56.8 | – |
| advantage | 49.6 | – | 49.6 | – | 49.5 | – | 51.2 | – | 48.8 | – |
| disadvantage | 50.4 | – | 50.4 | – | 50.5 | – | 48.8 | – | 51.2 | – |
| *Wage gap* | | | | | | | | | | |
| gap | 0.1154 | 0.1383 | 0.1118 | 0.134 | 0.1415 | 0.1686 | 0.1433 | 0.151 | 0.1042 | 0.1579 |
| explained | 63.3 | 59 | 62 | 57.8 | 75 | 68.6 | 89.2 | 71.3 | 70.3 | 71.7 |
| unexplained | 36.7 | 41 | 38 | 42.2 | 25 | 31.4 | 10.8 | 28.7 | 29.7 | 28.3 |
| advantage | 46 | 46.5 | 46.1 | 46.7 | 42.9 | 44.4 | 29.8 | 42.5 | 46.3 | 46 |
| disadvantage | 54 | 53.5 | 53.9 | 53.3 | 57.1 | 55.6 | 70.2 | 57.5 | 53.7 | 54 |
| *Wage gap BMZ* | | | | | | | | | | |
| gap | 0.1153 | 0.14 | 0.1111 | 0.1355 | 0.1444 | 0.1715 | – | – | – | – |
| inter–category | 0.005 | 0.008 | 0.005 | 0.007 | 0.012 | 0.013 | – | – | – | – |
| explained | −321.65 | −182.7 | −401.75 | −212.4 | −106.48 | −48.35 | – | – | – | – |
| unexplained | 421.65 | 282.7 | 501.75 | 312.4 | 206.48 | 148.35 | – | – | – | – |
| intra–category | 0.1095 | 0.1316 | 0.106 | 0.1276 | 0.1324 | 0.1581 | – | – | – | – |
| explained | 58.9 | 56.28 | 58.66 | 55.7 | 61.15 | 60.3 | – | – | – | – |
| advantage | 19.65 | 21.4 | 19.83 | 21.6 | 18.27 | 19.5 | – | – | – | – |
| disadvantage | 21.44 | 22.32 | 21.52 | 22.6 | 20.59 | 20.2 | – | – | – | – |
| Total explained | 39.83 | 42 | 37.51 | 40.1 | 47.21 | 51.8 | – | – | – | – |
| Total unexplained | 60.17 | 58 | 62.49 | 59.9 | 52.79 | 48.2 | – | – | – | – |

*Table 1A.2* Discrimination measures in the entry path for young people who changed jobs during integration: summary table

| | Total population men–women | | French origin population men–women | | Foreign origin population men–women | | Maghreb origin population men–women | | South Europe origin population men–women | |
|---|---|---|---|---|---|---|---|---|---|---|
| | *first job* | *current job* | *first job* | *current job* | *first job* | *current job* | *first job* | *current job* | *first job* | *current job* |
| *Job access gap* | | | | | | | | | | |
| gap | 0.059 | – | 0.052 | – | 0.106 | – | 0.128 | – | 0.053 | – |
| explained | 20.74 | – | 23.8 | – | 22.4 | – | 15.7 | – | 45 | – |
| unexplained | 79.26 | – | 76.2 | – | 77.6 | – | 84.3 | – | 55 | – |
| advantage | 48 | – | 48.6 | – | 44.6 | – | 45.5 | – | 43 | – |
| disadvantage | 52 | – | 51.4 | – | 55.4 | – | 54.5 | – | 57 | – |
| *Wage gap* | | | | | | | | | | |
| gap | 0.1138 | 0.1102 | 0.1098 | 0.1088 | 0.1484 | 0.1284 | 0.1718 | 0.1367 | 0.13 | 0.1423 |
| explained | 70.1 | 52.3 | 70.1 | 54.5 | 72.7 | 49.9 | 85.5 | 66.2 | 90.3 | 54.6 |
| unexplained | 29.9 | 47.7 | 29.9 | 45.5 | 27.3 | 50.1 | 14.5 | 33.8 | 9.7 | 45.4 |
| advantage | 44.6 | 45.1 | 45.2 | 45.6 | 40 | 40.6 | 34 | 37.2 | 31.5 | 40.7 |
| disadvantage | 55.4 | 54.9 | 54.8 | 54.4 | 60 | 59.4 | 66 | 62.8 | 68.5 | 59.3 |
| *Wage gap BMZ* | | | | | | | | | | |
| gap | 0.1157 | 0.1103 | 0.1117 | 0.1087 | 0.1509 | 0.1296 | – | – | – | – |
| inter-category | −0.011 | −0.01 | −0.01 | −0.008 | −0.015 | −0.02 | – | – | – | – |
| explained | 220.7 | 356.65 | 243.75 | 495.25 | 71.88 | 112.76 | – | – | – | – |
| unexplained | −120.7 | −256.65 | −143.75 | −395.25 | 28.12 | −12.76 | – | – | – | – |
| intra-category | 0.127 | 0.1211 | 0.122 | 0.1168 | 0.166 | 0.15 | – | – | – | – |
| explained | 70.17 | 55.47 | 69.36 | 55.91 | 75.14 | 55.94 | – | – | – | – |
| advantage | 13.8 | 21.11 | 14.48 | 21.18 | 10.12 | 18.93 | – | – | – | – |
| disadvantage | 16.03 | 23.42 | 16.16 | 22.91 | 14.74 | 25.13 | – | – | – | – |
| Total explained | 55.1 | 25.97 | 52.9 | 23.12 | 75.47 | 46.76 | – | – | – | – |
| Total unexplained | 44.9 | 74.03 | 47.1 | 76.88 | 24.53 | 53.24 | – | – | – | – |

## References


Blinder, A.S. (1973) 'Wage Discrimination: Reduced Form and Structural Estimates', *Journal of Human Resources*, 8(4).

Brown, R.S., Moon, M. and Zoloth, B.S. (1980) 'Incorporating Occupational Attainment in Studies of Male/Female Earnings Differentials', *Journal of Human Resources*, 15(1), pp. 3–28.

Céreq (2001) *Quand l'école est finie … Premiers pas dans la vie active de la Génération 98*, Enquête Génération 98, première interrogation.

Cotton, J. (1988) 'On the Decomposition of Wage Differentials', *Review of Economics and Statistics*, 70, pp. 236–43.

Dupray, A. and Moullet, S. (2003) 'Quelles discriminations à l'encontre des jeunes d'origine maghrébine à l'entrée sur le marché du travail en France?', seminar communication 'Marché du travail et genre dans les pays du Maghreb', Rabat, 11, 12 April.

Frickey, A. and Primon, J.L. (2003) 'L'insertion professionnelle après des études supérieures des jeunes femmes issues des familles d'immigrés des pays du Maghreb: une inégalité redoublée?' seminar communication 'Marché du travail et genre dans les pays du Maghreb' Rabat, 11, 12 April.

Heckman, J.J. (1979) 'Sample Selection Bias as a Specification Error', *Econometrica*, 47, pp. 153–61.

Joseph, O. and Lemière, S. (2004) 'La discrimination de genre et d'origine à l'encontre des jeunes sur le marche du travail: mesures a partir de differents aspects des situations professionnelles', *Document de travail Céreq Doc.net.*

Lemière, S. (2002) 'Mesure de la discrimination entre hommes et femme dans les primes salariales en France', *Cahiers Economiques de Bruxelles*, 45(2), Summer.

Meurs, D. and Ponthieux, S. (1999) 'Les inégalités salariales entre hommes et femmes dans les années 90', *Documents d'études*, 28, June.

Meurs, D. and Ponthieux, S. (2000) 'Une mesure de la discrimination dans l'écart de salaire entre hommes et femmes', *Économie et Statistique*, pp. 337–8.

Neuman, S. and Silber, J. (ed) (1994) 'The Econometrics of Labour Market Segregation and Discrimination', *Journal of Econometrics*, 61(1), March.

Oaxaca, R.L. and Ransom, M.R. (1994) 'On Discrimination and the Decomposition of Wage Differentials', *Journal of Econometrics*, 61, pp. 5–21.

Plassard, J.M. (1987) *Discrimination sur le marché du travail et information imparfaite*, Paris: editions du CNRS.

Reimers, C. (1983) 'Labour Market Discrimination against Hispanic and Black Men', *Review of Economics and Statistics*, 65, pp. 570–9.

# 2

# High-Performance Work Practices, Incentive Pay Schemes, Worker Evaluation Systems and Male–Female Wages*

*Nabanita Datta Gupta and Tor Eriksson*

## Introduction

A growing area of research these days focuses on the reorganization of work taking place in the modern-day organization, away from a task-specialized structure towards a more task-integrated organizational structure (Lindbeck and Snower, 2000). The new organizational structure has introduced work practices such as job rotation and learning across tasks, teamwork, decentralization of responsibility and worker participation in decision-making. The adoption of new work practices has led to a breakdown of traditional occupational barriers and the establishment of flatter organizational structures. Moreover, high-performance work practices are usually accompanied and sustained by performance-based pay, giving rise to new payment schemes.

In terms of their adoption, such practices diffused slowly in the decades of the 1970s and 1980s but began to be widely adopted starting from the early 1990s, and by 1997 approximately 71 per cent of US firms had adopted some form of innovative human-resource management practices (Osterman, 1994, 2000). In Europe considerably fewer employers have implemented these practices (see OECD, 1999), although, in Scandinavia, including Denmark, the new practices have been adopted more frequently than in the rest of Europe.

A great deal of the previous research in this area has focused on the effect of high-performance workplace practices on establishment-level outcomes such as total labour costs, and firm productivity (see Ichniowski and Shaw, 2003, for a recent survey). Relatively less is known about their effects on workers' wages, and in particular whether these practices affect groups of workers differently.[1] This is largely due to a lack of micro data on workers matched to firm-level data on the adoption of high-performance work practices. Even when wage outcomes are considered, previous studies have assumed that the returns to these practices do not vary by gender, race or other group characteristics, the typical outcome under study being total labour compensation or average establishment level earnings (a notable exception is Bauer and Bender, 2001, who examine the consequences of changing work organizations for wage differences between different skill groups). In this chapter we test whether the introduction of innovative human-resource management practices in recent times has had an impact on male and female wages.

By combining a unique 1999 survey of employers in Denmark to register data on their employees, we have matched data on a total of 224,262 workers working in 1,387 of the firms that were surveyed. Further, the firms that were surveyed were asked to provide information on the adoption of innovative work practices as well as new incentive-based pay practices. This allows us to estimate the wage impacts of new workplace practices on groups of male and female workers in the private sector in Denmark. Although sectoral affiliation has a significant impact on the overall gender wage gap in Denmark, we focus on the private sector only, where the gender wage gap has been found to be even larger than in the public sector (Deding and Wong, 2004).

High-performance work practices boost female productivity and thereby females' relative wages in a number of ways: first, practices such as job rotation and quality circles give women an entry into the production and design side, traditionally men's domain, allowing for learning and skill accumulation in tasks that may be more remunerative than traditionally female tasks. Secondly, decentralization of supervisory authority and increased worker participation in decision-making within the organization give women greater bargaining power and control over wages compared to hierarchical organizational structures. Further, practices such as job rotation could give women more flexibility in their daily schedules, allowing them to more effectively balance home and work responsibilities. Finally, in some recent studies, cognitive and social psychologists have explored whether women have an enhanced ability to multitask or superior communicative and collaborative skills, giving them a relative advantage in the modern workplace

(Williams *et al.*, 1991; Rubenstein *et al.*, 2001; Hannah and Murchaver, 1999; Underwood *et al.*, 1990, 1994).

On the other hand, the new economy and its new practices may widen gender wage differentials if women, because of lower labour force attachment and shorter expected tenures, find it costlier to make the needed investments to fully take advantage of these practices. Or, if firms find it necessary to give supervisors (mostly male) pay rises in exchange for their cooperation in supporting and disseminating these practices within their units (Black and Lynch, 2004). Thus, the overall effect of male–female wage differentials is an empirical question and our purpose is to estimate the effects of these practices on male and female wages, controlling for other human capital and firm characteristics known to affect wages.

As we will see below, new work practices are often introduced in bundles. Moreover, changes in how work is organized or jobs are designed are in many cases accompanied by changes in remuneration systems. This is only natural, as for instance organizing work in teams while paying employees for their individual performances would obviously be counterproductive. But, at least in some firms, some new work practices can be introduced without changes in pay practices, and the same is true also for the introduction of new pay practices in the firm. Thus, taking both new work and pay practices into account may be important.

Most of the new pay practices implemented in Danish firms in the nineties have in common that they introduce a stronger link between the individual's (or group's) performance and the compensation received. Moreover, an increasing of Danish firms have adopted performance pay in form of bonus schemes or stock compensation for their employees. According to two surveys carried out by the Center of Corporate Performance in Aarhus, in 1999 and 2003, respectively, the proportion of private-sector firms using performance pay increased from 40 to 63 per cent during the four-year period. Clearly, this is a potential source of major changes in firms' wage structures. Therefore, it seems natural to ask: What are the likely consequences of performance pay schemes such as team or individual bonuses, stock or option programmes, on the male–female wage differentials? Surprisingly enough, there are, however, very few studies looking at the effects of performance pay on wages in general (three exceptions are Booth and Frank, 1999; Lazear, 2000; and Parent, 1999), and the gender gap in particular, that could guide us in answering that question.[2] Zetterberg (1994) examined the impact on the gender wage differential in the Swedish public sector of the changes in the wage system in the late 1980s towards a more individualized wage-setting. He found that this change led to a marked increase in the gender wage gap. As many of the new pay practices adopted in Danish firms in recent years also imply an increased element of individualized pay, it is of considerable interest to learn whether these changes have had a profound impact on wage differences also in Denmark.

Performance pay systems may improve women's position to bargain for matching wage increases, thanks to the increased transparency in pay-setting, which could increase women's power to extract some of the benefits from the higher productivity created by the new work organizations. Of course, here it is crucial to distinguish between pay systems based on objective, quantifiable performance criteria and more subjective ones. Other factors that affect different groups' relative strength in rent sharing are the extent to which workers work together and therefore are able to discuss, organize and coerce, and the length of the workers' relationships with the firm (see Freeman and Lazear, 1995, for a theoretical analysis). We expect profit-sharing schemes to be gender-neutral. As a consequence of negotiations with the trade unions, in the 1990s several Danish firms introduced a so-called qualification pay system, which links the employee's pay more closely to qualifications obtained both before and after joining the current employer. The expectation when the system was introduced was that it would improve the relative wage position of female workers. Whether this has occurred or not depends on the extent to there are differences between the genders in the acquisition of these skills and in the skills that were considered important. Finally, in the discussion of the effects on male–female wages of new pay systems, an important development is that new forms of incentive-based pay and greater decentralization of pay negotiation replace centrally-determined wage floors which have historically been rather effective in increasing women's wages relative to men's in Denmark.

The rest of the chapter is organized as follows. The next section provides a brief review of the earlier literature, followed by a description of the data at our disposal. We then describe the empirical model, discuss some methodological issues and present the empirical estimates, respectively. A final section concludes.

## Previous research

Only a few previous studies have had access to data on work practices at the individual or firm level. A study of the impact of work practices on productivity by Black and Lynch (2001) estimates production functions using both GMM (Generalized method of moments) and within-estimator techniques on a representative panel data-set of businesses over the period 1987–93. They find that it is not so much the type of work practice but rather how it is implemented that matters for productivity. For example, productivity is higher in unionized establishments which adopt work practices giving workers greater decision-making authority, together with pay practices such as incentive-based pay schemes, compared to non-union establishments.

Another study on the relationship between workplace innovations and wages by Black and Lynch (2004) matches plant-level practices with plant-level productivity and average establishment wages and estimates production functions and wage functions using both cross-sectional and longitudinal data drawn from a survey of US establishments from 1993 and 1996. The study finds that the reorganization of workplaces to incorporate high-performance work practices leads to an increase in average establishment wages of about 6 per cent. But, at the same time, profit-sharing and/or stock options lead to lower regular pay for workers, particularly technical and clerical/sales workers. Their study is based on a sample size of 766 establishments in 1996 (cross-section) and 193 establishments in the panel (1993–96). Further, the sample is limited to the manufacturing sector only and is therefore not necessarily representative of the economy as a whole.

Cappelli and Neumark (2001) use a national probability sample of establishments that includes comparable measures of performance and work practices across organizations and are able to, by virtue of its longitudinal design, incorporate data stemming from a period preceding the introduction of these practices. This allows them to purge their estimates for firm or establishment-level heterogeneity that may arise due to high-performing firms having a greater ability to adopt such practices ('best practices'). Their findings point to higher labour costs per employee and therefore increased employee compensation from adopting these practices, but weak productivity effects so that the overall effect on profitability is inconclusive.

Caroli and van Reenen (2001) study organizational changes which imply a delayering of work organizations in a panel of French firms. They find that these changes had a positive impact on productivity. In addition, they find that the new work practices were biased against unskilled labour.

A paper by Bailey, Berg and Sandy (2001) examines the relationship between high-performance work systems (HPWS) and earnings of 4,000 management employees in 45 establishments in the steel, apparel and medical electronics and imaging industries in the period 1995–97. They find that, except in the case of medical electronics, management workers employed in industries that have more high- performance practices do earn more than those in traditional workplaces, after controlling for gender, race, education, experience and tenure. The lack of an effect in the medical industries probably reflects the importance of formal qualifications and education for pay in that industry.

We are aware of only a few micro studies examining the question of whether workplace practices can explain a significant part of the gender wage gap. Drolet (2002) using matched employer–employee data on 24,302 workers from the 1999 Canadian Workplace and Employee Survey find that without industry and occupation, workplace characteristics account for 27.9 per cent and worker characteristics for 10.8 per cent of the pay gap. However, the largest contributor of workplace characteristics is the workplace part-time rate, which alone accounts for 17.7 per cent of the pay gap. In terms of measures of high-performance workplace practices, Drolet (2002) has access to two measures, which are whether or not the worker participates in self-directed workgroups and whether or not the worker receives performance-based pay. These two variables account for 2.5 per cent and 2.3 per cent of the pay gap when occupation and industry are not included, and 2.1 per cent and 2.2 per cent when they are included. When occupation and industry are included, respectively, in worker and workplace characteristics the part of the pay gap explained by these components increases to 18.6 per cent and 42.6 per cent. Thus, while overall 61.2 per cent of the gender wage gap is explained in this study, the contribution of the two new workplace practice measures is minor and the largest single contributing factor explaining gender differences in pay between men and women in Canada appears to be industry.

Another recent paper by Garcia *et al.* (2002) investigates the relationship between job characteristics and the gender wage gap using data from a Spanish survey from 1991. They estimate the effect of individual and job characteristics on male and female wages, after controlling for selection due to participation and occupational choice. In terms of job characteristics they distinguish between five types of measures. These relate respectively to the degree of worker autonomy in the workplace, the degree of control by others over the worker's output, the degree of supervisory power over other employees, the power to decide on issues related to other employees and the degree of educational mismatch. Their results show that taking into account these types of 'job-quality' measures can explain a fraction of the wage gap that would otherwise have been attributed to discrimination. Still, a substantial portion of the wage gap (81%) remains unexplained in Spain.

Two previous Danish studies have used matched employer–employee data to study the effect of firm and job level factors on the gender wage gap. Lausten (2001) examines the gender earnings gap at the executive level using a data-set of Danish executives in the period 1992–95. Findings show that the gender wage gap among Danish executives is explained by individual, job, occupation and industry differences. In terms of job characteristics, there is information on CEO status, headship of division, an index of the level of authority held and board membership. Decomposition of wage equations into inter- and intra-occupational differences shows that two-thirds of the wage gap of executives is due to differences between occupations, while individual-specific characteristics contribute negatively, that is in favour of female executives. The gender wage gap among executives is found to be strongly influenced by the real level of authority.

Datta Gupta and Rothstein (2005) use matched employer–employee cross-sectional data from 1983 and 1995 for full-time private-sector workers in Denmark to examine how segregation of women by occupation, industry, establishment and job cells impacts the male–female wage differential. For both salaried and manual workers, job cells are found to be the most segregated, followed by occupation, while segregation is less evident at the industry and establishment levels. Based on fixed effects wage regressions, they find that occupation differences account for much of the wage gap between male and female salaried, but not manual employees in Denmark. Second, differences in actual experience, industry, and establishment explain much of the gender wage differential for manual, but not salaried employees. And, finally, even in the fullest specification, which includes human-capital characteristics and job-cell fixed effects, both salaried and manual male and female employees earn different wages within job cells.

None of these previous studies has, however, been able to examine the effect of a wide array of high performance work and incentive pay practices on male and female wages. By having access to an unique survey of the extent of adoption of high performance work and pay practices among firms in Denmark matched to a large employer–employee data base, ours is one of the few studies to be able to quantify the impact of such practices on the wages of male and female full-time employees in the private sector, controlling for other measurable individual and firm-level characteristics known to affect wages.

## Data description

The analysis uses a data-set on Danish private-sector firms with more than 20 employees, which has been constructed by merging information from two sources. The first source is a questionnaire directed at firms that contains information about their work and compensation practices. The other is a longitudinal employer–employee data-set[3] that provides information about firm characteristics and performance as well as about the firms' employees.

The survey was administered by Statistics Denmark as a mail questionnaire survey in May and June 1999, which was sent out to 3,200 private sector firms with more than 20 employees. The firms were chosen from a random sample, stratified according to size (as measured by the number of full-time employees) and industry. The survey over-sampled large and medium-sized firms: all firms with 50 employees or more were included, and 35 per cent of firms in the 20–49 employees range. The response rate was 51 per cent, which is relatively high for a rather long and detailed questionnaire of the type that was used.[4]

The survey represents a unique source of information on Danish firms' internal labour markets and changes therein. Besides some background information about the firm, the firm was asked about its work organization, compensation systems, recruitment, internal training practices and how it evaluates its employees. For a brief description of the questionnaire and the main results (in Danish), see Eriksson *et al.* (2000). Owing to the high response rate, the survey provides us with responses from 1,605 firms. For the questions concerning work design and practices, the firms were asked to differentiate between hourly paid and salaried employees.

Using unique firm identification numbers within Statistics Denmark, the survey data were supplemented with information about the firms as well as about their workforces. This information is taken from a large employer–employee linked database, which covers all private-sector firms and all the employees who worked in them (in Denmark) in any year during the period 1980 to 2000.[5] The panel contains detailed information about employee characteristics[6] (and hence, firms' workforces in any year) and about their labour earnings and other income. In addition, the panel has economic information about the firms, with 20 or more full-time equivalent employees, for the years 1992 to 2000.

Firms' use of work (and pay) practices can be measured along several dimensions. The measure adopted in the survey questionnaire is whether a firm has implemented one of six work designs:

1 *Self-managed teams*. Self-managed teams is a work organization which gives its members authority over decisions regarding how to perform tasks or even, which tasks to perform. Important aspects of team working is pooling of skills and skills development of individual workers.
2 *Job rotation*. Job rotation is a system where the workers are explicitly required to rotate between different jobs. This increases the variety of tasks to be performed by the employee and is also likely to enhance the employee's understanding of the operation.
3 *Quality circles*. Groups of workers who meet regularly to solve problems concerning productivity and people and to discuss aspects of performance and quality.
4 *Total quality management* (TQM). An important element of TQM programmes, of which ISO9000 is probably the best-known, that they include employee involvement.
5 *Benchmarking*. Benchmarking is a formal system of learning about practices in other firms and organizations.
6 *Project organization*. Groups of workers are organized in projects with defined targets, timetables, budgets and frequently considerable authority with respect to how to perform tasks.

It is important to note that the firms were also asked about when each work practice (if any) was adopted. However, one important piece of information we do not have regarding the implementation of the practices is the proportion of employees affected by the particular work designs.[7] Nor were the respondents asked to rank the practices according to some notion of their importance. The firms were also asked a corresponding question regarding the implementation of performance related pay (PRP) practices. More precisely the firms were asked whether they had adopted one of four PRP methods – team bonus, individual bonus, stock and stock options and profit sharing – for four different categories of employees: top managers, middle-management, other white collar workers and blue collar workers; see Eriksson (2001), for details. Unlike for the work practices, the firms were unfortunately not asked about when they had implemented the different pay practices. The questionnaire only asked the firms whether they had made considerable changes in their payment systems in recent years, without being more specific as to when or to which payment system.[8]

About every second firm in our sample has the so-called qualification pay system – a formalized wage-setting system where extra pay is given to an employee based on qualifications such as education, experience of a certain job or tasks, skills acquired through on-the-job training, and so on; 25–30 per cent of the firms have team or individual bonuses. The proportion of females is the same in firms with and without the performance-related pay systems, save stock and stock options where there are more women working in firms that have them, and profit schemes that are more common in firms with relatively more female workers. For both genders the following pattern can be observed[9]: with the exception for qualification pay, the average wage is higher in firms without the new pay practices than in those which have introduced them, and the differences are typically quite large. The pattern is rather peculiar as the qualification pay system is supposed to tie wages to qualifications and hence reduce differentials for other reasons, whereas the other payment schemes do not have that type of goals. As for the firm gender gaps, they are smaller in firms with a qualification pay system, whereas they are larger in firms with bonus systems, stock and stock-option schemes and profit-sharing schemes.

The questionnaire contains a number of questions regarding the firm's use of formal evaluations of its workers' performance. For this chapter we make use of the information about whether the firm has a regular, formal evaluation system and, if so, whether this is based on objective, that is, quantifiable, criteria, or more subjective assessments of the employees' performance.

Our sample is restricted to full-time workers only. This is to ensure that the males and females being considered are as homogeneous as possible and have about the same degree of labour market attachment. The full-time definition is based upon annual hours of work. Annual hours of work are calculated from the supplementary pension payment, or ATP register, which contains information on annual mandatory employer payments. The ATP payment is a step-wise function of weekly or monthly hours. We define full-time as working 1,166 or more annual hours, thus combining ATP definitions with a selection criterion based on inspection of the bimodal hours distribution. The hourly wage measure for both salaried and manual workers is computed based on annual labour earnings and annual hours of work calculated as a function of employer contributions (see above). The wage measure includes all paid-out supplements such as overtime pay, bonuses, premiums for shift work, night work and so on, but excludes fringes such as holiday pay or sickness pay.

Table 2.1 shows descriptive statistics for the full sample of private-sector employees attached to the surveyed firms.[10] Means are calculated separately by gender. Full-time males earn more than their counterpart females, the gender wage gap being 24.6 per cent. Males are also about a year and a half older, have slightly more education and tenure and less likely to live in Copenhagen. There are no big gender differences in firm size, firm age distribution or foreign ownership, but the average skill level of the workforce is higher among females than males. In terms of work practices, except for TQM and project organization, a higher

*Table 2.1* Means of variables by gender, full-time private-sector employees

| | *Females* | *Males* |
|---|---|---|
| Hourly wage rate | 154.823 (58.440) | 205.392 (113.831) |
| Age | 38.637 (10.368) | 40.163 (11.122) |
| Age-squared | 16.003 (8.378) | 17.368 (9.148) |
| Education | 12.333 (2.543) | 12.825 (2.718) |
| Tenure | 7.349 (6.358) | 7.565 (6.689) |
| Residence in Copenhagen | 0.455 (0.498) | 0.339 (0.473) |
| Firm size | 6.260 (1.818) | 6.038 (1.774) |
| Firm age 1–10 yrs | 0.100 (0.300) | 0.133 (0.339) |
| Firm age 11–20 yrs | 0.102 (0.303) | 0.098 (0.297) |
| Foreign-owned | 0.244 (0.429) | 0.247 (0.431) |
| Skill composition of workforce | 0.612 (0.296) | 0.548 (0.302) |
| Teamwork | 0.331 (0.471) | 0.243 (0.429) |
| Job rotation | 0.227 (0.419) | 0.209 (0.209) |
| Q. circles | 0.052 (0.222) | 0.043 (0.204) |
| TQM | 0.089 (0.285) | 0.092 (0.290) |
| Benchmarking | 0.103 (0.303) | 0.097 (0.296) |
| Project org. | 0.198 (0.399) | 0.198 (0.399) |
| Team bonus | 0.423 (0.494) | 0.358 (0.479) |
| Individual bonus | 0.467 (0.499) | 0.425 (0.494) |
| Stocks | 0.199 (0.400) | 0.207 (0.405) |
| Profit-sharing | 0.097 (0.295) | 0.103 (0.304) |
| Qualifications pay | 0.574 (0.494) | 0.576 (0.494) |
| Evaluation | 0.431 (0.495) | 0.380 (0.485) |
| *N* | 42,407 | 107,011 |

*Note*: Standard deviations in parentheses.

percentage of the females in our sample work in firms with these practices. The same is not, however, true for the incentive pay schemes where we see that while females have greater access to both individual and team bonuses, men have greater access to stock options and profit-sharing. Both sexes have about equal access to qualifications pay. Finally, a higher share of females works in firms which carry out performance evaluations of their employees.

Thus, Table 2.1 suggests that there may be sufficient differences in the composition and skills structures of the workforces of the firms in which women work compared to the firms in which men work, and that these differences should be controlled for when calculating the wage impacts of new work and pay schemes. This may be very important as the new work and pay practices are likely to be complementary to skilled labour, and hence neglecting firm differences in workforce composition may result in upward biased estimates of the impact of the adoption of the practices on wages.

Another issue to keep in mind is that the gender differentials in the wage effects of these new pay practices may reflect the sorting effect (see Lazear, 2000) – that pay systems rewarding good performance attract the best workers, and that these incentive effects may differ by gender. But there are also two other reasons why gender sorting may arise. One, emphasized by Goldin (1986), is that because female employees have shorter expected tenure in their jobs than men, they are less motivated by deferred compensation and other internal labour market incentives, and therefore firms employing relatively many women instead make use of contemporaneous incentive schemes like piece rates. Although gender differences in job tenure have decreased considerably over time in countries like Denmark, women's labour-force attachment may still be lower owing to women's need for more flexibility between work and home. Heywood and Wei (1997) argue that a greater share of female workers will in particular increase the costs of firms that rely on team production. Thus, women are expected to be disproportionately often paid according to individual-based payment schemes; see Heywood and Jirhahn (2002) for some empirical evidence from Germany on these hypotheses.

## Empirical model

The dependent variable in the analysis is the log of hourly wages of full-time male and female workers in 1999.[11] Separate regressions are run for salaried and manual workers. Thus, log hourly wages of individual *i* of job type *j* (salaried, manual) belonging to sex group *s* is given by:

$$\log W_{ijs} = \alpha_{js} + \beta_{js} X_{ijs} + \gamma_{js} F_{ijs} + \delta_{js} HPWP_{ijs} + \eta_{js} IPS_{ijs} \\ + \theta_{js} E_{ijs} + \varepsilon_{ijs}, \qquad (1)$$

where $X$ is a vector of individual characteristics, $F$ denotes firm characteristics, *HPWP* is an indicator for high performance workplace practices, *IPS* an indicator for incentive pay schemes, and $E$ a dummy variable for whether the individual is working in a firm which carries out performance evaluations of its workers. All full-time individuals employed in the firms that responded are included in the analysis, provided that the firm employed at least five male (or female) employees. Firms that had less than five male or female employees are dropped from the analysis. All regressions are estimated with robust standard errors, taking into account that the same firm appears multiple times in our data-set, thereby allowing for dependence in wage outcomes of employees within these firms.

As mentioned earlier, one factor that may impact the returns to practices in a wage regression is that more productive workers self-select into jobs characterized by high-performance work practices or where pay is tied to performance (see for example Parent, 1999; Lazear, 2000). While this type of selection may bias the return to practices upwards in a wage regression, it will in general have no consequences for the male–female gap in pay unless there is differential self-selection by males and females to firms offering workplace practices.[12]

## Estimation results

Wage regression estimates for full-time private sector female employees for a number of specifications are collected in Table 2.2 while the same for the male sample are presented in Table 2.3. In each of these tables, specification (1) only allows for individual productivity-enhancing characteristics to affect wages. The second specification (2) adds the effect of certain firm characteristics, namely (log) firm size (number of employees), firm age (captured by age range indicators) and the skill composition of the workforce, which is the share of skilled workers in the firm – including both white collar and skilled blue-collar. Specification (3) introduces the high performance work practices and specification (4), the additional impact of incentive pay schemes. In the last specification (5) we test the importance of worker evaluations on pay.

A little more than a third of the variation in wages of full-time private-sector females is explained by human-capital characteristics.

*Table 2.2* Wage regressions, full-time, private-sector female employees

| | (1) | (2) | (3) | (4) | (5) |
|---|---|---|---|---|---|
| Constant | 2.727 (0.085)*** | 2.595 (0.082)*** | 2.599 (0.074)*** | 2.617 (0.071)*** | 2.626 (0.069)*** |
| Age | 0.074 (0.004)*** | 0.074 (0.004)*** | 0.073 (0.004)*** | 0.073 (0.003)*** | 0.073 (0.003)*** |
| Age-squared | −0.081 (0.004)*** | −0.080 (0.004)*** | −0.080 (0.004)*** | −0.079 (0.004)*** | −0.079 (0.004)*** |
| Education | 0.046 (0.002)*** | 0.045 (0.002)*** | 0.045 (0.002)*** | 0.044 (0.002)*** | 0.044 (0.002)*** |
| Tenure | 0.005 (0.001)*** | 0.005 (0.001)*** | 0.005 (0.001)*** | 0.005 (0.001)*** | 0.005 (0.001)*** |
| Residence in Copenhagen | 0.161 (0.015)*** | 0.146 (0.01)*** | 0.146 (0.01)*** | 0.141 (0.01)*** | 0.140 (0.010)*** |
| Firm size | | 0.020 (0.008)** | 0.020 (0.007)*** | 0.023 (0.005)*** | 0.022 (0.005)*** |
| Firm age 1–10 yrs | | 0.052 (0.035) | 0.049 (0.028)* | 0.056 (0.023)** | 0.056 (0.024)** |
| Firm age 11–20 yrs | | 0.029 (0.013)** | 0.024 (0.013)* | 0.026 (0.012)** | 0.025 (0.130)** |
| Foreign-owned | | 0.039 (0.015)*** | 0.042 (0.015)*** | 0.046 (0.016)*** | 0.045 (0.016)*** |
| Skill composition of workforce | | 0.028 (0.036) | 0.034 (0.034) | 0.033 (0.028) | 0.039 (0.028) |
| Teamwork | | | 0.019 (0.025) | 0.015 (0.021) | 0.018 (0.021) |
| Job rotation | | | 0.046 (0.02)** | 0.053 (0.019)*** | 0.054 (0.018)*** |
| Q. circles | | | −0.085 (0.024)*** | −0.068 (0.022)*** | −0.066 (0.022)*** |
| TQM | | | 0.000 (0.018) | −0.009 (0.017) | −0.016 (0.017) |
| Benchmarking | | | −0.046 (0.025)* | −0.046 (0.023)* | −0.040 (0.021)** |
| Project org. | | | −0.007 (0.02) | 0.006 (0.018) | 0.005 (0.017) |
| Team bonus | | | | −0.027(0.019) | −0.033 (0.018) |
| Individual bonus | | | | 0.015 (0.013) | 0.012 (0.013) |
| Stock options | | | | 0.022 (0.015) | 0.022 (0.014) |
| Profit-sharing | | | | 0.052 (0.017)*** | 0.056 (0.016)*** |
| Qualifications pay | | | | −0.051 (0.017)*** | −0.051 (0.017)*** |
| Evaluation | | | | | −0.033 (0.014)** |
| Evaluation*objective | | | | | 0.037 (0.016)** |
| Adj. $R^2$ | 0.3665 | 0.3793 | 0.3842 | 0.3924 | 0.394 |
| $N$ | | | 42,407 | | |

*Note*: * Statistically significant at the 0.10 level; ** at the 0.05 level; *** at the 0.01 level.

*Table 2.3* Wage regressions, full-time, private-sector male employees

| | (1) | (2) | (3) | (4) | (5) |
|---|---|---|---|---|---|
| Constant | 2.552 (0.062)*** | 2.431 (0.054)*** | 2.431 (0.053)*** | 2.442 (0.051)*** | 2.437 (0.053)*** |
| Age | 0.087 (0.002)*** | 0.086 (0.002)*** | 0.085 (0.002)*** | 0.085 (0.002)*** | 0.085 (0.002)*** |
| Age-squared | −0.089 (0.002)*** | −0.088 (0.002)*** | −0.087 (0.002)*** | −0.087 (0.002)*** | −0.087 (0.002)*** |
| Education | 0.050 (0.003)*** | 0.047 (0.002)*** | 0.047 (0.002)*** | 0.047 (0.002)*** | 0.047 (0.002)*** |
| Tenure | 0.003 (0.003)*** | 0.004 (0.001)*** | 0.004 (0.001)*** | 0.004 (0.001)*** | 0.004 (0.001)*** |
| Residence in Copenhagen | 0.158 (0.014)*** | 0.121 (0.01)*** | 0.123 (0.01)*** | 0.119 (0.01)*** | 0.119 (0.010)*** |
| Firm size | | 0.018 (0.006)*** | 0.019 (0.006)*** | 0.020 (0.005)*** | 0.021 (0.005)*** |
| Firm age 1–10 yrs | | 0.066 (0.043) | 0.051 (0.034) | 0.056 (0.029)* | 0.056 (0.029)* |
| Firm age 11–20 yrs | | 0.040 (0.015)*** | 0.040 (0.014)*** | 0.042 (0.014)*** | 0.042 (0.014)*** |
| Foreign-owned | | 0.034 (0.014)** | 0.032 (0.014)** | 0.037 (0.014)*** | 0.037 (0.014)*** |
| Skill composition of workforce | | 0.130 (0.03)*** | 0.135 (0.025)*** | 0.121(0.022)*** | 0.119 (0.022)*** |
| Teamwork | | | −0.018 (0.015) | −0.018 (0.013) | −0.021 (0.013) |
| Job rotation | | | 0.052 (0.026)*** | 0.053 (0.023)** | 0.053 (0.023)** |
| Q. circles | | | −0.060 (0.029)** | −0.046 (0.027)* | −0.047 (0.027)* |
| TQM | | | −0.036 (0.018)** | −0.045 (0.016)*** | −0.043 (0.017)*** |
| Benchmarking | | | −0.014 (0.027) | −0.014 (0.024) | −0.015 (0.024) |
| Project org. | | | 0.015 (0.015) | 0.020 (0.015) | 0.021 (0.015) |
| Team bonus | | | | −0.027 (0.017) | −0.025 (0.017) |
| Individual bonus | | | | 0.034 (0.014)** | 0.035 (0.015)** |
| Stocks | | | | 0.026 (0.013)* | 0.025 (0.014)* |
| Profit-sharing | | | | 0.044 (0.016)*** | 0.043 (0.017)*** |
| Qualifications pay | | | | −0.038 (0.011)*** | −0.038 (0.011)*** |
| Evaluation | | | | | 0.016 (0.016) |
| Evaluation*objective | | | | | −0.015 (0.019) |
| Adj. $R^2$ | 0.3944 | 0.4093 | 0.4125 | 0.4169 | 0.4171 |
| *N* | 107,011 | | | | |

These are all highly significant and have the expected signs. The wage–age profile is concave.[13] Returns to education are around 5 per cent, while returns to tenure are minor. Residence in Copenhagen gives a 16 per cent wage premium compared to living in the provinces. When adding firm characteristics, fit improves only marginally, but older firms and foreign-owned firms pay significantly higher wages – 3 and 4 per cent respectively – to females employed in these firms. The next specification introduces high performance work practices.[14] Again, jointly, these factors increase the fit slightly, and in terms of individual practices, job rotation significantly increases female wages by about 5 per cent, while working in firms which have quality circles and project organization reduces them almost 9 per cent and 5 per cent respectively. The other practices do not have significant impacts.

However, as argued earlier, these practices more often than not are accompanied by pay practices as well which may be imparting omitted variable bias to these estimates. The simplest way to capture this is to sequentially add the effect of pay practices to the regression. Although there are correlations, the work practices in general retain their magnitudes and significances (although the negative effect of quality circles is mitigated), while among incentive pay schemes, profit-sharing raises females wages 5 per cent while qualifications pay, in which increases are tied to formal qualifications attainment, surprisingly reduce them by 5 per cent. Wage-setting in the firms that have adopted the qualification pay system is characterized by rules rather than discretion, and pay is not used as a motivator to the same extent as in other firms. (From the correlation matrix in Appendix Table 2A-1, we may note that the correlations between the qualification pay indicator and the indicators for the other payments systems are very small and negative.) By adopting the qualification system the firm commits itself to reward its employees for the skills they acquire. In return, the employees receive a lower base pay than what is received by similar workers in other firms.

Having worker evaluation procedures has a significant impact on female wages; it turns out to be very important to distinguish between the criteria used in the performance evaluations. Female employees in firms that utilize objective criteria[15] gain, *ceteris paribus*, a little less than 4 per cent relative to their colleagues in firms that do not carry out employee evaluations. On the other hand, evaluations based on subjective criteria – typically evaluations made by the employee's supervisor – have a negative effect on women's wages, both relative to employees in firms that use objective criteria and those that do not have performance evaluations.

For males, results are similar with respect to human capital characteristics, although the returns to age and education are higher for males than females, a result that is typically also found elsewhere, indicating perhaps gender differences in the type of obtained education or accumulated experience. Individual firm characteristics also turn out important for men although jointly the fit improves only slightly. For example, firm size and firm age 11–20 have positive and significant impacts, as does foreign ownership. In fact the return to working in a firm between 11–20 years of age is about twice that for females. Also, as in the case of females, the higher the share of skilled workers, the higher are male wages, and this effect is very strong, around 13 per cent, about four times that for women. Adding work and pay practices only marginally improves fit for men as well. Again, many of these have negative wage impacts, particularly quality circles and TQM, −6 per cent and −4 per cent, while job rotation also raises male wages by 5 per cent. Adding incentive pay schemes does not change the effect of work practices, suggesting low correlations between the two sets of factors, although the negative effect of quality circles again is reduced from 6 per cent down to 5 per cent. Among pay schemes, men gain 3.4 per cent from individual bonuses (but not team bonuses), 2.6 per cent from stocks, and 4.4 per cent from profit sharing. This is in contrast to the results found for full-time women, where only profit sharing gave a significant wage gain. Qualifications pay also reduces male wages but somewhat less than female wages. In general, it can be said that males seem to reap more wage benefits from incentive pay schemes than women. Finally, having formal worker evaluation practices does not impact male wages.

So far it seems that new work and pay practices only have modest effects on workers' wages. However, this could be a result of pooling together salaried and manual workers for whom the wage setting process could be quite different. Thus, in Table 2.4 we split the sample according to these groups and re-run the most general specification (5). Some interesting results obtain from this exercise: First, looking at human capital characteristics, in many respects, salaried females and males are indeed close while manual females and males share certain features, hinting at independent wage-setting processes for these groups. For example, the returns to education and tenure and residence in Copenhagen are about the same within these two groups, the only exception being that all males enjoy a higher return to age than females, both salaried and manual. Firm size and firm age effects also break out by salaried versus hourly pay status. Manual males and females seem to benefit from working in medium-aged firms, while salaried males and females benefit from working in older firms. Similarly, the gains to working in foreign-owned firms accrue mainly to salaried workers and the skill composition of the workforce gives a sizable premium to salaried workers but none to manual workers.

*Table 2.4* Wage regressions, salaried versus manual private-sector employees

| | *Salaried females* | *Manual females* | *Salaried males* | *Manual males* |
|---|---|---|---|---|
| Constant | 2.530 (0.152)*** | 3.206 (0.068)*** | 2.712 (0.147) *** | 2.754 (0.056) *** |
| Age | 0.078 (0.006)*** | 0.061 (0.003)*** | 0.084 (0.005) *** | 0.089 (0.002) *** |
| Age-squared | −0.083 (0.007)*** | −0.067 (0.003)*** | −0.085 (0.006) *** | −0.100 (0.002)*** |
| Education | 0.046 (0.003)*** | 0.020 (0.002)*** | 0.036 (0.002)*** | 0.023 (0.002) |
| Tenure | 0.003 (0.001)*** | 0.005 (0.001)*** | 0.002 (0.001)** | 0.006 (0.001)*** |
| Residence in Copenhagen | 0.149 (0.013)*** | 0.102 (0.012)*** | 0.121 (0.010) *** | 0.056 (0.013)*** |
| Firm size | 0.014 (0.004)*** | 0.020 (0.007)*** | 0.014 (0.006)** | 0.023 (0.007)*** |
| Firm age 1–10 yrs | 0.025 (0.020) | 0.067 (0.033)** | 0.042 (0.021)** | 0.076 (0.032)** |
| Firm age 11–20 yrs | 0.035 (0.019) * | 0.016 (0.013) | 0.046 (0.019)** | 0.028 (0.013)** |
| Foreign-owned | 0.045 (0.015)*** | 0.031 (0.016)* | 0.037 (0.015)** | 0.009 (0.017) |
| Skill composition of workforce | 0.104 (0.025)*** | −0.029 (0.030) | 0.102 (0.023)*** | −0.019 (0.033) |
| Teamwork | −0.003 (0.017) | 0.034 (0.026) | −0.025 (0.018) | −0.017 (0.021) |
| Job rotation | 0.044 (0.021)** | 0.055 (0.021)** | 0.002 (0.016) | 0.053 (0.028)** |
| Q. circles | −0.055 (0.042) | −0.060 (0.026)** | −0.020 (0.035) | −0.072 (0.029)** |
| TQM | −0.003 (0.022) | −0.021 (0.016) | −0.056 (0.02)*** | −0.045 (0.024)* |
| Benchmarking | −0.086 (0.035)** | −0.019 (0.022) | 0.009 (0.028) | −0.002 (0.039) |
| Project org. | 0.019 (0.024) | −0.017 (0.017) | 0.029 (0.018)* | 0.018 (0.021) |
| Team bonus | −0.014 (0.017) | −0.043 (0.021)* | −0.024 (0.016) | −0.031 (0.020) |
| Individual bonus | 0.014 (0.014) | 0.020 (0.017) | 0.040 (0.018)** | 0.035 (0.019)* |
| Stocks | 0.026 (0.017) | 0.007 (0.015) | 0.016 (0.017) | 0.021 (0.018) |
| Profit-sharing | 0.089 (0.020)*** | 0.034 (0.021) | 0.065 (0.026)*** | 0.015 (0.022) |
| Qualifications pay | −0.033 (0.011)*** | −0.057 (0.021)*** | −0.036 (0.013)*** | −0.048 (0.015)*** |
| Evaluation | −0.025 (0.018) | −0.034 (0.015)** | 0.023 (0.022) | −0.010 (0.020) |
| Evaluation*objective | 0.058 (0.020)*** | 0.025 (0.018) | 0.014 (0.026) | −0.023 (0.023) |
| $R^2$ | 0.4061 | 0.2866 | 0.3183 | 0.3863 |
| $N$ | 16,344 | 23,458 | 38,040 | 58,253 |

This pattern breaks down a bit when it comes to the new work practices. Here, it seems that salaried males are set apart from the others. For example, looking only at the significant effects all groups, except salaried males, obtain about a 5 per cent gain from job rotation schemes and the manual worker groups obtain a 5 per cent cut from quality circles. Salaried males get a 6 per cent cut in pay from TQM and a 3 per cent benefit from project organization while the other groups do not. So, in relative terms, these practices seem to hurt salaried males compared to the other groups.

Interestingly, for pay practices, we observe an opposite pattern in which salaried employees (particularly males) fare relatively better than manual employees, obtaining large gains from profit sharing, almost 9 per cent for females and 7 per cent for males. The gains from individual bonus and team bonus are, however, more evenly spread, while no group seems to gain significantly from stock options when disaggregating the sample, although the coefficient is positive in each case. Here too, we find that qualification pay has strongly significant and negative effects across the board.

Finally, we can note that the subjective evaluations have a negative effect on female manual workers' wages, whereas there is no impact from objective evaluations nor from the absence of performance evaluations. For female salaried employees, the pattern is the other way around. For them, working in firms that carry out evaluations based on objective performance criteria is associated with a six per cent wage gain as compared to those working in firms with other criteria or no evaluations. For both categories of male employees, evaluations have no statistically significant impact on their wages.

## Conclusions

This chapter has investigated the effect of high-performance work practices, incentive pay schemes and formal worker performance evaluation procedures on the wages of full-time private-sector male and female employees by combining information on the adoption of an array of workplace and pay practices obtained from a unique survey on firms to matched panel data on the population of workers within these firms. Thus, this is one of few studies to explore the issue of whether such practices affect the wage of individual workers within the firm, in contrast to the previous literature that is largely focused on establishment-wide earnings outcomes.

We find that the wage gains from work practices are in general modest, but especially job rotation and project organization seem to be schemes that impart positive effects, presumably through the increased learning across tasks, variation in responsibility and greater authority and control over task definition and planning implied by such practices. On the other hand, a relative wage disadvantage arises from schemes such as quality circles, which may impose time demands that are difficult to accord with other responsibilities.

However, these gains and losses are not evenly distributed across all groups in the workforce. It seems that salaried males is the group that gains the least from high-performance work practices, a not wholly unexpected finding as this is the group that stands to lose the most from the delayering of management levels and greater dispersion of authority following the move to a more horizontal organizational structure.

In terms of incentive pay schemes, all males gain from individual bonuses while salaried males and females reap benefits from profit-sharing. Thus, manual females tend not to be able to capture any gains from incentive pay schemes, a factor that might widen male–female wage differentials.

Finally, we find evidence that women working for employers having regular, formal evaluation systems based on objective criteria are paid higher wages. Distinguishing between salaried and manual females workers, we furthermore find that this still holds for the former, whereas for the latter subjective evaluations are particularly harmful. For males, we find no traces of wage effects of the performance evaluations.

In general, the gains and losses from new work and pay schemes are in many cases the same for men and women, so that we may not expect that they would generate large changes in the gender gap in pay. From a gender equality perspective, is this then, bad or good news? On one hand, the new practices do not seem to contribute much to a reduction in the gender gap. On the other hand, especially the increased used of incentive pay schemes which in conjunction with the decentralization of wage bargaining and wage setting is likely to have increased individualized pay setting, could have led to increased male–female wage differentials as in the Swedish public sector documented in Zetterberg's (1992) study. But it has not. From other perspectives, such as differences between skill groups, the picture may be different. At least, our estimations indicate that that high-performance practices narrow wage differentials between salaried males and other groups, while incentive pay schemes benefit salaried workers, particularly males, more than those on hourly pay, suggesting that further implementation of new pay and work practices would certainly affect wage differences between skill groups but that the overall effect may difficult to predict. Performance evaluation systems, however, particularly those in which evaluation is based on objective criteria, emerges as a way to narrow the wage gap between male and female salaried workers in the private sector.

# Appendix

*Table 2A.1* Correlation matrix of work and pay practices

| | *Teamwk.* | *Job rot.* | *Circles* | *TQM* | *Benchmk.* | *Proj. org.* | *Team bonus* | *Ind. bonus* | *Stocks* | *Profit sharing* | *Qual. pay* | *Eval.* | *Obj. eval.* |
|---|---|---|---|---|---|---|---|---|---|---|---|---|---|
| Teamwk. | 1.0000 | | | | | | | | | | | | |
| Job. rot. | 0.2662 | 1.0000 | | | | | | | | | | | |
| Circles | 0.1434 | 0.1851 | 1.0000 | | | | | | | | | | |
| TQM | 0.1693 | 0.2026 | 0.2227 | 1.0000 | | | | | | | | | |
| Benchmk. | 0.1288 | 0.2232 | 0.1739 | 0.2377 | 1.0000 | | | | | | | | |
| Proj. org. | 0.3011 | 0.2589 | 0.1172 | 0.2253 | 0.2433 | 1.0000 | | | | | | | |
| Team bonus | 0.0490 | 0.0690 | 0.0582 | 0.0667 | 0.0826 | 0.0288 | 1.0000 | | | | | | |
| Ind. bonus | 0.0316 | 0.0443 | 0.0653 | 0.0780 | 0.0672 | 0.0709 | 0.1687 | 1.0000 | | | | | |
| Stocks | −0.0401 | −0.0184 | −0.0272 | −0.0443 | −0.0050 | −0.0326 | −0.1540 | −0.1291 | 1.0000 | | | | |
| Profit shar. | 0.0785 | −0.0108 | 0.0143 | 0.0216 | 0.0093 | 0.0587 | −0.0244 | −0.0364 | −0.1173 | 1.0000 | | | |
| Qual. pay | 0.1331 | 0.1061 | 0.0227 | 0.0465 | 0.0080 | 0.0940 | −0.0256 | −0.0552 | −0.0387 | −0.0197 | 1.0000 | | |
| Eval. | 0.1420 | 0.1080 | 0.0530 | 0.1339 | 0.0994 | 0.1375 | 0.1241 | 0.1331 | −0.1019 | 0.0495 | 0.0504 | 1.0000 | |
| Obj. eval. | 0.0780 | 0.0852 | 0.0089 | 0.1255 | 0.0815 | 0.1091 | 0.1950 | 0.1945 | −0.1210 | 0.0287 | 0.0377 | 0.5627 | 1.0000 |

## Notes

* We are grateful to the Danish Social Science Research Council for financial support and to Jens Therkelsen for able research assistance.

1 And, yet, it is very important to account for individual skill differences as the new work practices are likely to be complementary to skilled labour. Otherwise, the gains of implementing the new practices may be overestimated.

2 The two main difficulties in studying the impact of new pay practices on individuals' wages are first that the switch from one compensation scheme to another can only rarely be considered as exogenous (and finding instrumental variables to correct for the endogeneity problem is close to impossible), and second, that data sources which have individual performance information under different pay schemes are very thin on the ground.

3 See www.ccp.asb.dk for a more detailed description.

4 The response rates for the size and one-digit industry cells vary only little: between 47 and 53 per cent. Thus, the representativeness of the sample is of no major concern.

5 The important feature of the panel is the link between firms and employees, which is consistent over time. The data originate from two separate registers maintained by Statistics Denmark: the integrated database for labour market research (IDA) and the business statistics database (BSD).

6 Worker characteristics at the person-year level include gender, age, ongoing tenure, and level and years of education.

7 If seems plausible to assume that the higher the number of practices used, the larger is the proportion of workers in the firm involved in some of the new work practices. Thus, the number of practices implemented can serve as a proxy for coverage.

8 More specifically, they were asked whether they had been working with the introduction of new payment schemes within the three previous years. 41 per cent of the firms answered the question affirmatively.

9 For details, see our companion paper, Datta Gupta and Eriksson (2004).

10 Note, these numbers in contrast to the discussion in the paragraph above, refer to the sample individuals, not the firms.

11 Although we know when work practices were introduced, since we lack information concerning the point in time when the pay practices were adopted, we are unable to exploit the panel aspect with respect to pay practices and instead we examine their impact on male and female wages by adopting simple cross-sectional regressions in the survey year, 1999.

12 We do not address this issue here, but in a companion paper based on firm-level data, Datta Gupta and Eriksson (2004), we address the selection issue by comparing establishment-level wage gains resulting from introducing at least one new work practice among incumbents only, i.e. those workers who were employed in the firm before practices were implemented, to those that arise among all workers, both incumbents and new entrants. Results show that while selection is present to some extent, but the large part of the gains is likely a result of rent-sharing.

13 All models have been estimated with actual labour market experience in place of age but age specifications produced a better fit and are reported here.

14 We have also estimated, albeit to save space not reported, the wage equations omitting the human capital variables. This yields larger coefficient estimates to the work and pay practice indicators, confirming our expectations that these practices are complementary to skills. This pattern seems to be more profound for female employees.

15 A little less than half (47.5%) of the firms that run performance evaluations are basing them on objective criteria.

## References

Bailey, T., Berg, P. and Sandy, C. (2001) 'The Effect of High-Performance Work Practices on Employee Earnings in the Steel, Apparel and Medical Electronics and Imaging Industries', *Industrial and Labor Relations Review*, 54, pp. 525–43.

Bauer, T. and Bender, S. (2001) 'Flexible Work Systems and the Structure of Wages: Evidence from Matched Employer–Employee Data', IZA Discussion Paper no. 353.

Bayo-Moriones, J., Galilea-Salvatierra, P. and Merino-Diaz de Cerio, J. (2001) 'Participation, Cooperatives and Performance: An Analysis of Spanish Manufacturing Firms', in T. Kato and J. Pliskin (eds), *The Determinants of the Incidence and the Effects of Participatory Organizations. Advances in the Economic Analysis of Participatory and Labor-Managed Firms*, Vol. 7. Amsterdam: Elsevier, pp. 31–56.

Black, S.E. and Lynch, L. (2001) 'How to Compete: The Impact of Workplace Practices and Information Technology on Productivity', *Review of Economics and Statistics*, 83, pp. 434–45.

Black, S.E. and Lynch, L. (2004) 'What's Driving the New Economy: The Benefits of Workplace Innovation', *Economic Journal*, 114, F97–F116.

Booth, A. and Frank, J. (1999) 'Earnings, Productivity and Performance-Related Pay', *Journal of Labor Economics*, 17(3), pp. 447–63.

Cappelli, P. and Neumark, D. (2001) 'Do "High-Performance" Work Practices Improve Establishment-level Outcomes?', *Industrial and Labor Relations Review*, 54, pp. 737–75.

Caroli, E. and van Reenen, J. (2001) 'Skill Biased Organizational Change? Evidence from a Panel of British and French Establishments', *Quarterly Journal of Economics*, 116, pp. 1449–92.

Datta Gupta, N. and Eriksson, T. (2004) 'New Workplace Practices and the Gender Wage Gap', Working Paper 04-18, Aarhus School of Business.

Datta Gupta, N. and Rothstein, D.S. (2005) 'The Impact of Worker and Establishment-level Characteristics on Male–Female Wage Differentials: Evidence from Danish Matched Employer–Employee Data', *Labour*, 19(1), pp. 1–34.

Deding, M. and Wong, K. (2004) 'Mænds og kvinders løn – En analyse af løngabet 1997–2001', the Danish National Institute of Social Research report 04:10.

Drolet, M. (2002) Can the Workplace Explain Canadian Gender Pay Differentials? Paper presented at the NZ Conference on Database Integration and Linked Employer–Employee Data in Wellington.

Eriksson, T. (2001) 'How Common are the New Compensation and Work Practices and Who Adopts Them?', Working Paper 01-8, Aarhus School of Business.

Eriksson, T. (2003) 'The Effects of New Work Practices: Evidence from Employer-Employee Data', in T. Kato and J. Pliskin (eds), *The Determinants of the*

*Incidence and the Effects of Participatory Organizations. Advances in the Economic Analysis of Participatory and Labor-Managed Firms*, Vol. 7. Amsterdam: Elsevier, pp. 3–30.

Eriksson, T., Poulsen, C.Ø. and Westergaard-Nielsen, N. (2000) 'Har nye arbejdsorganisationer og aflønningsformer fundet plads i Danske virksomheder?', CLS report, March.

Freeman, R. and Lazear, E. (1995) 'An Economic Analysis of Works Councils', in J. Rogers and W. Streeck (eds), *Works Councils: Consultation, Representation, and Cooperation in Industrial Relations*. University of Chicago Press.

Garcia, J., Hernández, P.J. and López, A. (2002) 'An Investigation of the Relationship between Job Characteristics and the Gender Wage Gap', unpublished working paper, May 2002.

Goldin, C. (1986) 'Monitoring Costs and Occupational Segregation by Sex: A Historical Analysis', *Journal of Labor Economics*, 4, pp. 1–27.

Hannah, A. and Murachver, T. (1999) 'Gender and Conversational Style as predictors of Conversational Behavior', *Journal of Language and Social Psychology*, 18, pp. 153–75.

Heywood, J. and Jirhahn, U. (2002) 'Payment Schemes and Gender in Germany', *Industrial and Labor Relations Review*, 56, pp. 44–64.

Heywood, J. and Wei, X. (1997) 'Piece-Rate Payment Systems and the Employment of Women: The Case of Hong Kong', *Journal of Comparative Economics*, 25, pp. 237–55.

Ichinowski, C. and Shaw, K. (2003) 'Beyond Incentive Pay: Insiders' Estimates of the Value of Complementary High Resource Management Practices', *Journal of Economic Perspectives*, 17, pp. 155–80.

Lausten, M. (2001) Gender Differences in Managerial Compensation – Evidences from Denmark. Aarhus School of Business Department of Economics working paper no. 01–4.

Lazear, E. P. (2000) 'Performance Pay and Productivity', *American Economic Review*, 90, pp. 1346–61.

Lindbeck, A. and Snower, D.J. (2000) 'Multi-task Learning and Reorganization of Work: From Tayloristic to Holistic Organization', *Journal of Labor Economics*, 18(3), pp. 353–76.

Organization for Economic Cooperation and Development (1999) *Employment Outlook*. Paris: OECD.

Osterman, P. (1994) 'How Common is Workplace Transformation and Who Adopts It?', *Industrial and Labor Relations Review*, 47, pp. 173–88.

Osterman, P. (2000) 'Work Reorganization in an Era of Restructuring: Diffusion and Effects on Employee Welfare', *Industrial and Labor Relations Review*, 53, pp. 179–96.

Parent, D. (1999) 'Methods of Pay and Earnings: A Longitudinal Analysis', *Industrial and Labor Relations Review*, 53, pp. 71–86.

Rubenstein, J., Meyer, D.E. and Evans, J.E. (2001) 'Executive Control in Cognitive Processes in Task Switching', *Journal of Experimental Psychology – Human Perception and Performance*, 27, pp. 763–97.

Underwood, C., Jindal, N. and Underwood, J. (1994) 'Gender Differences and Effects of Co-operation in a Computer-based Task', *Educational Research*, 36, pp. 63–74.

Underwood, C., McCaffrey, M. and Underwood, J. (1990) 'Gender Differences in a Cooperative Computer-based Task', *Educational Research*, 32, pp. 44–49.

Williams, C.L. and Meck, W.H. (1991) 'Organizational Effects of Gonadal Steroids on Sexually Dimorphic Spatial Ability', *Psychoneuroendocrinology*, 16, pp. 157–77.

Zetterberg, J. (1994) 'Effects of Changed Wage Setting Conditions on Male–female Wage Differentials in the Swedish Public Sector', *Public Administration Quarterly*, 18, pp. 342–58.

# Part II

# Promotions and Wage Growth

# 3

# Return to Internal Mobility in the Spanish Labour Market: Differences by Gender*

*Dolores García-Crespo*

## Introduction

Interest in intra-firm mobility and its incidence by gender has been increasing in the labour market literature. Theoretical models of promotions have explicitly incorporated gender into the promotion process by assuming that relative opportunities inside and outside the firm differ for men and women. Empirical studies of the relationship between gender and promotions use either specific firm samples or nationally representative surveys – as well as panel data and cross-sectional data-sets – although their results are not unambiguous. In an earlier work for Spain, García-Crespo (2001), it was found that women have a lower probability than comparable men of receiving a promotion, similar to the finding of Olson and Becker (1983) for the US labour market and by Pekkarinen and Vartiainen (2004) with data from the Finnish metal industry.

Recently, in a study for the British labour market, Booth *et al.* (2003) find, after controlling for observed and unobserved individual heterogeneity, that women are promoted at the same rate as men, in line with results obtained previously by Groot and Van den Brink (1996) also for the UK. Nevertheless, Hersch and Viscusi (1996), with data for a single firm, find that women receive more promotions than men. The large disparity of results can be explained because the studies differ on a number of dimensions, including the time period, the data-set analysed and the econometric method.

On the other hand, the wage gender gap is a stylized fact shared by all labour markets and well-documented in the empirical literature on this topic.[1] From an empirical point of view, the main challenge in discrimination analysis has been modelling the salary process in order to decompose the wage gender gap into two parts: a component due to differences in productivity-related characteristics by gender, and a component due to differences in the returns to characteristics. Moreover, previous empirical studies have emphasized the importance of the promotions as a source of wage growth. In fact, according to McCue (1996), internal mobility defined as promotion or other position change accounts for approximately 15 per cent of wage growth over the life-cycle for white and black men in the US labour market. However, notwithstanding the potential role of promotion patterns in explaining gender differences in earnings, there have only been a few empirical studies of this relationship, and the findings in the literature are also mixed.

In particular, with data from single firms, Hersch and Viscusi (1996) obtained that the wage payoff for promotions is greater for men and is not statistically significant for women, while Pekkarinen and Vartiainen (2004) found that women's promotion premium is higher than for men. These findings provide a somewhat different perspective than the studies based on national samples such as Olson and Becker (1983), who found no gender differences in the estimated return to promotion, or Booth *et al.* (2003) according to whom women obtain less wage gains upon promotion.

Combining these results, we conclude that to assess the role of gender in the promotion process, one must assess not only differences in the frequency of promotions but also their average wage effects. In this sense, the incidence of promotions on gender wage differentials can arise in two ways: first, women are less promoted than comparable men, and, second, they receive lower wages upon promotion. Therefore if women are less likely to be promoted than comparable men, these differences in promotion patterns may contribute to gender inequality in earnings. Even when men and women are promoted at the same rate, women can receive smaller wage increases consequent upon promotion.

Taking the previous evidence on incidence of promotions by gender in Spain (García-Crespo, 2001), this chapter focuses on the gender differences in returns to internal labour mobility. To date, no study has examined the impact of promotions on earnings, or its effect by gender. This study extends the previous empirical literature on promotion in Spain focusing specially on the following questions: are wage payoffs on promotion different by gender? How do gender differences in promotion translate into differences in wages? To what extent does the promotion gap contribute to the gender wage gap? In answering these questions, earnings functions are estimated by using a nationally representative Spanish household survey and by using Oaxaca's decomposition method.

The rest of the chapter is organized as follows. The next section briefly discusses the most relevant developments in the theoretical literature on promotions, which serve as the conceptual basis for this study. I then describe the data used in the empirical analysis, followed by a presentation and discussion of the main estimation results concerning the earnings equations and wage decomposition. The final section summarizes my main conclusions.

## Theoretical background

The model developed by Lazear and Rosen (1990) provides the first unified theory in which training, promotion and pay are endogenized. Their theory is driven by two key ideas. First, promotion decisions are not costless to a firm. Promoted workers have to be trained to fit their new roles, and training takes time that could otherwise be devoted to production. The return to investment is obtained in the future through enhanced productivity of the promoted workers, and is uncertain because the existence of turnover implies that some workers may leave the firm before it is reached. The second assumption of the model is that the only thing that distinguishes women from men is their comparative advantage in non-market activities, and so in their probability to quit. Consider two workers one of whom has a higher propensity to quit the firm than the other, but who are otherwise identical. The firm's expected net return to promotion will be lower for the worker with the high risk of turnover. Lazear and Rosen argue that women generally have higher productive opportunities in the household sector than men, thus have a higher risk of turnover, and for that lower rates of promotion and training, which contribute to observed pay differential. The Lazear and Rosen model also predicts that pay differentials should be favourable to women throughout the hierarchy. Moreover, since there is a group of promoted men who are less able than the least able promoted woman, the conditional mean ability both pre- and post-training is larger for promoted women than for promoted men.

As already noted, recently Booth *et al.* (2003), based on a study of the British Household Panel Survey 1991–95, found that women are promoted at roughly the same rate as men, but may receive smaller wage increases consequent upon promotion. To explain these phenomena, they constructed a 'sticky-floors' model of pay and promotion. In their model, women are just as likely as men to be promoted, but find themselves 'stuck at' the bottom of the wage scale for the new grade.

Their framework allows them to explore not only why women and men might have different promotion rates, but also why women might gain different rewards over time to promotion. The driving force is that women and men differ in their market and non-market outside options, or in the firm's response to these outside offers. Women may be disadvantaged in the outside market opportunities either because of discrimination in the outside market leading to fewer opportunities, or because family commitments limit female mobility.

If the driving assumption is that women have worse market opportunities than men, their model predicts that women: (i) are more likely to be promoted than men, (ii) less likely to quit to new jobs, and (iii) are likely to receive lower wage gains than men.

Booth *et al.* use the term 'sticky floors' to refer to the situation – arising either due to worse market alternatives or to less-favourable firm responses to outside offers for women – where women are promoted as often as men but receive lower wage gains consequent upon promotion. This means that in firms with formal wage scales, women remain stuck to the lower wage points on the wage scale of their new and higher job grade, thus gaining lower wage increases from promotion. The sense of the discrimination could be of the 'glass-ceiling' form, that is the discrimination occurs in the high-level but not lower-level jobs.

## Data and empirical model

In Spain there does not exist any survey designed for analysing either the incidence of internal mobility by gender or the influence of promotions on wages. Currently, however, eight waves of the European Community Household Panel Survey conducted over the period 1994–2001 are available. Like the British Panel this is a nationally representative random sample survey of private households in Spain. The Spanish Panel provides annual information on the timing and type of job changes made by a worker, but in contrast to the British one it does not cover job changes at the same employer.

For this reason, in this chapter I use data from the Encuesta de Estructura, Conciencia y Biografia de Clase (ECBC) for examining the wage effect of promotions and their incidence on the gender wage gap. The ECBC is a rich cross-sectional data-set, nationally representative, which contains individual information concerning personal, educational and training characteristics and work histories. A feature of this data-set is that it contains self-reported information about the internal mobility of workers at the firm.

In particular, workers answered the following question: 'How many promotions have you received since you began working for your current employer?', where to have received a promotion means to work at a superior level with more responsibility or authority. From the ECBC data-set we restricted the analysis sample to currently employed men and women in the time of survey aged 19–65. Then, the final sample to undertake the analysis contains 1,096 men and 689 women with complete information about all the independent variables use in the regression analysis.

There are advantages and disadvantages in using ECBC data to study the promotions and its influence on wages. A limitation is that we are not able to take into account the initial task assignment of workers. Since career advancement is an essentially dynamic phenomenon, the initial position would be important in this kind of study. However, a possible positive aspect of the data is that individuals report the number of promotions received, so we do not have to construct any measure of mobility but can use it directly from the survey. It is also worthwhile to note that using a representative group of workers is important in order to draw conclusions about all the labour market.

In Table 3.1 we present average wages[2] and sample size by promotion status for men and women referred to 1991. We distinguish workers who declared that they have not received any promotion at their current firm from those who have received at least one promotion. Looking at this table we see that about 32 per cent of all workers reported at least one promotion at their firm, but this figure is very different by gender. In particular, only 22 per cent of women declare to have received a promotion, while for men this figure is almost double. Moreover, for both men and women we confirm that intra-firm mobility plays a significant role in their earnings process. Overall, and on average, workers promoted have wages 26 per cent higher than the non-promoted. Nevertheless, this premium is higher for men.

The previous figures show the potential role of promotions patterns in explaining gender differences in earnings. So, in order to assess the importance of gender in the wage formation process and the consequences of promotion in the gender wage gap we outline two equations that incorporate intra-firm mobility variables in their specification. These equations are conditioned by the nature of our data, that is, we use the accumulated number of promotions at the current firm as a proxy of intra-firm mobility of workers.

*Table 3.1* Average hourly wage by sex (pesetas) and promotion status (standard deviations in parentheses)

| | *Mean* | *(S.D)* | *N* | *% overall* |
|---|---|---|---|---|
| Overall | 665.73 | (415.43) | 1785 | |
| Females | 610.34 | (382.60) | 689 | |
| Males | 693.88 | (428.57) | 1096 | |
| Females/males | 0.88 | | | |
| No promotion (1) | 609.87 | (417.57) | 1207 | 67.6% |
| Females | 584.12 | (389.73) | 539 | 78.2% |
| Males | 626.71 | (434.26) | 668 | 60.9% |
| Females/males | 0.93 | | | |
| At least one promotion | 791.23 | (382.21) | 578 | 32.4% |
| Females | 723.85 | (327.81) | 150 | 21.8% |
| Males | 808.63 | (393.46) | 428 | 39.1% |
| Females/males | 0.87 | | | |
| $\Delta$ Wage [(2)/(1)] | | | | |
| Females | 26.0% | | | |
| Males | 23.9% | | | |
| Females/males | 29.0% | | | |

*Source*: Encuesta de Estructura, Conciencia y Biografía de Clase (1991).

Specifically we first introduce in the usual semi-log wage formulation the number of promotions received in the firm, so the equation of interest would be the following:

$$\ln W_i = X_i\beta + \gamma_1 Nprom_i + u_i \tag{3.1}$$

where $W_i$ is the hourly wage for individual $i$, $X$ is a vector that picks up the individual human-capital and job-related characteristics and $u$ is a error term normally distributed, $u \sim N(0, \sigma_u)$.

The variable *Nprom* can be interpreted as a proxy for the acquisition of human capital that leads to higher productivity and wages in the future, and $\gamma_1$, in turn, picks up the wage returns to these investments.[3] Hence, the comparison between monetary returns of intra-firm mobility for men and women would be carried out through the estimated coefficients of the variable *Nprom* for both genders. Nevertheless this comparison has some limitations.

First, as already noted, the initial job occupation and the size of the promotions are not known in our data-set, so that different coefficients $\gamma_1$ could indicate a smaller return of the same ascent or also a promotion of inferior size, in the sense that it supposes a short distance from the individual position occupied before the ascent. For this reason, when interpreting the coefficient of the variable number of promotions, it will be assumed that it picks up the pecuniary yield that the workers obtain for upward professional changes of the same characteristics.

A second problem that appears in equation (3.1) is the known problem of sample selection. That is, if the observations that compose the sample have not been selected in the population in an random way, this implies that the error term of the equation (3.1) do not have mean equal to zero and the estimated parameters of the independent variables are not consistent. To overcome this problem, we use the usual procedure of estimation in two stages developed by Heckman (1979), in which in a first stage we estimate a participation probit model, and by using the estimated coefficients we build an auxiliary variable ($\lambda$) that, in a second stage, is incorporated as an additional regressor in the wage function estimated for OLS. Then, the equation to estimate would be:

$$\ln W_i = X_i\beta + \gamma_1 Nprom_i + \psi\lambda_i + u_i \tag{3.2}$$

In an alternative specification to pick up the return to intra-firm mobility, we introduce an interaction term to allow us to distinguish the return to tenure among promoted and non-promoted workers. Then, the variable called *Tenprom* is built as the product of the variable tenure at the current employer and a dummy variable that takes a value 1 if the individual has been promoted. In this way the equation to estimate is the following:

$$\ln W_i = X_i\beta + \gamma_2 Tenprom_i + \psi\lambda_i + u_i \tag{3.3}$$

## Promotions and wages

Table 3.2 presents estimates of wage equations for men and women following the two-stage Heckman procedure. The obtained results confirm many of the usual findings.

As expected, more education is associated with higher wages, for men and women, and there is not a significant difference in this return between sexes. The participation in job-related training at the current firm has a positive impact only on male wages, but has no effect for women.

Wages rise with previous experience of workers with other employers and with tenure, but at a decreasing rate. By gender, the wage experience

*Table 3.2* Two-stage wage equation estimates (I)

| | *Dependent variable*: ln*W* | |
|---|---|---|
| *Independent variables* | *Males* | *Females* |
| Intercept | 5.026 (15.87)* | 5.897 (17.19)* |
| Education | 0.048 (6.79)* | 0.046 (4.14)* |
| On-the-job training | 0.075 (2.91)* | 0.051 (1.13) |
| Experience | 0.011 (2.55)* | 0.015 (3.52)* |
| Experience²/100 | −0.039 (2.55)* | −0.037 (2.91)* |
| Tenure | 0.006 (1.71)** | 0.012 (1.69)** |
| Tenure²/100 | −0.003 (1.77)** | −0.018 (1.67)** |
| Number of promotions | 0.044 (4.77)* | 0.044 (2.32)* |
| Partial time | 0.296 (3.42)* | 0.307 (5.47)* |
| Fixed-term | −0.192 (4.68)* | −0.141 (3.14)* |
| Public sector | 0.123 (3.92)* | 0.232 (4.51)* |
| Manager | 0.366 (7.69)* | 0.332 (4.50)* |
| Professional | 0.341 (5.03)* | 0.256 (1.23) |
| Clerical | 0.157 (4.42)* | 0.179 (2.76)* |
| Sales | 0.090 (1.38) | −0.081 (0.91) |
| Other services | −0.003 (0.07) | 0.123 (1.36) |
| Non-qualified | 0.238 (0.96) | −0.267 (0.97) |
| Industry | 1.028 (3.35)* | −0.018 (0.05) |
| Service | 0.926 (3.06)* | −0.159 (0.43) |
| Construction | 1.006 (3.15)* | −0.078 (0.23) |
| 'Female's occupation' | −0.077 (1.57) | −0.134 (2.66)* |
| Inverse Mills ratio (λ) | −0.153 (3.78)* | −0.111 (2.56)* |
| $\bar{R}^2$ | 0.472 | 0.385 |
| *N* | 1096 | 689 |

*Note*: Standard errors corrected by White's estimator. Absolute-*t* in parentheses.
* Indicates that the coefficient is significant at the .05 level; ** at the .10 level.

profile for women is substantially steeper than for men. Moreover, an additional year in the firm is rewarded more for women than for men. These results, then, seem to reflect that both portable general human capital as the job-specific human capital increase especially female wages, a finding also obtained in the previous empirical literature (Hersch and Viscusi, 1996).

As for the central variable in the analysis, the number of promotions, the obtained evidence confirms that intra-firm mobility increases wages in a significant way. Nevertheless, the most striking finding in these equations is the absence of gender difference in the impact of number of promotions on wages. That is, the estimated coefficients $\gamma_1$ are equal in the male and female equations. As mentioned before, in a earlier work using the same data-set, García-Crespo (2001) found that women are held to higher promotion standards than men with equal measured abilities. Taken together, these results suggest that although the return from promotion is largely the same for men and for women, the promotion process is quite different for the two groups. So, unequal access to opportunities, rather than unequal rewards, constitutes the principal source of male–female differences in employment outcomes. Our findings are also found in Olson and Becker (1983) for the US market, and although they do not fit totally with either of the discussed theoretical models, they seem to be closer to the prediction of the Lazear and Rosen framework in which differences in promotion rates are explained because women have better outside opportunities in non-market activities.

In relation to the rest of variables, we find that having a part-time job or working in the public sector implies higher wage levels and this premium is higher for women.[4] Working with a fixed-term contract reduces wages, especially for men. Among occupations, the results show that manager-level and clerical occupations raise wages for both genders and professional occupations increase wages of men only. Moreover, there is no difference by economic sector among women but we observe important differences for men.

The coefficient of the variable that picks up the effect of sex within the wages effect shows a negative sign. This variable takes the value 1 when the individual is in an occupation in which female employment is higher than 50 per cent of the overall employment.[5] The negative coefficient obtained is consistent with the occupational segmentation hypothesis developed by Sorensen (1989) in the sense that working in a female's occupation implies lower wages. This effect, stronger among women, would be in line with previous research for Spain that suggested that intra-occupational earnings differences are an important source of the long-standing earnings gap between men and women (Hernandez, 1996).

Lastly, the coefficient for sample selection $\lambda$ is negative and significant for both men and women. The negative sign is usual in empirical literature and means that those individuals with more probability of being in work also expect bigger wages in the market (Heckman, 1979). It is also the interpretation offered by Dolton and Makepeace (1986) and Ermisch and Wright (1994).

As mentioned before, in a second wage specification we include a variable that allows us to distinguish the return to tenure for promoted and non-promoted workers. Table 3.3 shows that there are significant

*Table 3.3* Two-stage wage equation estimates (II)

| | *Dependent variable*: ln$W$ | |
|---|---|---|
| *Independent variables* | *Males* | *Females* |
| Intercept | 5.045 (15.92)* | 5.909 (17.35)* |
| Education | 0.049 (7.19)* | 0.047 (4.40)* |
| On-the-job training | 0.084 (3.28)* | 0.046 (1.01) |
| Experience | 0.010 (2.22)* | 0.016 (3.50)* |
| Experience$^2$/100 | −0.036 (2.34)* | −0.038 (3.02)* |
| Tenure | 0.007 (1.65)** | 0.010 (1.67)** |
| Tenure$^2$/100 | −0.008 (1.69)** | −0.018 (1.72)** |
| Tenure*promotion(yes = 1) | 0.004 (2.45)* | 0.089 (3.07)* |
| Partial time | 0.300 (3.44)* | 0.308 (5.48)* |
| Fixed-term | −0.191 (4.65)* | −0.144 (3.22)* |
| Public sector | 0.116 (3.66)* | 0.222 (4.28)* |
| Manager | 0.350 (7.25)* | 0.324 (4.44)* |
| Professional | 0.339 (4.98)* | 0.221 (1.06) |
| Clerical | 0.155 (4.19)* | 0.159 (2.44)* |
| Sales | 0.080 (1.22) | −0.092 (1.04) |
| Other services | −0.003 (0.05) | 0.107 (1.19) |
| Non-qualified | 0.219 (0.88) | −0.279 (1.02) |
| Industry | 1.017 (3.32)* | −0.029 (0.09) |
| Service | 0.921 (3.05)* | −0.164 (0.51) |
| Construction | 0.992 (3.01)* | −0.082 (0.24) |
| 'Female's occupation' | −0.089 (1.80)** | −0.129 (2.53)* |
| Inverse Mills ratio ($\lambda$) | −0.164 (4.04)* | −0.104 (2.41)* |
| $\bar{R}^2$ | 0.466 | 0.387 |
| $N$ | 1096 | 689 |

*Note*: Standard errors corrected by White's estimator. Absolute-*t* in parentheses.
* Indicates that the coefficient is significant at the .05 level; ** at the .10 level.

differences in the tenure *premium* according to internal mobility, and even that the coefficient for the interaction term is much bigger for women than for men. Again, this result would be interpret in the Lazear and Rosen theory in the following way: since women are held to higher promotion standards than men, the bigger wage *premium* reflects that promoted women are more productive than promoted men. Combined with the results obtained for the specification including the number of promotions, it would seem, at least, that they are not sufficient evidence against the main predictions of Lazear and Rosen's theory.

## Decomposition of the gender wage differential

In order to find the contribution of various factors to the gender wage differential, I apply a variant of Oaxaca's (1973) wage decomposition to my regression results in Table 3.2 in order to separate out the percentage of the observed wage differential that may be attributable to: (1) selection bias; (2) differences in the observed characteristics of the employees by gender and (3) differences in the treatment of, or returns to, these characteristics by gender. We can then write the following decomposition equation:

$$\overline{\ln W_m} - \overline{\ln W_f} = (\hat{\psi}_m \lambda_m - \hat{\psi}_f \lambda_f) + (\overline{X}_m - \overline{X}_f)\hat{\beta}_m + \overline{X}_m(\hat{\beta}_m - \hat{\beta}_f) \quad (3.4)$$

Table 3.4 reports the results of this decomposition applied to the selectivity corrected regression in Table 3.2. In our data, the male–female wage estimated differential is 0.135. Looking at this table we see that around 37 per cent of this gap is due to selection bias and 63 per cent is attributable either endowments or returns to such as endowments. Moreover, we see that differences in the coefficients are more important factors in accounting for wage differentials by gender than are differences in the endowments. Note that a negative sign for a component of the decomposition means that women have a comparative advantage in this component. Therefore, we can see that the majority of the observed gap, 93.8 per cent, is due to differences in treatment of endowments, that is male endowments are rewards to higher wages than female ones. Therefore, differences in endowments are favourable to women, and for this reason we obtain a negative sign for this component.

We are interested in the mechanisms behind this result. More precisely, we study the relative contribution of some selected regressors to the observed gender gap. Table 3.5 presents the same previous

*Table 3.4* Oaxaca's decomposition of the gender wage gap

| | *Bias* | *Δ Endowment* | *Δ Return endowment* |
|---|---|---|---|
| *Wage gap* | $(\hat{\psi}_m\lambda_m - \hat{\psi}_f\lambda_f)$ | $(\overline{X}_m - \overline{X}_f)\hat{\beta}_m$ | $\overline{X}_m(\hat{\beta}_m - \hat{\beta}_f)$ |
| 0.1354<br>(100%) | 0.0497<br>(36.71%) | −0.0413<br>(−30.5%) | 0.1270<br>(93.8%) |

*Note*: A negative sign means a female comparative advantage.

*Table 3.5* Contribution of the human-capital variables to the gender wage gap

| *Variables* | *Δ Endowment* $(\overline{X}_m - \overline{X}_f)\hat{\beta}_m$ *(1)* | *Δ Return endowm.* $\overline{X}_m(\hat{\beta}_m - \hat{\beta}_f)$ *(2)* | *Net contribution* *(3) = (1) + (2)* | *% gap* |
|---|---|---|---|---|
| Education | −0.0254 | 0.0191 | −0.0063 | −4.7% |
| Training | 0.0036 | 0.0081 | 0.0117 | 8.8% |
| Experience | 0.0374 | −0.0260 | 0.0114 | 8.6% |
| Tenure | 0.0206 | −0.0459 | −0.0253 | −19.1% |
| Promotions | 0.0210 | 0.0000 | 0.0210 | 15.8% |
| Total gap | −0.0413 | 0.1270 | 0.1354 | 100% |

*Note*: A negative sign means female comparative advantage.

decomposition for some human capital indicators. Again, note that a negative signs means a comparative advantage for women.

One of the most striking findings in this table is that education endowment and experience and tenure wage premiums are higher for women. The rest of the endowments and returns are more favourable to men. In particular, it is worthwhile to remark that the average education level is higher for women, and although the return to education is higher for men the net effect is favourable to women, being 4.7 per cent of the overall gap. The same net effect appears with tenure although for the reverse reason: women are rewarded more in tenure but this is lower than for men. Again, these findings can suggest that since women are more educated than men but are held to higher promotion standards than comparable men, their payoff for the permanent human capital is higher after promotion has happened.

Finally, we find that the intra-firm mobility component can explain 15.8 per cent of the gender wage differential. Then, since returns by gender are comparable, this means that if women were to have the same promotions patterns than men the wage differential would reduce by 15.8 per cent.

## Concluding remarks

In this chapter I have tried to add some empirical evidence in relation to intra-firm mobility in the Spanish labour market. Previous empirical evidence has found that women are held to higher promotion standards than men, and therefore receive fewer promotions than men with equal measured abilities according to an earlier analysis (García-Crespo, 2001).

Following this line of research I have focused here on an aspect of the wage determination process often suggested but little tested as an important source of male–female earnings differences: the influence of promotions on the gender wage gap.

With data from a nationally representative survey, the Encuesta de Estructura, Conciencia y Biografía de Clase, the effect of promotions on wages for men and women has been estimated and the magnitude of their contributions assessed, as incidence and return by gender, to the overall gender wage gap.

The empirical evidence in this study indicates that the promotion process has an important influence on male and female wages. However, after controlling for job-related and human-capital characteristics, we find no significant gender difference in the effect of promotions on wages. In fact, the payoff for an additional promotion is 4 per cent for men and women. Therefore, promotions contribute to higher wage levels for both genders. Our findings are the same as Olson and Becker (1983) with US panel data: a higher male promotion rate, but after controlling for human-capital and job-related characteristics the returns to promotions are comparable for men and women. Therefore, on average, in Spain there are differences in promotion rates by gender but not in returns to promotion.

Taking all the results together, they suggest that although the return from promotions is largely the same for men and for women, the promotion process is quite different for the two groups. More precisely, our findings seem to indicate that unequal access to opportunities, rather than unequal returns, constitutes the principal source of male–female difference in employment outcomes. In particular, the decomposition analysis of the gender wage gap shows that intra-firm mobility can explain 15.8 per cent of the net gender wage differential. Since returns by gender are comparable, this means that if women were to have the same promotions patterns than men, the wage differential would reduce by 15.8 per cent.

Theoretically, although our results do not fit totally with either of the discussed theoretical models, than seem to be closer to the prediction of the Lazear and Rosen framework.

## Notes

* Financial support of the project, SEC2003-08855-C01-01, is gratefully acknowledged. The author would like to thank María Lucía Navarro, María Isabel Aguilar and an anonymous referee for helpful comments and suggestions. The usual caveat applies.

1 Recent surveys are Altonji and Blank (1999) and Blau and Kahn (1996).
2 The hourly wage is derived from information about monthly net wage and the number of hours worked in a week. This wage includes neither premia nor bonuses.
3 We follow Hersch and Viscusi (1996) who consider that the history of promotions affects wages and therefore assume a recursive model. In their study they analysed a cross-section sample with promotions as an accountable data variable as we do.
4 Lassibille (1998) also finds that the mean wage is higher in the Spanish public sector for both sexes by using the Household Survey (1990–91). Moreover, he notes that the public–private earnings differential is much larger for females than for males.
5 According to the information of the Labour Force Survey (1991).

## References

Altonji, J. and Blank, R. (1999) 'Race and Gender in the Labor Market', in O. Aschenfelter and R. Card (eds), *Handbook of Labor Economics*, Vol. 3C, ch. 38. Netherlands: Elsevier, North-Holland.

Blau, F.D. and Kahn, L.M. (1996) 'Wage Structure and Gender Earnings Differentials: An International Comparasion', *Economica*, 63, pp. S29–S62.

Booth, A., Francesconi, M. and Frank, J. (2003) 'A Sticky Floors Model of Promotion, Pay and Gender', *European Economic Review*, 47(2), pp. 295–322.

Dolton, P.J. and Makepeace, G.H. (1988) 'Interpreting Sample Selection Effects', *Economics Letters*, 24, pp. 373–9.

Encuesta sobre Estructura, Conciencia y Biografía de Clase (1991). Madrid: Instituto Nacional de Estadística, Instituto de la Mujer y Comunidad de Madrid.

Ermisch, J.F. and Wright, E.R. (1994) 'Interpretation of Negative Sample Selection Effects in Wage Offer Equation', *Applied Economics Letters*, 1, pp. 187–9.

García-Crespo, D. (2001) 'Promotions in the Spanish Labour Market: Differences by Gender', *Oxford Bulletin of Economics and Statistics*, 63(5), pp. 599–615.

Groot, W. and Van den Brink, H.M. (1996) 'Glass Ceilings or Dead Ends: Job Promotions of Men and Women Compared', *Economics Letters*, 53, pp. 221–6.

Heckman, J. (1979) 'Sample Selection Bias as a Specification Error', *Econometrica*, 47, pp. 153–61.

Hernández, P.J. (1996). 'Segregación ocupacional de la mujer y discriminación salarial', *Revista de Economía Aplicada*, 4, pp. 57–80.

Hersch, J. and Viscusi, W.K. (1996) 'Gender Differences in Promotions and Wages', *Industrial Relations*, 35(4), pp. 461–72.

Jones, D.R. and Makepeace, G.H. (1996) 'Equal Worth, Equal Opportunities: Pay and Promotion in an Internal Labour Market', *The Economic Journal*, 106, pp. 401–9.

Labour Force Survey (1991) Madrid: Instituto Nacional de Estadística.

Lassibille, G. (1998) 'Wage Gaps between the Public and Private Sectors in Spain', *Economics of Education Review*, 17(1), pp. 83–92.

Lazear, E.P. and Rosen, S. (1990) 'Male–Female Wage Differentials in Job Ladders', *Journal of Labor Economics*, 8, pp. S106–S123.

McCue, K. (1996) 'Promotions and Wage Growth', *Journal of Labor Economics*, 14(2), pp. 175–209.

Oaxaca, R.L. (1973). 'Male–Female Wage Differentials in Urban Labor Markets', *International Economic Review*, 14, pp. 693–709.

Olson, C.A. and Becker, B.E. (1983) 'Sex Discrimination in the Promotions Process', *Industrial and Labor Relations Review*, 36(4), pp. 625–41.

Pekkarinen, T. and Vartiainen, J. (2004) 'Gender Differences in Job Assignment and Promotions in a Complexity Ladder of Jobs', *IZA Discussion Paper*, no. 1184.

Sorensen, E. (1989) 'Measuring the Pay Disparity between Typically Female Occupations and Other Jobs: A Bivariate Selectivity Approach', *Industrial and Labor Relations Review*, 42(4), pp. 624–39.

# 4
# Gender Differences in Wage Growth and Promotion in Luxembourg

*Philippe Van Kerm*

## Introduction

There is no dispute about the fact that women tend to fare worse than men in the labour market; evidence of a wage gap in pay is abundant. This chapter attempts to complement this static picture with an examination of gender differences in promotion and wage growth. These issues relate to the ongoing debate about the existence (or otherwise) of a 'glass ceiling' above women in the labour market – an invisible barrier that inhibits promotion opportunities for women (but not men) and prevents women from reaching top-level (high-wage) positions in firms. Do such 'glass ceilings' exist and exacerbate the male–female wage differential? Or, on the contrary, are women able to take advantage of promotions and other opportunities for wage growth to catch up partially to male wage rates?

The majority of studies addressing this question have relied on personnel record data (see Hersch and Viscusi, 1996, for an oft-cited example). The data-sets typically analysed provide detailed information on individual wages, on the evolution thereof, and on internal promotions as well as on institutional context (for example on the pay schedule in use in the firm). However, the conclusions drawn are not easily generalized as firm idiosyncratic features may impact on the results. There is therefore interest in complementary analysis using survey data.

Existing evidence based on surveys representative of large populations (rather than based on personnel record data) remains relatively scarce, and results are mixed. The majority of recent studies have focused on

Britain (Groot and van den Brink, 1996; Booth and Francesconi, 2000; Francesconi, 2001; Booth *et al.*, 2003; Manning and Robinson, 2004). Analysis of US data can also be found in McCue (1996) and Cobb-Clark (2001). In general, gender differences have not been reported to be large and there is no strong support for the standard 'glass-ceiling' hypothesis: promotion probabilities and wage growth often turn out to be similar between men and women.[1] Note that the wage return to promotion has been reported to differ more substantially between men and women (Cobb-Clark, 2001; Booth *et al.*, 2003).[2] Overall, no clear stylized facts have yet been established. Further investigation of new data sources is therefore of interest.

This chapter provides additional empirical evidence using panel-survey data, that is data collected at repeated interviews, for a sample of individuals representative of the population residing in Luxembourg, the Panel Socio-Économique 'Liewen zu Lëtzebuerg' for the period 1998–2001. This data-set proved valuable for the problem at hand since (i) it is nationally representative of the population (rather than focused on a single firm) thereby allowing firm specificities to be averaged out, (ii) it contains direct information on whether workers have been promoted in the last year, (iii) it permits to identify wage growth over time, and finally (iv) it contains data on a large set of covariates so that it is possible to control for differences in workers' and jobs' attributes.

As a first step, the analysis attempts to identify if there are observable differences in promotion rates between males and females. Differences in wage growth are then considered. In a second step, local kernel weighting methods are applied to assess men's and women's wage growth rates, as well as promotion probabilities, conditionally on the base period wage level. It makes it possible to examine the issue in greater detail and identify what happens at different points on the wage scale. If 'glass ceilings' are in effect, we may anticipate differences in wage growth and promotion probabilities to appear more strikingly for high-wage workers. Similarly, some of the forces at play in the 'sticky-floors' model of Booth *et al.* (see note 2) are very likely to have different effects for men and women at different points on the wage scale (for example the distribution of outside offers, or of non-market opportunities). Looking at the mean only, as typically done in empirical analyses, may therefore return a mitigated picture of this issue.

The chapter is structured as follows. The next section describes the data used, followed by a brief presentation of the raw differences in wages, promotion and wage growth between men and women. I then examine the differences after controlling for sample composition differences, before reexamining the results for varying levels of wage. A final section concludes.

## Data

The data are drawn from the second Panel Socio-Economique 'Liewen zu Lëtzebuerg' (PSELL II) survey collected by CEPS/INSTEAD. PSELL II is a large-scale annual longitudinal survey representative of the population residing in the Grand-Duchy of Luxembourg. It is a multi-purpose survey gathering information on activity status and employment, wages and income, family structure, accommodation, and so on. The first interview was conducted in 1995, and the sample has been followed up to 2002. Refreshment samples of immigrants were added every two years.

In PSELL II, the information collected in survey year $y$ refers either to the whole preceding year, or to the situation at 31 December of year $y - 1$. In particular, detailed information on wages and employment conditions are available for all interviewees employed at 31 December of year $y - 1$. It is therefore possible to track, for example, wage changes for all individuals at work in December of consecutive years. From wave four onwards, that is for survey years 1998 to 2002, workers were asked to report if they experienced a promotion or if they changed job at some time during the preceding year ($y - 1$). From wave five onwards, it is also possible to identify whether the change of job is voluntary or unvoluntary (that is due to dismissal or firm closing). The present analysis consequently concentrates on survey years 1999–2002 (covering data for the period 1998–2001).[3]

The basic sub-sample used for estimation includes all men and women aged between 17 and 65 who are not enrolled in full-time education. In order to concentrate on people with strong labour-market attachment, only people reporting 'work' as main activity and reporting working more than 32 hours per week are considered as 'at work'. Self-employed and unpaid workers, for whom wage growth is ill-defined, are also discarded from the 'at work' sample.

The wage variable is the monthly wage deflated to the base year 2000 using consumer price indices and expressed in euros. The reported wage is net of taxes and social security contributions (data on gross wage are only available from survey year 2001 onwards). The fact that wages are reported net of taxes is a limitation of the analysis as wage increases may be due to changes in the tax treatment, due, for example, to household composition change, and not necessarily changes in the gross wage. Bias in gender comparisons might be introduced if tax treatment changes are not equally distributed between men and women. Results should be interpreted in terms of the 'disposable earnings' of workers and not in terms of the 'price of labour' paid by the employers. Throughout the chapter, wage growth is defined as $100^*(\ln(w_{it}) - \ln(w_{it-1}))$, where $t$ refers to 31 December of year $y - 1$, and $w_{it}$ is the real net monthly wage. This percentage wage growth indicator is estimated for the sub-sample of respondents who remained in the 'at work' group for two consecutive waves.

Additional covariates selected for the analysis are the age and gender of respondents, their education level, nationality, and their work experience (respondents provide an estimate of their number of years of professional activity).[4] For 'at work' individuals, the job-related variables are years of tenure with current employer, type of contract (fixed-term or permanent), one-digit ISCO codes of worker's occupation, one-digit NACE codes of employer's activity, and three firm size dummies (1–50, 51–200, and 200+ employees). Data on marital status, household composition, and father's and mother's occupation when finished full-time education for all sample members are also used to control for non-random selection in the 'at work' sample.

All analyses are based on the pooled sample of survey waves 1999 to 2002. Each interviewee can therefore contribute up to four person-year observations. After removing observations with incomplete data, the available sample consists of 14,123 person-years in total (6,869 for men and 7,254 for women), of which 6,404 are for people 'at work' at two consecutive waves (4,571 for men and 1,833 for women). These 6,404 person-years observations are obtained from 2,351 distinct interviewees (1,614 men and 737 women) who provide at least one person-year observation.

## Raw gender differences in promotion and wage growth rates

Raw statistics on wages, wage growth and promotion are reported in Table 4.1. The well-known gap in average pay between working men and working women is evident: women's mean wage is 26 per cent lower than men's mean wage in our sample, which is in line with the estimates of Lejealle (2002) for the year 2000. Similarly, differences between quintile points remain relatively constant near this same value; both low-wage women and high-wage women are paid about 26 per cent less than low-wage men and high-wage men respectively.[5]

*Table 4.1* Raw statistics on gender differences in monthly wage, promotion and job change rates, and annual wage growth

| | *Men* (1) | *Women* (2) | *Difference* (1)–(2) |
|---|---|---|---|
| *Monthly wage (in constant 2000 euros)* | | | |
| Mean | 2,770 | 2,051 | 719* |
| Bottom quintile | 1,653 | 1,260 | 393* |
| Top quintile | 3,622 | 2,702 | 920* |
| *Percentage promoted/changing job each year* | | | |
| Promotion | 18.1 | 14.7 | 3.4* |
| Job change (all) | 6.2 | 8.3 | −2.1* |
| Job change (unvoluntary only) | 1.1 | 1.5 | 0.5 |
| *Real wage growth rate (in per cent)* | | | |
| Mean | 2.84 | 3.92 | −1.08* |
| 1st decile | −8.95 | −8.22 | −0.73 |
| 2nd decile | −3.12 | −2.86 | −0.26 |
| 3rd decile | −1.06 | −0.99 | −0.70 |
| 4th decile | −0.43 | 0.70 | −1.13* |
| 5th decile | 1.78 | 2.37 | −0.60* |
| 6th decile | 3.78 | 4.36 | −0.58 |
| 7th decile | 6.05 | 6.66 | −0.62 |
| 8th decile | 9.59 | 10.61 | −1.02 |
| 9th decile | 17.17 | 17.75 | −0.59 |
| *Promotion/job change wage growth* | | | |
| Mean wage growth upon promotion | 5.88 | 5.78 | 0.11 |
| Mean wage growth upon job change | 7.55 | 10.98 | −3.43 |

*Notes*: Asterisks indicate that the difference between men and women is statistically significant at the 5 per cent significance level. Wages are expressed in constant 2000 euros. Sample consists of full-time workers at two consecutive interviews from PSELL II with data from survey years 1999–2002 pooled.

Turning to differences in promotion and wage growth rates provides a different picture. The first observation is that men are promoted at a higher rate than women. The promotion rate of women is 19 per cent lower than men's. This figure can therefore be added to the general picture of the disadvantage of women in the labour market. (Note, however, that this observation is not in line with previous research on Britain or the United States.)

The second observation is that women are more likely to have changed job between two interviews. This is a surprising result as women are generally considered as less flexible because of family-related commitments, and therefore less able to take advantage of opportunities of changing employers. Women are more likely to have changed jobs for unvoluntary reasons, but that is only a small part of all job changes. This seems to suggest that women on the Luxembourg labour market are not less flexible than men once they pass the participation hurdle – keep in mind that we only look at a sample of full-time workers and female participation in the labour market in Luxembourg remains low in comparison with other European countries (Statec, 2003). It is important, however, to bear in mind the geographical concentration of jobs in the Grand-Duchy of Luxembourg. It is possible that geographical mobility constraints are not as binding for women as in larger markets where more distant moves may be associated with employer changes.

The third observation is that, by contrast to promotion statistics, wage-growth statistics are generally more favourable to women. The mean annual percentage growth of real monthly wage is 2.84 for men against 3.92 for women. Wage growth is highly variable across individuals, as statistics for the different deciles of the wage growth distribution show. Ten per cent of men and women experience real wage losses of more than 8 per cent, whereas 10 per cent of men and women experience real wage gains of more than 17 per cent. However, the situation of women is better at all deciles (although the difference is only statistically significant near the median): worse-off women tend to lose less than worse-off men and better-off women tend to win more than better-off men. The differences, however, are relatively small in view of the overall distribution of wage growth.

## What does remain after controlling for sample composition differences?

Drawing conclusions about the degree of 'discrimination' against (or in favour of) women as far as promotion and wage growth are concerned obviously requires that the different characteristics of men and women in the sample are controlled for.

Two sets of control variables are distinguished. The first set contains 'human capital' variables: education level, age (and age squared), years of employment experience (and its square), and nationality. The second set contains job-related characteristics: firm size (number of workers), sector of activity (one-digit NACE classification), whether private or public employer, occupation (one-digit ISCO classification), type of contract (permanent or not), and tenure with the current employer (and its square).

The rationale for separating control variables into two sets is that whereas human-capital variables could be seen here as 'gender neutral', it is likely that job-related characteristics are themselves gender-determined. This may impact on the analysis if women are found in jobs with fewer promotion opportunities than men. This phenomenon is documented for Britain by Groot and van den Brink (1996). Controlling for detailed job characteristics potentially results in 'over-controlling' and therefore hiding some gender differences. All the estimations have therefore been repeated with and without the job characteristics controls.

Various regression models have been estimated. For promotion, a standard probit model was chosen, and the model has been estimated with the two sets of control variables presented above. For each case, two specifications were implemented to identify gender differences: a constrained version merely adds a 'female dummy' to the control variables, and an unconstrained version lets all variables (and the constant) have a different effect on men and women. For wage growth, classical OLS regressions have been estimated for the same four combinations as for the promotion models. Dummy variables indicating the experience (or otherwise) of a promotion and/or a change of employer since the last interview were added to all specifications in order to capture the effect of promotions and employer changes on wage growth. In all models, standard errors are adjusted to take into account the repetition of observations for the same respondents in the pooled sample (Huber, 1967; StataCorp, 2003). Test statistics are similarly corrected (Eltinge and Sribney, 1996).

As explained earlier, promotion and wage growth are only observed for a sample of people who are in full-time employment at two consecutive survey interviews. This is clearly a highly selective sub-sample of the population, and the classical problem of sample selection bias may be suspected to affect the results of the regression models just described (see for example Heckman, 1990, and Vella, 1998, for an overview of sample selection issues). Selectivity-corrected equations were also run (assuming joint normality of the error terms in the equation of sample selection and in the promotion/wage growth equations).[6] Surprisingly, no strong evidence of selectivity problems was found. The null hypothesis of no correlation in the error terms in the selection equation and in the main equation was not rejected at conventional significance levels in all models of wage growth, and was only rejected in some particular versions of the promotion models.

The salient observations from inspection of the regression coefficients are as follows.[7] Education and age are strongly associated with promotion, promotions being, *ceteris paribus*, more frequent the higher the education level is, and the older the person is. The job-related characteristics that appear to affect promotion opportunities are the type of occupation (as measured by ISCO codes of occupational status) and the size of the firm (promotion being more frequent in large firms). Unexpectedly, *ceteris paribus* (controlling for age in particular), tenure with the same employer does not seem to have a statistically significant effect on promotion. Determinants of wage growth are less clearly identifiable. Of the human capital variables, only years of experience appear to influence (negatively) wage growth significantly. Of the job characteristics, only some occupations dummies and types of firm activity are associated with different levels of wage growth, as well as the type of employment contract (workers on fixed-term contracts achieve lower wage-growth rates).

In order to assess the performance of women relative to men controlling for differences in sample composition, I follow common practice and compare the average promotion probability of women in our sample with the average promotion probability that the above-mentioned models predict these women would have if their human capital and job characteristics were 'rewarded' as men's. In other words, I compare the prediction from the models when men's regression coefficients are used instead of women's. This simple procedure eliminates differences due to sample composition (see for example Jones and Makepeace, 1996, for an example in a similar context). The same procedure is applied to the wage growth equations. Tables 4.2 and 4.3 summarize these results for the promotion and wage growth models respectively. Raw estimates (as in Table 4.1) are reported in the first line. The predicted promotion/wage growth when men's model coefficients are applied to the sample of women is reported in the third column for four different models (with or without job characteristics covariates, and with or without sample selection correction). (Note that for the selectivity-corrected models, it is the promotion probability (or expected wage growth) *conditionally on participation* that is reported.) The difference between the third column and the unconditional average promotion/wage growth of women provides an estimate of the net disadvantage of women relative to men. A negative value indicates a relative advantage. The last column gives the *p*-values for Wald tests of equality of model coefficients between men and women (or for a classical difference-of-means *t*-test in the first line). The null hypothesis is that all characteristics included in the model are 'rewarded' identically for men and women. Rejection is therefore an indication that there is some gender difference in the process of promotion or wage growth.

*Table 4.2* Gender differences in average promotion probabilities. Unconditional estimates (col.1, col.2), counterfactual estimates if women's attributes were rewarded exactly as men's (col.3), difference thereof, and tests for gender differences in model coefficients (col.4)

| *Model* | *Men* (1) | *Women* (2) | *Women (with men's model)* (3) | *Difference* (3)–(2) | *Wald test p-values* (4) |
|---|---|---|---|---|---|
| *Unconditional estimates ('female dummy only' model)* | | | | | |
| | 18.1 | 14.7 | 18.1 | 3.4 | 0.011 |
| *Models with distinct coefficient vectors (no sample selection correction)* | | | | | |
| Human capital vars. | – | – | 19.9 | 5.2 | < 0.0005 |
| + Job characteristics | – | – | 20.4 | 5.7 | < 0.0005 |
| *Models with distinct coefficient vectors and sample selection correction* | | | | | |
| Human capital vars. | – | – | 18.5 | 3.8 | 0.002 |
| + Job characteristics | – | – | 19.6 | 4.9 | < 0.0005 |

*Notes*: The reported *p*-values are for Wald tests of equality of model coefficients for men and women. Sample consists of full-time workers at two consecutive interviews. Sample selection correction assumes joint normality of the error terms in a participation equation and in the promotion equation. Estimation is by maximum likelihood. Non-sample observations (i.e. non-participants) are all observations not full-time workers at $t-1$ and $t$.

*Table 4.3* Gender differences in average percentage wage growth. Unconditional estimates (col.1, col.2), counterfactual estimates if women's attributes were rewarded exactly as men's (col.3), difference thereof, and tests for gender differences in model coefficients (col.4)

| *Model* | *Men* (1) | *Women* (2) | *Women (with men's model)* (3) | *Difference* (3)–(2) | *Wald test p-values* (4) |
|---|---|---|---|---|---|
| *Unconditional estimates ('female dummy only' model)* | | | | | |
| | 2.84 | 3.92 | 2.84 | −1.08 | 0.004 |
| *Models with distinct coefficient vectors (no sample selection correction)* | | | | | |
| Human capital vars. | – | – | 3.41 | −0.51 | 0.020 |
| + Job characteristics | – | – | 3.32 | −0.60 | 0.045 |
| *Models with distinct coefficient vectors and sample selection correction* | | | | | |
| Human capital vars. | – | – | 3.28 | −0.64 | 0.028 |
| + Job characteristics | – | – | 3.24 | −0.68 | 0.054 |

*Notes*: See Table 4.2.

As far as promotion is concerned, controlling for sample composition differences exacerbates the estimate of women's disadvantage, rather than 'explains' it. Women's average promotion probability is between 3.8 and 5.7 percentage points lower than it would be if they were men; that is, women's average promotion probability would be 26 to 38 per cent higher if their attributes were rewarded as men's. Interestingly, comparing the results with and without the job characteristics variables does not support the argument that much of the difference is explained by the choice of job – women ending up in jobs offering less promotion opportunities (Groot and van den Brink, 1996) – since controlling for job characteristics further increases the estimated disadvantage. The Wald tests clearly emphasize the differences in treatment between men and women.

The observations for the wage-growth equations go in the opposite direction. First of all, observe that women remain advantaged after controlling for sample composition, but the advantage is reduced almost by half. In particular, controlling for differences in human capital reduce the estimated gap: on average, working women have human-capital characteristics that are more highly rewarded than men's as far as wage growth is concerned. Job characteristics seem to favour men, but their effect is limited. Finally, note that the impact of promotion and job change on wage growth did not turn out to be significantly different between men and women. Wald tests support the evidence of a difference in treatment between men and women, but the estimated *p*-values are not much below conventional significance levels.

## Does the level of wage matter?

Many of the potential forces that are at play in models of promotion and of gender differences thereof (see Booth *et al.*, 2003) are likely to be of different significance for different locations in the wage ladder. What is relevant at the bottom of the distribution may not be relevant for high wage earners. Think, for example, of non-market opportunities which are emphasized by Lazear and Rosen (1990). The attractiveness of non-market activities such as houseworking and caring for children is higher for women with low earnings potential as they face a lower opportunity cost of quitting their job. It is also conceivable that high-earnings women are more able to bear the cost of external childcare and thereby have more incentives to remain on the labour market. Consequently, incentives to invest in human capital and to make the effort to acquire the skills required for promotion (or more general career development inside or outside the firm), as well as gender differences thereof, are likely to vary across different earnings levels. There is therefore interest in looking at differences in promotion and wage growth rates between men and women at different points along the wage distribution.

The results presented in this section are replications of those of the previous section when conditioning on varying levels of base-period wage. A simple local weighting procedure is applied to condition the analysis on the wage level. The procedure bears similarity to density function estimation by the kernel method. It can also be thought of as an extension of the practice of cutting the sample into a fixed number of quantile groups and replicating the analysis on the different sub-samples separately (just as the kernel method is an extension of the histogram approach). The various statistics of interest are estimated when conditioning on a base-period wage located at (or near) the $p$th quantile of the base period wage distribution ($0 < p < 1$). To do so, all observations in the sample are used, but they are reweighted so that observations with wage near the quantile of interest receive a high weight whereas observations with substantially different wages receive a small or zero weight. The first step is to estimate the quantile position of each observation in the distribution of base wages ($w_{it-1}$) when the men and women samples are merged. Call it $p_{it-1}$. In a second step, kernel weights based on the distance of $p_{it-1}$ from the $p$th quantile of interest are computed for all observations. The kernel weight used here is $k_{it-1}(p) = 1/h\ K((p-p_{it-1})/h)$ where $K$ is the Epanechnikov kernel function, and $h$ is a bandwidth parameter that controls the degree of smoothness of the resulting estimates over the grid points. A small $h$ gives a large weight to $p_{it-1}$ very close to $p$ but the weight declines rapidly with $|p - p_{it-1}|$. On the contrary, a large $h$ gives weights that are positive over a much larger range of $p_{it-1}$ values around $p$. In the application, $h$ is set to 0.18. This results in the Epanechnikov kernel weight functions illustrated in Figure 4.1.

Once kernel weights are computed for all observations, standard weighted estimation methods are used to construct the various statistics and regression models conditional on base wage level at $p$.[8] The whole procedure is repeated across a range of fixed quantile points spanning the wage range so as to depict variations along the wage distributions.

To fix ideas, Figure 4.2 describes the position of women in the distribution of base-period wages. The unfavourable position of women shows up clearly. The left panel presents the proportion of women at various points along the distribution (estimated using the local weighting procedure just described). The proportion of women is decreasing substantially as we move from low-wage positions to high-wage positions: 42 per cent of workers at the 10th percentile are women, but they only represent 17 per cent of workers at the 90th percentile. The right panel illustrates this point further by plotting the cumulative

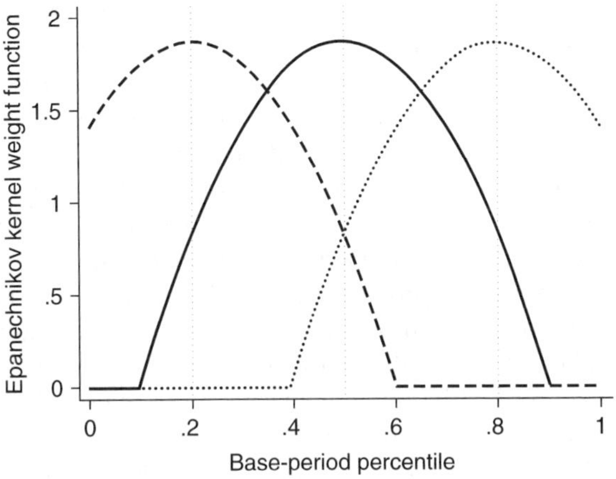


*Figure 4.1* Epanechnikov kernel weighting functions with bandwidth of 0.18 and centred on 0.20, 0.50 and 0.80

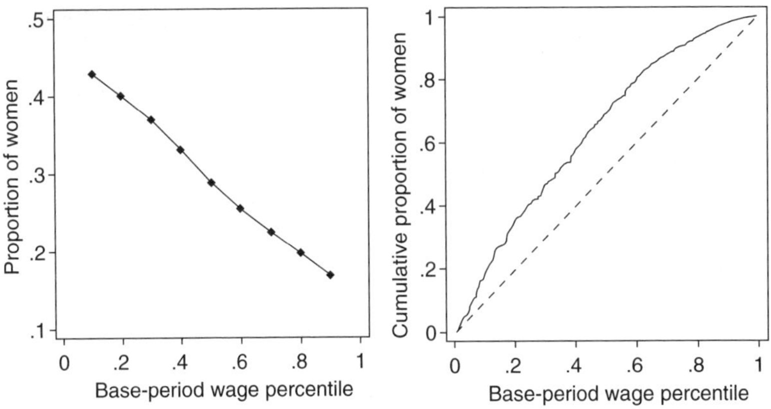


*Figure 4.2* Distribution of women along the base-period wage levels

proportion of women against the cumulative proportion of workers as we move from low to high wages. It is blatant that women are disproportionately concentrated at low wages since, for example, almost 40 per cent working women are in the bottom fifth of the overall distribution of workers, and more than 70 per cent of working women are in the bottom half.[9] Gender differences in promotion and wage growth at the bottom of the wage distribution therefore have a more important impact on the overall situation of women than differences at the top, where they affect a smaller fraction of working women.

Results for promotion are presented in Figure 4.3. Consider first the left panel. The solid line shows the raw promotion probability of women for different positions in the base-period wage distribution. The dotted line gives the raw probabilities for men. The dashed lines are the predicted promotion probabilities of women as if they were men for two distinct models. The distance between these dashed lines and the solid line indicates the net disadvantage of women. The line with cross-nodes is for a model with only human capital variables and the line with bullet-nodes is for a model with both human capital and job characteristics variables. The models do not take sample selection into account as the estimations performed did not show evidence of correlation between the error terms in the selection and promotion equations. These estimates are the counterparts of the statistics reported in Table 4.2 estimated conditionally on varying base-period wage percentiles.

The right panel of Figure 4.3 shows the *p*-values of *t*-tests of equality of raw promotion probabilities between men and women (solid line).

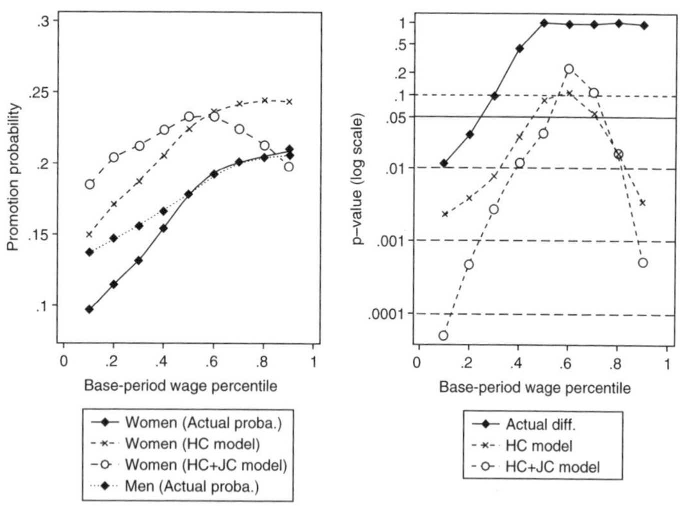


*Figure 4.3* Promotion probabilities for different base-period wage levels. Men's probability, women's probability and women's probability 'as if' they had men's model coefficients (left); *p*-values of Wald tests of equality of model coefficients across gender (right)

Points below the solid horizontal line indicate rejection of the null hypothesis at the 5 per cent confidence level. The horizontal dashed lines show thresholds for alternative confidence levels. (Note that the vertical axis is in logarithmic scale.) It indicates, for example, that the difference between the raw promotion probabilities is significant at the 5 per cent confidence level when conditioning on $p = 0.10$ or $p = 0.20$ but not for higher wage levels. Similarly, the two dashed lines with cross- and bullet-nodes present the *p*-values for Wald tests of equality of the estimated model coefficients between men and women in the two estimated models. These are the local variants of the *p*-values reported in the last column of Table 4.2.

Promotion probabilities clearly increase with the level of wage. Raw gender differences are large at the bottom of the distribution but women catch up to men's raw promotion rates in the upper half of the distribution. Just as in the results of the previous section, controlling for sample composition exacerbates the disadvantage of women. Women would achieve higher promotion rates if they were as rewarded as men. The evolution of the net gap depends on the models. According to the 'human-capital only' model, women have a lower promotion probability of about 5 percentage points throughout the whole wage range. The second model suggests that the gap is large at the bottom of the distribution, where women would almost double their promotion probability if they were men, but then the gap decreases gradually with the increase in wage. Accounting for the fact that women may hold jobs that offer different promotion opportunities than men provides an important insight: the net disadvantage of women at the bottom of the wage scale should not be attributed to differences in job characteristics, whereas the net disadvantage of women at the top (if we only consider human capital controls) can be explained by the type of jobs that women hold.

Wald tests suggest that the reward associated to women's characteristics varies significantly from that of men for wage levels below the 40th percentile and above the 80th percentile. Between these two regions of the wage distribution, the evidence of a net disadvantage of women is only weakly supported.

Figure 4.4 reports the estimates for the wage-growth equations. The interpretation of the plots is the same as for the promotion models. Wage growth follows the opposed trend from promotion. Estimated percentage wage growth rates fall dramatically with the level of wage from near 5 at the bottom decile to about 1.5 at the top decile. Except at the very bottom, the raw wage-growth rate of women exceeds that of men. However, the difference is only significant in the middle of the wage

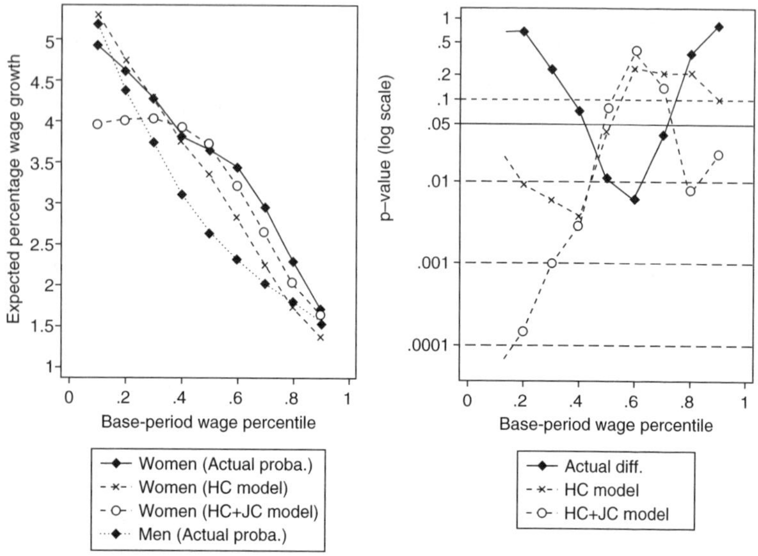


*Figure 4.4* Expected percentage wage growth for different base-period wage levels. Men's expected value, women's expected value and women's expected value 'as if' they had men's model coefficients (left); *p*-values of Wald tests of equality of model coefficients across gender (right)

distribution. Controlling for sample composition differences tends to reduce the advantage of women. In the upper half of the wage distribution, the net advantage of women is small, and the Wald tests often do not support (or support weakly) the hypothesis that women and men's characteristics are rewarded differently. By contrast, at the lowest wage levels, if controls for job characteristics are used women appear to fare significantly better than men. It is worth stressing that the actual magnitudes of differences in percentage wage growth remain small (less than one percentage point on an annual basis).

One potential drawback of the approach used so far is that the base-period wage level is potentially endogenous to subsequent wage growth. The main risk of endogeneity arises because of measurement error and takes the form of a regression-to-the-mean problem: respondents whose wage is underestimated in $t-1$ (and thereby located at a too low percentile position $p_{it-1}$) are more likely to experience high wage growth between $t-1$ and $t$ as they catch up to their actual wage level (see Friedman, 1992). To address this issue, the analysis has been repeated using the percentile position in a distribution of *predicted* base-period wages (rather than actual base-period wages). The prediction is based on a standard earnings equation (which does *not* include gender as explanatory variable). This correction is akin to 'instrumenting' base-period wage with a linear combination of a set of predictors. Figures 4.5 and 4.6 are the counterparts of Figures 4.3 and 4.4 with this alternative definition of base period percentile.

The results for promotion are not affected by the correction; all broad conclusions remain valid. However, as was expected, the results for the wage growth models are substantially altered. Most striking is the disappearance of the steep gradient between wage growth and wage level. Men's wage growth still falls with the predicted base-period wage, but women's wage growth tends to increase. Interestingly, the raw difference between men and women is larger than previously estimated. Again, controlling for sample composition differences accounts for more than half of women's advantage in most locations. A noticeable net

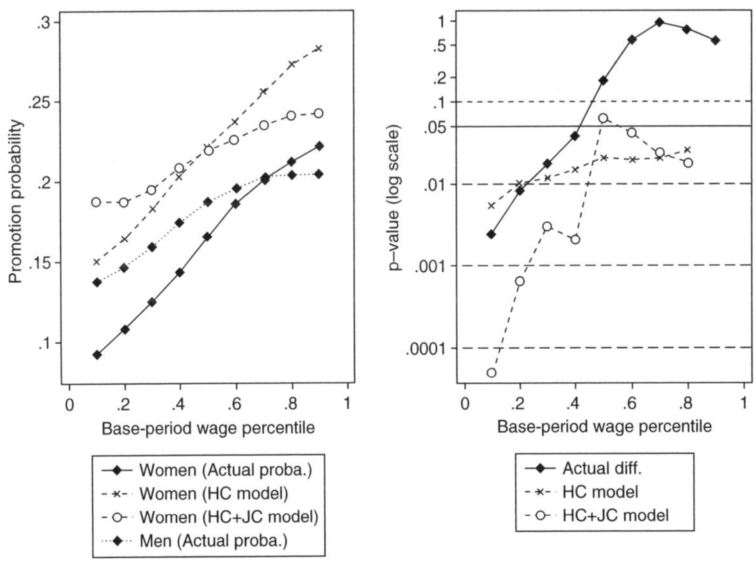


*Figure 4.5* Promotion probabilities for different *predicted* base-period wage levels. Men's probability, women's probability and women's probability 'as if' they had men's model coefficients (left); *p*-values of Wald tests of equality of model coefficients across gender (right)

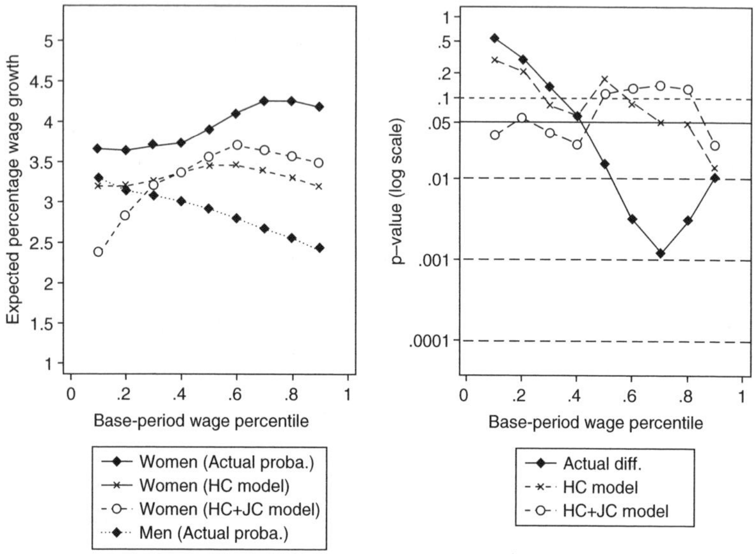


*Figure 4.6* Expected percentage wage growth for different *predicted* base-period wage levels. Men's expected value, women's expected value and women's expected value 'as if' they had men's model coefficients (left); *p*-values of Wald tests of equality of model coefficients across gender (right)

advantage for women yet remains at the very bottom of the predicted wage distribution when job characteristics are taken into account. Wald tests generally provide even weaker support to the hypothesis of differences in model coefficients between men and women.

## Conclusion

Are women able to take advantage of promotions and other opportunities for wage growth to catch up partially to male wage rates? Evidence on gender differences in promotion rates and wage growth among a sample of working people from the panel survey Panel Socio-Économique 'Liewen zu Lëtzebuerg' provides ambiguous answers. The process of promotion seems to sustain the advantage of men. Women experience a lower promotion rate, in particular among low-pay workers. As it is also observed that promotion is associated with a wage-increase premium, gender differences in promotions tend to depress the wage growth of women relative to men. However, overall, the average wage growth of women turns out to be no lower than that of men – or even possibly higher, although the robustness of this result to sampling variability is not strong. Other factors therefore appear to influence wage growth and balance the disadvantage associated with lower promotion opportunities. A possible explanation for this might be the higher mobility of women between jobs, as we also observed that job mobility is associated with a wage-growth premium too. This is a topic for further research. Note that in both promotion and wage-growth statistics, the situation of women worsens relative to men after controlling for differences in sample composition. In sum, even if women are disadvantaged in the process of promotion – admittedly a source of concern in itself – their overall performance in wage growth suggests that women who remain in employment do not lose ground relative to men or even tend to catch up gradually to men's wage rates. However, differences in wage growth are nothing compared to differences in wage *levels*, and the dynamics of pay in continuous employment does not appear to be a strong determinant of male–female wage differences.

The methodological lesson of this analysis is that it appears useful to augment the classical approach to an analysis conditioning on the level of wage. The magnitude of gender differences in promotion turns out to vary widely along the wage range, and, in particular, no evidence of a 'glass ceiling' above highly skilled women is found. On the contrary, the most striking gender differences are in promotion opportunities for workers at the bottom of the wage distribution. In addition, wage growth, if anything, is higher for high-wage women than for high-wage men. Note, finally, that taking regression-to-the-mean effects into account in this approach had an important impact on the resulting wage-growth profile.

## Notes

1 I consider directly wage growth and promotion rates to assess the 'glass-ceiling' hypothesis. An alternative strand of literature has assessed 'glass ceilings' by comparing the top quantiles of men's wage distribution with the top quantiles of women's wage distribution; see Albrecht *et al.* (2003). Evidence of a 'glass ceiling' with this alternative approach is generally strong (see also Machado and Mata, 2005).

2 Booth *et al.* (2003) coin the term 'sticky floors' (as opposed to 'glass ceiling') to describe such a situation. They develop a model of promotion and wage growth allowing such (and other) patterns to emerge by combining elements of the classical Lazear and Rosen (1990) model (women having better non-market opportunities), discrimination in the form of different reaction to outside offer threats, and gender differences in the distribution of outside offers.

3 In addition, survey year 1998 is used to estimate the wage growth of workers from 31 December 1997 to 31 December 1998, the period which is referred to in the 'promotion' question in the 1999 survey.

4 Missing data on the 'experience' variable have been partly imputed with data on education, activity status in previous years, age, and age at first job.

5 Note in passing that this observation does not support the idea of a 'glass ceiling' in raw estimates according to the definition of Albrecht *et al.* (2003) (see note 1), as this would imply the wage gap to be larger between high-wage men and women.

6 The sample selection equation included the human capital variables as well as information on parental activity when the respondent left school, marital status and household composition.

7 For the sake of brevity, detailed regression results are not reported here but are available from the author on request.

8 More precisely, sample weights used in the unconditional estimators of the preceding sections are multiplied by the kernel weights.

9 The corresponding concentration coefficient is −0.237.

## References

Albrecht, J., Björklund, A. and Vroman, S. (2003) 'Is There a Glass Ceiling in Sweden?', *Journal of Labour Economics*, 21(1), pp. 145–77.

Booth, A.L. and Francesconi, M. (2000) 'Job Mobility in 1990s Britain: Does Gender Matter?', *Research in Labour Economics*, 19, pp. 173–89.

Booth, A.L., Francesconi, M. and Frank, J. (2003) 'A Sticky Floors Model of Promotion, Pay and Gender', *European Economic Review*, 47(2), pp. 99–126.

Cobb-Clark, D. (2001) 'Getting Ahead: The Determinants of and Payoffs to Internal Promotion for Young Men and Women', *Research in Labour Economics*, 20, pp. 339–72.

Eltinge, J.L. and Sribney, W.M. (1996) 'Estimates of Linear Combinations and Hypothesis Tests for Survey Data', *Stata Technical Bulletin*, 31, pp. 31–42.

Francesconi, M. (2001) 'Determinants and Consequences of Promotions in Britain', *Oxford Bulletin of Economics and Statistics*, 63(3), pp. 279–310.

Friedman, M. (1992) 'Do Old Fallacies Ever Die?', *Journal of Economic Literature*, 30(4).

Groot, W. and van den Brink, H.M. (1996) 'Glass Ceilings or Dead Ends: Job Promotion of Men and Women Compared', *Economics Letters*, 53, pp. 221–6.

Heckman, J.J. (1990) 'Varieties of Sample Selection Bias', *American Economic Review*, 80(2), pp. 313–18.

Hersch, J. and Viscusi, W.K. (1996) 'Gender Differences in Promotions and Wages', *Industrial Relations*, 35(4), pp. 461–72.

Huber, P.J. (1967) 'The Behaviour of Maximum Likelihood Estimators under Non-Standard Conditions', in *Proceedings of the Fifth Berkeley Symposium in Mathematical Statistics and Probability*. Berkeley, USA: University of California Press.

Jones, D.R. and Makepeace, G.H. (1996) 'Equal Worth, Equal Opportunities: Pay and Promotion in an Internal Labour Market', *Economic Journal*, 106(435), pp. 401–9.

Lazear, E.P. and Rosen, S. (1990) 'Male–Female Wage Differentials in Job Ladders', *Journal of Labour Economics*, 8(2), pp. S106–S123.
Lejealle, B. (2002) 'Les écarts de salaire entre hommes et femmes', CEPS/INSTEAD, Differdange, G.-D. Luxembourg.
Machado, J.A.F. and Mata, J. (2005) 'Counterfactual Decomposition of Changes in Wage Distributions using Quantile Regression', *Journal of Applied Econometrics*, 20(4), pp. 445–65.
Manning, A. and Robinson, H. (2004) 'Something in the Way She Moves: A Fresh Look at an Old Gap', *Oxford Economic Papers*, 56(2), pp. 169–88.
McCue, K. (1996) 'Promotions and Wage Growth', *Journal of Labour Economics*, 14(2), pp. 175–205.
StataCorp (2003) *Stata Statistical Software: Release 8.0*, Stata Corporation, College Station, USA.
Statec (2003) *Portrait économique et social du Luxembourg*, Luxembourg: Statec.
Vella, F. (1998) 'Estimating Models with Sample Selection Bias: A Survey', *Journal of Human Resources*, 33(1), pp. 127–69.

# Part III

# Sectors, Profits and Rent-Sharing

# 5
# The Gender Pay Gap in Belgium: How Much do Sectors Matter?

*François Rycx and Ilan Tojerow*

## Introduction

The existence of sectoral effects on workers' wages is well-documented in the economic literature (Araï *et al.*, 1996; Krueger and Summers, 1988; Lucifora, 1993; Rycx, 2002; Vainiomäki and Laaksonen, 1995). Although their exact scale is still questionable (Abowd *et al.*, 1999; Björklund *et al.*, 2004; Gibbons and Katz, 1992; Goux and Maurin, 1999), there is some agreement on the fact that these effects are fairly persistent, closely correlated from one country to another (Helwege, 1992), and of varying dimensions in the industrialized countries (Hartog *et al.*, 1997). A number of studies suggest in addition that sectoral effects are significantly weaker in strongly corporatist countries (Edin and Zetterberg, 1992; Hartog *et al.*, 2000; Kahn, 1998; Rycx, 2003; Teulings and Hartog, 1998; Zanchi, 1992; Zweimüller and Barth, 1994). Moreover, while various explanations based on efficiency wage mechanisms or rent sharing have been put forward (Benito, 2000, Krueger and Summers, 1988, Lindbeck and Snower, 1990, Thaler, 1989, Walsh, 1999), the existence of industry wage differentials remains a complex and unresolved puzzle.

Since Becker's (1957) seminal paper on the economics of discrimination, studies on the magnitude and sources of the gender wage gap have proliferated (see for example Blau and Kahn, 2000). Numerous studies have in particular focused on the relationship between labour market segregation and the gender wage differential (for example Groshen, 1991; MacPherson and Hirsch, 1995; Fields and Wolff, 1995; Carrington and Troske, 1998; Bayard *et al.*, 2003). These papers basically examine to what extent the observed sex wage gap can be explained by occupational and sectoral segregation. Although the evidence is still inconclusive, recent findings show that a large fraction of the gender wage gap is accounted for by segregation of women in lower-paying occupations, industries and occupations within establishments. Nevertheless, in contrast to previous research (in particular Groshen, 1991), Bayard *et al.* (2003) suggest, on the basis of a large matched employer–employee data-set covering all industries and occupations across all regions of the USA in 1990, that a substantial part of the sex wage gap remains attributable to the individual's sex.

Surprisingly little is known about the interaction between inter-industry wage differentials and the gender wage gap. The main contribution to this field of research has been provided by Fields and Wolff (1995). Using the 1988 US Current Population Survey, the authors find significant industry wage differentials for women and men, after controlling for productivity-related individual characteristics. These differentials are highly correlated and their dispersion is of the same order of magnitude for both sexes. In spite of these similarities, the authors report significant gender wage gaps within industries. Moreover, their results suggest that around one-third of the overall gender wage gap is explained by industry effects. While thorough and convincing, this study has several shortcomings: (i) the standard errors of the inter-industry wage differentials are wrong (Haisken-DeNew and Schmidt, 1997; Reilly and Zanchi, 2003), (ii) the industry wage gaps are not identified (Horrace and Oaxaca, 2001), and (iii) the level of significance of the different components of the gender wage gap is not reported (Oaxaca and Ransom, 1998).

The purpose of this chapter is to examine the interaction between inter-industry wage differentials and the gender wage gap in the Belgian private sector. The existence of inter-industry wage differentials in the Belgian economy has been recently highlighted by Rycx (2002, 2003). The author shows *inter alia* that their structure is comparable to that observed in the other industrialized countries and that they result in part from the characteristics of the employers in each sector. Moreover, results fit in with findings from earlier studies on the existence of a negative relation between the dispersion of inter-industry wage differentials and the degree of corporatism that characterizes a country. What is more, the current evidence regarding the level and sources of the gender wage gap in Belgium is still incomplete. Jepsen (2001) shows, on the basis of the 1994 and 1995 Panel Study of Belgian Households (PSBH), that the sex wage gap between full-time workers stands at around 15 per cent and that only a very small part of it can be explained by gender differences in endowments. In contrast, using the 1995 Structure of

Earnings Survey, Plasman *et al.* (2002) suggest that the wage gap between (all) men and women working in the Belgian private sector reaches almost 22 per cent and that half of it is attributable to gender differences in working conditions, individual and firm characteristics. Finally, Sissoko (2004) shows that occupational segregation accounts for 13 per cent of the overall gender wage gap in Belgium. As far as we are aware, little is known about the interaction between sectors and the gender pay ratio.

This chapter aims to partially fill this gap by investigating, on the basis of the 1995 Structure of Earnings Survey, how inter-industry wage differentials interact with the gender wage gap in the Belgian economy. The following questions are addressed: (1) Can we observe inter-industry wage differentials for male and female workers, even when controlling for productivity-related factors? (2) Is the magnitude and dispersion in inter-industry wage differentials alike for men and women? (3) Are male and female industry wage differentials highly correlated? That is, are the same sectors offering high or low wages to male and female workers? (4) Even if industry wage differentials are highly correlated, are there significant differences between them? To put it differently, what is the magnitude of the wage gap between male and female workers within sectors? (5) Of the overall gender wage gap, what proportion can be attributed to: (a) differences in the distribution of male and female workers across sectors, (b) differences by gender in the structure of industry wage premia, and (c) differences by gender in all other factors, that is intercepts, working conditions, individual and firm characteristics?

The remainder of the chapter is organized as follows. The next section describes the data-set, and subsequent sections present the methodology and the empirical results. The last section concludes.

## Description of the data

The present study is based upon the 1995 Structure of Earnings Survey carried out by Statistics Belgium. This large matched employer–employee data-set covers establishments employing at least 10 workers and whose economic activities fall within sections C to K of the Nace Rev. 1 nomenclature.[1] The survey contains a wealth of information, provided by the management of the establishments, both on the characteristics of the latter (for example sector of activity, region, size of the establishment, level of wage bargaining) and on the individuals working

*Table 5.1* Means (standard deviations) of selected variables

| *Variables* | *Overall sample* | *Men* | *Women* |
|---|---|---|---|
| Gross hourly wage (in ECU)[a] | 15.0 | 16.0 | 12.8 |
| | (7.9) | (8.5) | (5.4) |
| Potential experience[b] | 9.6 | 9.8 | 9.1 |
| | (8.3) | (8.2) | (8.6) |
| Seniority in the establishment | 10.4 | 11.0 | 8.9 |
| | (9.5) | (9.7) | (8.7) |
| Number of paid hours[c] | 162.1 | 168.1 | 147.5 |
| | (26.0) | (16.9) | (36.4) |
| Per cent permanent contract | 96.7 | 97.5 | 95.0 |
| Size of the establishment[d] | 669.4 | 777.7 | 406.3 |
| | (1,525.7) | (1,681.7) | (1,007.2) |
| Number of observations | 80,265 | 58,166 | 22,099 |

*Notes*: Descriptive statistics refer to the weighted sample.
[a] Includes overtime paid, premiums for shift work, night work and/or weekend work, and bonuses (i.e. irregular payments which do not occur during each pay period, such as pay for holiday, 13th month, profit sharing, etc.). 1 ECU = 1.23 USD (in 1995).
[b] Experience (potentially) accumulated on the labour market before the last job. It has been computed as follows: age − 6 − years of education − seniority.
[c] Number of hour paid in the reference period (October 1995), including overtime paid.
[d] Number of workers in the establishment.

there (for example education, potential experience, gross hourly wages, bonuses, number of working hours paid, gender, occupation).

Table 5.1 sets out the means and standard deviations of selected variables for women and men. We note a clear-cut difference between the average characteristics of male and female workers. The point is that on average men earn significantly higher wages (including bonuses), work a larger number of (paid) hours, have more seniority and potential experience, are employed in larger establishments, and more frequently have a permanent contract.

## Inter-industry wage differentials by gender

The methodology adopted to estimate the inter-industry wage differentials by gender is consistent with that of Krueger and Summers (1988). However, the standard errors of these differentials have been corrected using the method proposed by Haisken-DeNew and Schmidt (1997).

The following semi-logarithmic wage equation has been estimated, separately for male and female workers, by ordinary least-squares (OLS):

$$\ln W_i = \alpha + \sum_{j=1}^{J} \beta_j X_{j,i} + \sum_{k=1}^{K} \psi_k Y_{k,i} + \sum_{l=1}^{L} \delta_l Z_{l,i} + \boldsymbol{\varepsilon}_i \qquad (5.1)$$

where $\ln W_i$ represents the Naperian logarithm of the gross hourly wage of the individual *i; X* is the vector of the individual characteristics of the workers and their working conditions (5 indicators showing the highest completed level of education; potential experience, its square and its cube; seniority within the establishment and its square; a dummy variable controlling for entrants, that is individuals with no seniority; number of hours paid; a dummy for extra paid hours; 22 occupational dummies; 2 regional dummies indicating where the establishment is located; 2 dummies for the type of contract; and an indicator showing whether the individual is paid a bonus for shift work, night-time and/or weekend work); $Y$ comprises dummy variables relating to the sectoral affiliation of the workers (at the Nace two-digit level); $Z$ contains employer characteristics (the size of the establishment and the level of wage bargaining); $\alpha$ is the intercept; $\psi$, $\beta$ and $\delta$ are the parameters to be estimated and $\varepsilon_i$ is an error term.[2]

Technically, the computation of the inter-industry wage differentials first of all involves calculating the average wage differential of all the sectors compared to the reference:

$$\pi = \sum_{k=1}^{K} s_k \widehat{\psi}_k \quad (\text{for } k = 1,\ldots, K) \qquad (5.2)$$

and then applying the formulae below:

$$\begin{aligned} \widehat{d}_k &= \widehat{\psi}_k - \pi \quad (\text{for } k = 1,\ldots, K) \\ \widehat{d}_{K+1} &= -\pi \end{aligned} \qquad (5.3)$$

where $\widehat{\psi}_k$ is the regression coefficient estimated for the industry dummy $k$ and $s_k$ is the proportion of the sample employed in industry $k$.

Table 5.2 reports the estimates of the industry wage differentials for male and female workers, as well as for the overall sample, at the Nace two-digit level. These are shown as deviations from the employment-weighted mean. Table 5.2 also records the range and the standard deviation of the inter-industry wage differentials, adjusted for sampling

*Table 5.2* Inter-industry wage differentials by gender, 1995

| *Industry (NACE two-digit)* | *Overall sample* | *Men* | *Women* |
|---|---|---|---|
| Other extractive industries (14) | 0 | 0 | 0 |
| Food industries (15) | 0 | −.01 | 0 |
| Tobacco industry (16) | +.03 | +.04 | +.04 |
| Textile industry (17) | −.12*** | −.10*** | −.14*** |
| Clothing and fur industry (18) | −.13*** | −.08*** | −.13*** |
| Leather and footwear industry (19) | −.05*** | −.07*** | −.01 |
| Woodwork and manufacture of articles in wood, cork, basketwork or esparto (20) | −.06*** | −.07*** | −.05*** |
| Paper and cardboard industry (21) | +.06*** | +.08*** | −.01 |
| Publishing, printing and reproduction (22) | +.06*** | +.08*** | +.02 |
| Coking, refining and nuclear industries (23) | +.23*** | +.23*** | +.15*** |
| Chemical industry (24) | +.09*** | +.09*** | +.07*** |
| Rubber and plastic industry (25) | 0 | −.01 | +.02 |
| Manufacture of other non-metallic mineral products (26) | +.01** | +.02*** | −.02 |
| Metallurgy (27) | 0 | 0 | +.04** |
| Metal work (28) | −.01** | −.02*** | +.01 |
| Manufacture of machinery and plant (29) | −.06** | −.06*** | −.07*** |
| Manufacture of office machinery and computers (30) | +.04 | 0 | +.10*** |
| Manufacture of electrical machinery and appliances (31) | −.03*** | −.02*** | −.04** |
| Manufacture of radio, television and comm. equip. (32) | −.03*** | −.01 | −.08*** |
| Manufacture of medical, precision, optical watch making instruments (33) | 0 | +.01 | −.02 |
| Manufacture of motor vehicles, trailers and semi-trailers (34) | 0 | 0 | −.02 |
| Manufacture of other transport materials (35) | −.03*** | −.03*** | +.01 |
| Manufacture of furniture; sundry industries (36) | −.09*** | −.10*** | −.06*** |
| Recovery of recyclable materials (37) | −.05*** | −.01 | −.06*** |
| Prod. and distr. of electricity, gas, steam and hot water (40) | +.28*** | +.28*** | +.26*** |
| Construction (45) | −.08*** | −.08*** | −.08*** |
| Dealing in and repairing motor vehicles and motorcycles; retail fuel trade (50) | −.04*** | −.04*** | −.03** |
| Wholesale and intermediaries in trade, excl. motor trade (51) | −.01** | −.02*** | +.01*** |
| Retail, excl. motor trade (52) | −.09*** | −.09*** | −.10*** |
| Hotels and restaurants (55) | −.17*** | −.20*** | −.15*** |
| Land-based transport (60) | −.04*** | −.04*** | −.03** |

*Continued*

*Table 5.2 continued*

| *Industry (NACE two-digit)* | *Overall sample* | *Men* | *Women* |
|---|---|---|---|
| Water-based transport (61) | +.13*** | +.13*** | +.15*** |
| Air transport (62) | +.14*** | +.13*** | +.16*** |
| Transport auxiliary services (63) | +.01 | 0 | +.03*** |
| Post and telecommunications (64) | −.10*** | −.12*** | −.02** |
| Financial intermediaries (65) | +.13*** | +.14*** | +.13*** |
| Insurance (66) | +.06*** | +.06*** | +.06*** |
| Financial auxiliaries (67) | −.03** | −.03 | −.03** |
| Property activities (70) | −.01 | −.01 | −.01 |
| Renting of machinery and equipment (71) | −.05*** | −.10*** | +.05 |
| Computer activities (72) | −.01 | −.01 | 0 |
| Other services to businesses (74) | −.01** | −.02*** | +.01** |
| Adjusted $R^2$ of wage regression | .68 | .67 | .63 |
| *F*-stat relative to the sectoral dummies | 2510*** | 138*** | 38*** |
| Per cent significant industry wage differentials at the .10 level | 74% | 67% | 64% |
| Spearman correlation coefficient between male and female wage differentials | | .74*** | |
| Per cent industry wage differentials significantly different for male and female workers at the .10 level | | 43% | |
| *F*-stat relative to Chow test on industry dummy variables | | 93*** | |
| Range of industry wage differentials | .45 | .47 | .41 |
| Weighted adjusted standard deviation of industry wage differentials | .08 | .08 | .08 |
| Number of industries | 42 | 42 | 42 |
| Number of observations | 80,265 | 58,166 | 22,099 |

*Notes*: Results are based on equation (5.1) in the text, estimated on the basis of the 1995 Structure of Earnings Survey. Standard errors of the industry wage differentials have been corrected according to Haisken-DeNew and Schmidt (1997).
* Statistically significant at the .10 level; ** at the .05 level; *** at the .01 level.

error and weighted by the sectoral employment shares (further referred in the text as WASD, that is weighted adjusted standard deviation). The WASD of the differentials is computed as follows:

$$WASD(\hat{d}_k) = \sqrt{\sum_{k=1}^{K+1} s_k \left( \hat{d}_k - \frac{\sum_{k=1}^{K+1} \hat{d}_k}{K+1} \right)^2 - \frac{\sum_{k=1}^{K+1} \text{var}(\hat{d}_k)}{K+1} + \frac{\sum_{k=1}^{K+1}\sum_{l=1}^{K+1} \text{cov}(\hat{d}_k, \hat{d}_l)}{(K+1)^2}} \quad (5.4)$$

Results in Table 5.2 show that for both sexes wage differentials exist between workers employed in different sectors, even when controlling for working conditions, individual and firm characteristics. *F*-statistics reveal that the industry dummy variables are jointly significant at the 0.01 level, independently of the sex considered. We also find for both sexes that more than 60 per cent of the industry wage differentials are significantly different from zero (at the 0.10 level). Moreover, we note that the hierarchy of the sectors in terms of wages is quite similar for male and female workers. Among the best paid sectors, we find the financial sector; the coking, refining and nuclear industry; and the production and distribution of electricity, gas steam and hot water. Wages are the lowest in the traditional sectors (hotels and restaurants, the textile industry, and retailing). Furthermore, if we look at the dispersion of the industry wage differentials (that is the range and the WASD), we find quite similar results for men and women.

Yet the apparent similarity between industry wage differentials is challenged by standard statistical tests. Indeed, simple *t*-tests, reported in Table 5.2, show that more than 40 per cent of the industry wage disparities are significantly different (at the 0.10 level) for women and men. Moreover, a Chow test indicates that sectoral wage differentials are significantly different (at the 0.01 level) as a group for both sexes.

## Gender wage gaps by industry

In this section, gender wage gaps within industries are estimated using the methodology developed by Horrace and Oaxaca (2001). According to this methodology, the gender wage gap in a particular sector can be defined as follows:

$$\hat{\theta}_k = (\hat{\psi}_k^f - \hat{\psi}_k^m) + (\hat{\alpha}^f - \hat{\alpha}^m) + \sum_{j=1}^{J} \overline{X}_j^f(\hat{\beta}_j^f - \hat{\beta}_j^m) + \sum_{l=1}^{L} \overline{Z}_l^f(\hat{\delta}_l^f - \hat{\delta}_l^m) \qquad (5.5)$$

where the index *k* identifies the sector ($k = 1, \ldots, K + 1$), and superscripts *f* and *m* represent female and male workers, respectively. $(\hat{\alpha}^f - \hat{\alpha}^m)$ is the difference between the estimates of the intercepts in the female and male wage regressions, $(\hat{\psi}_k^f - \hat{\psi}_k^m)$ is the difference between the regression coefficients associated to the *k*th industry dummy for women and men, $\overline{X}^f$ is the vector of mean female individual characteristics and working conditions, and $\overline{Z}^f$ contains mean characteristics of female workers' employers. $\beta$ and $\delta$ are the vectors of regression coefficients.

By including the mean characteristics of female workers and the difference between female and male coefficients, equation (5.5) tends to overcome the identification problem encountered by Fields and Wolff (1995).[3] It shows how a randomly selected female worker would do if she were treated as a man with the same characteristics. For this reason, it is also referred to as the identified wage gap evaluated at the mean characteristics of all women in the sample.

To 'sweep out' the effect of the intercepts, we also computed the *relative* wage gap in each industry. In other words, we estimated the difference between the gender wage gap in a particular sector and the largest sectoral wage gap. To do so, we applied the following formulae:

$$\hat{\gamma}_k = \max_{n=1,\ldots,K+1} \hat{\theta}_n - \hat{\theta}_k \tag{5.6}$$

Since $\hat{\gamma}_k \geq 0$, it can be shown that $e^{-\hat{\gamma}_k} \in (0,1)$ measures the wage gap in sector $k$ as a percentage of the largest sectoral wage gap. From this normalized estimator we tested the significance of the ordered industry wage gaps.

The measures of $\hat{\theta}_k$, $\hat{\gamma}_k$ and $e^{-\hat{\gamma}_k}$ are reported in Table 5.3. Results show that almost all gender wage gaps ($\hat{\theta}_k$), computed at the Nace two-digit level, are statistically different from zero (at the 0.01 level). The average industry gender wage gap stands at −0.11. This means that on average women have an inter-industry wage differential of 11 per cent below that of men. The range of the industry gender wage gaps is equal to 0.24. To put it differently, the size of the industry gender wage gaps fluctuate between +0.03 and −0.20. Among the sectors with the smallest gender wage gaps we find: (i) the renting of machinery and equipment industry, (ii) the manufacture of office machinery and computers, and (iii) the post and telecommunications industry. The largest gender wage gaps are found in: (i) the paper and cardboard industry, (ii) the coking, refining and nuclear industries, and (iii) the manufacture of radio, television and communication equipment. Also noteworthy is that 98 per cent of the relative gender wage gaps ($\hat{\gamma}_k$) are statistically significant (at the 0.01 level). This result implies that the ranking of the gender wage gaps, reported in Table 5.3, has a statistical meaning.

*Table 5.3* Identified wage gaps evaluated at women sample mean characteristics

| *Industry (NACE two-digit)* | $\hat{\theta}_k$ | $\hat{\gamma}_k$ | $e^{-\hat{\gamma}_k}$ |
|---|---|---|---|
| Renting of machinery and equipment (71) | +.03 | .00 | 1.000 |
| Manufacture of office machinery and computers (30) | −.01 | .05*** | .954 |
| Post and telecommunications (64) | −.02 | .05 | .952 |
| Leather and footwear industry (19) | −.05* | .09** | .917 |
| Manufacture of furniture; sundry industries (36) | −.07*** | .10*** | .903 |
| Hotels and restaurants (55) | −.07** | .10*** | .903 |
| Manufacture of other transport materials (35) | −.07*** | .11*** | .899 |
| Metallurgy (27) | −.08*** | .11*** | .897 |
| Wholesale and intermediaries in trade, excl. motor trade (51) | −.08*** | .12*** | .890 |
| Air transport (62) | −.09 | .12*** | .888 |
| Other services to businesses (74) | −.09*** | .12*** | .887 |
| Rubber and plastic industry (25) | −.09*** | .12*** | .886 |
| Water-based transport (61) | −.09* | .12*** | .885 |
| Metal work (28) | −.09*** | .13*** | .882 |
| Woodwork and manufacture of articles in wood, cork, basketwork or esparto (20) | −.10*** | .13*** | .877 |
| Transport auxiliary services (63) | −.10*** | .13*** | .877 |
| Food industry (15) | −.10*** | .14*** | .873 |
| Dealing in and repairing motor vehicles and motorcycles; retail fuel trade (50) | −.10*** | .14*** | .872 |
| Land-based transport (60) | −.10*** | .14*** | .872 |
| Computer activities (72) | −.10*** | .14*** | .871 |
| Construction (45) | −.11*** | .14*** | .870 |
| Insurance (66) | −.11*** | .14*** | .866 |
| Tobacco industry (16) | −.11*** | .15*** | .864 |
| Retail, excl. motor trade (52) | −.11*** | .15*** | .862 |
| Property activities (70) | −.11** | .15*** | .862 |
| Other extractive industries (14) | −.12*** | .15*** | .861 |
| Manufacture of machinery and plant (29) | −.12** | .15*** | .859 |
| Financial auxiliaries (67) | −.12*** | .15*** | .859 |
| Financial intermediaries (65) | −.12*** | .16*** | .856 |
| Prod. and distr. of electricity, gas, steam and hot water (40) | −.13*** | .16*** | .851 |
| Chemical industry (24) | −.13*** | .17*** | .847 |
| Manufacture of electrical machinery and appliances (31) | −.14*** | .17*** | .845 |
| Manufacture of motor vehicles, trailers and semi-trailers (34) | −.14*** | .17*** | .843 |
| Manufacture of medical, precision, optical watch making instruments (33) | −.15*** | .18*** | .836 |
| Manufacture of other non-metallic mineral products (26) | −.15*** | .18*** | .832 |

*Continued*

*Table 5.3 continued*

| *Industry (NACE two-digit)* | $\widehat{\theta}_k$ | $\widehat{\gamma}_k$ | $e^{-\widehat{\gamma}_k}$ |
|---|---|---|---|
| Textile industry (17) | −.16*** | .19*** | .827 |
| Clothing and fur industry (18) | −.16*** | .20*** | .821 |
| Recovery of recyclable materials (37) | −.17*** | .20*** | .818 |
| Publishing, printing and reproduction (22) | −.18*** | .21*** | .810 |
| Manufacture of radio, television and comm. equip. (32) | −.18*** | .22*** | .806 |
| Coking, refining and nuclear industries (23) | −.20*** | .23*** | .794 |
| Paper and cardboard industry (21) | −.20*** | .24*** | .788 |
| Average wage gap | −.11 | | |
| Range of wage gaps | .24 | | |
| Standard deviation of wage gaps | .05 | | |
| Per cent significant gender wage gaps at the .01 level | 90% | 98% | |
| Number of industries | 42 | 42 | |

*Notes*: Results are based on equation (5.1) in the text, estimated on the basis of the 1995 Structure of Earnings Survey.
* Statistically significant at the .10 level; ** at the .05 level; *** at the .01 level.

## Decomposition of the overall gender wage gap

To complete our analysis, we have decomposed the overall gender wage gap in order to assess what proportion is due to: (a) differences in the distribution of male and female workers across sectors, (b) differences by gender in the structure of industry wage premia, and (c) differences by gender in all other factors, that is intercepts, working conditions, individual and firm characteristics. Therefore, we applied the Oaxaca (1973) and Blinder (1973) decomposition technique as follows:

$$\overline{\ln W_i^m} - \overline{\ln W_i^f} = \sum_{g=1}^{G} \overline{\hat{\lambda}}_g(\overline{V}_g^m - \overline{V}_g^f) + \sum_{g=1}^{G} \overline{V}_g(\hat{\lambda}_g^m - \hat{\lambda}_g^f)$$

$$+ \sum_{k=1}^{K} \overline{\hat{\psi}}_k(s_k^m - s_k^f) + \sum_{k=1}^{K} \overline{s}_k(\hat{\psi}_k^m - \hat{\psi}_k^f) \qquad (5.7)$$

where the superscripts $m$ and $f$ refer respectively to male and female workers; $\overline{\ln W}$ represents the average (Naperian logarithm) of the hourly wage; $\overline{V}$ is a vector containing the mean values of the intercept, working

*Table 5.4* Decomposition of the overall gender wage gap

| Overall gender wage gap | Percentage of overall gender wage gap due to differences in | | |
|---|---|---|---|
| | Employment distribution | Industry coefficients | |
| $\overline{\ln W_i^m} - \overline{\ln W_i^f}$ | $\sum_{k=1}^{K} \overline{\hat{\psi}}_k (s_k^m - s_k^f)$ | $\sum_{k=1}^{K} \overline{s}_k (\hat{\psi}_k^m - \hat{\psi}_k^f)$ | All other factors |
| .20 | 3.1*** | 3.8 | 100.8 |

*Notes*: The level of significance of the different components of the gender wage gaps has been computed according to Oaxaca and Ransom (1998). Estimations are based on the 1995 Structure of Earnings Survey.
* Statistically significant at the .10 level; ** at the .05 level; *** at the .01 level.

conditions, individual and firm characteristics; $s_k$ is the share of employment in sector $k$; $\hat{\lambda}$ and $\hat{\psi}$ are the regression coefficients associated respectively to the vector $V$ and the industry dummy variables:

$$\overline{\lambda}_g = (\hat{\lambda}_g^m - \hat{\lambda}_g^f)/2; \ \overline{\psi}_k = (\hat{\psi}_k^m - \hat{\psi}_k^f)/2; \ \text{and} \quad \overline{s}_k = (s_k^m - s_k^f)/2$$

The significance of the different components of the overall gender wage gap has been tested according to the methodology developed by Oaxaca and Ransom (1998).

Table 5.4 shows that the overall gender wage gap, measured as the difference between the mean log wages of male and female workers, is equal to 0.20. This means that the average female worker earns about 80 per cent of the mean male wage in the Belgian private sector. Further results indicate that only 3 per cent of the overall gender wage gap can be explained by differences in the distribution of male and female workers across sectors. To put it differently, only a very small fraction of the gender wage gap is explained by the segregation of women into lower paying industries. Besides, results show that around 4 per cent of the gender wage gap is accounted for by gender differences in industry wage premia. However, this result is not significantly different from zero (at the 0.10 level). In sum, findings in Table 5.4 suggest that industry effects do not very much contribute to of the overall gender wage gap. This result derives at least partially from the fact that industry wage premia are relatively small in Belgium as compared to other industrialized countries (for example Rycx, 2002).

## Conclusion

In this chapter we have simultaneously analysed the gender wage gap and the inter-industry wage differentials in the Belgian private sector. On the basis of the 1995 Structure of Earnings Survey, we estimated the inter-industry wage differentials by gender and the gender wage gap by industry. Moreover, we decomposed the overall gender wage gap in order to assess what proportion is due to: (a) differences in the distribution of male and female workers across sectors, (b) differences by gender in the structure of industry wage premia, and (c) differences by gender in other productivity-related factors.

Empirical results emphasize the existence of inter-industry wage differentials for both male and female workers, even when controlling for working conditions, individual and firm characteristics. Moreover, we find that, *ceteris paribus*, sectors offering high or low wages are similar for men and women. Findings also indicate that the dispersion of inter-industry wage differentials is of the same order of magnitude for both sexes. Yet the apparent similarity between male and female industry wage differentials is challenged by standard statistical tests. Indeed, simple *t*-tests show that 43 per cent of the industry wage disparities are significantly different for women and men. Moreover, a Chow test indicates that sectoral wage differentials are significantly different as a group for both sexes.

In addition, we found that almost all gender wage gaps within two-digit industries are statistically different from zero (at the 0.01 level). On average women have an inter-industry wage differential of 11 per cent below that of men. Among the sector with the smallest gender wage gaps we find: (1) the renting of machinery and equipment industry, (2) the manufacture of office machinery and computers, and (3) the post and telecommunications industry. The largest gender wage gaps are found in: (i) the paper and cardboard industry, (ii) the coking, refining and nuclear industries, and (iii) the manufacture of radio, television and communication equipment.

Final results show that the overall gender wage gap, measured as the difference between the mean log wages of male and female workers, is equal to 0.20. This means that the average female worker earns about 80 per cent of the mean male wage in the Belgian private sector. Only 3 per cent of this wage gap can be explained by the segregation of women into lower paying industries. Moreover, results suggest that differences by gender in industry wage premia do not significantly contribute to the overall gender wage gap. In sum, findings show that industry effects do not very much account for the overall gender wage gap.

# Appendix

*Table 5A.1* Means (standard deviations) of selected variables

| *Variables* | *Overall sample* | *Women* | *Men* |
|---|---|---|---|
| *Gross hourly wage*: (in ECU), includes overtime paid and bonuses for shift work, night work and/or weekend work, and bonuses (i.e. irregular payments which do not occur during each pay period, such as pay for holiday, 13th month, arrears, advances, travelling expenses, etc.). 1 ECU = 1.23 USD (in 1995). | 15.0 (7.9) | 12.8 (5.4) | 16.0 (8.5) |
| *Education* | | | |
| Primary or no degree: 0–6 years | 12.2 | 9.7 | 13.2 |
| Lower secondary: 9 years | 22.5 | 21.5 | 22.9 |
| Upper secondary: 12 years | 40.8 | 42.4 | 40.1 |
| Higher non-university degree: 14 years | 14.6 | 18.6 | 12.9 |
| University degree: 16 years | 9.4 | 7.4 | 10.2 |
| Post-graduate degree: 17 years or more | 0.6 | 0.4 | 0.6 |
| *Female (yes)* | 29.2 | | |
| *Potential experience*: (years), experience accumulated on the labour market before the last job. | 9.6 (8.3) | 9.1 (8.6) | 9.8 (8.2) |
| *Seniority in the company*: (years) | 10.4 (9.5) | 8.9 (8.7) | 11.0 (9.7) |
| *Region*: location of the establishment | | | |
| Brussels | 19.9 | 25.7 | 17.6 |
| Flanders | 60.7 | 57.0 | 62.2 |
| Wallonia | 19.4 | 17.3 | 20.2 |
| *Hours*: number of hours paid in the reference period, including overtime paid | 162.1 | 147.5 | 168.1 |
| *Type of contract*: | | | |
| Permanent employment contract | 96.7 | 95.0 | 97.5 |
| Fixed-term employment contract | 2.6 | 4.0 | 2.0 |
| Other employment contract | 0.6 | 1.0 | 0.5 |
| *Bonus for shift work, night work, and/or weekend work (yes)* | 16.9 | 6.0 | 21.4 |

*Continued*

*Table 5A.1 continued*

| *Variables* | *Overall sample* | *Women* | *Men* |
|---|---|---|---|
| *Overtime paid (yes)* | 8.1 | 2.9 | 10.2 |
| *Size of the establishment*: number of workers | 669.4 | 406.3 | 777.7 |
| | (1,525.7) | (1,007.2) | (1,681.7) |
| *Level of collective wage bargaining* | | | |
| Only national/sectoral | 45.1 | 48.7 | 43.6 |
| National/sectoral and local | 40.9 | 34.2 | 43.7 |
| Other | 14.0 | 17.1 | 12.7 |
| Number of observations | 80,265 | 22,099 | 58,166 |

*Notes*: Descriptive statistics, computed from the 1995 Structure of Earnings Survey, refer to the weighted sample. Descriptive statistics relative to other variables included in the regression model (e.g. occupation, sectoral affiliation) are available upon request.

*Table 5A.2* Results of the wage regressions

| *Variables/models* | *Overall sample* | *Women* | *Men* |
|---|---|---|---|
| Intercept | 5.384** | 5.412** | 5.189** |
| | (108.6) | (86.9) | (61.9) |
| Education: | | | |
| Primary or no degree | Reference | Reference | Reference |
| Lower secondary | 0.089** | 0.072** | 0.091** |
| | (23.0) | (6.8) | (24.2) |
| Upper secondary | 0.197** | 0.192** | 0.195** |
| | (46.3) | (16.3) | (45.8) |
| Higher non-university degree | 0.306** | 0.310** | 0.300** |
| | (55.8) | (23.2) | (50.5) |
| University degree | 0.511** | 0.499** | 0.513** |
| | (76.5) | (32.3) | (69.4) |
| Post-graduate degree | 0.639** | 0.600** | 0.646** |
| | (33.9) | (19.4) | (28.9) |
| Female (yes) | −0.112** | | |
| | (−39.1) | | |
| Potential experience (years): | | | |
| Simple | 0.019** | 0.024** | 0.019** |
| | (22.3) | (15.1) | (18.3) |
| Squared/$10^2$ | −0.040** | −0.068** | −0.038** |
| | (−6.2) | (−5.8) | (−5.0) |
| Cubed/$10^3$ | 0.002 | 0.005* | 0.002 |
| | (1.2) | (2.0) | (1.3) |

*Continued*

*Table 5A.2 continued*

| *Variables/models* | *Overall sample* | *Women* | *Men* |
|---|---|---|---|
| Seniority in the company (years) | | | |
| Simple | 0.022** | 0.023** | 0.021** |
| | (60.3) | (30.2) | (51.6) |
| Squared/$10^2$ | −0.025** | −0.023** | −0.025** |
| | (−22.9) | (−9.4) | (−20.0) |
| Region: | | | |
| Brussels | Reference | Reference | Reference |
| Flanders | −0.042** | −0.061** | −0.032** |
| | (−13.0) | (−10.6) | (−8.6) |
| Wallonia | −0.046** | −0.044** | −0.045** |
| | (−12.3) | (−6.3) | (−10.2) |
| Hours (ln) | 0.035** | 0.007 | 0.074** |
| | (3.7) | (0.6) | (4.6) |
| Type of contract: | | | |
| Permanent employment contract | Reference | Reference | Reference |
| Fixed-term employment contract | −0.082** | −0.109** | −0.065** |
| | (−9.0) | (−6.2) | (−7.4) |
| Other employment contract | −0.179** | −0.146** | −0.207** |
| | (−5.0) | (−2.9) | (−4.1) |
| Bonus for shift work, night work, and/or weekend work (yes) | 0.064** | 0.048** | 0.066** |
| | (23.0) | (5.7) | (22.4) |
| Overtime paid (yes) | 0.006 | 0.032** | 0.000 |
| | (1.9) | (3.1) | (0.1) |
| Size of the establishment (ln) | 0.030** | 0.029** | 0.030** |
| | (37.4) | (19.5) | (32.1) |
| Level of wage bargaining: | | | |
| National/sectoral | Reference | Reference | Reference |
| National/sectoral and local | 0.018** | 0.030** | 0.014** |
| | (6.6) | (5.9) | (4.3) |
| Other | −0.035** | −0.040** | −0.031** |
| | (−8.7) | (−5.7) | (−6.4) |
| Adjusted $R^2$ | 0.684 | 0.629 | 0.668 |
| *F*-test | 1,423.8** | 341.8** | 1,120.4** |
| Number of observations | 80,265 | 22,099 | 58,166 |

*Notes*: The dependent variable is the (Naperian) logarithm of the individual gross hourly wage. *t*-statistics are reported between brackets. Model estimated by ordinary least squares. White (1980) heteroscedasticity consistent standard errors. A dummy controlling for entrants (i.e., individuals with no seniority), 22 occupational dummies, and 43 indicators of the sectoral affiliation have also been included in the regression. Estimations based on the 1995 Structure of Earnings Survey.

* Statistically significant at the .10 level; ** at the .05 level; *** at the .01 level.

## Notes

1 It thus covers the following sectors: (i) mining and quarrying (C), (ii) manufacturing (D), (iii) electricity, gas and water supply (E), (iv) construction (F), (v) wholesale and retail trade, repair of motor vehicles, motorcycles and personal and household goods (G), (vi) hotels and restaurants (H), (vii) transport, storage and communication (I), financial intermediation (J), and (viii) real estate, renting and business activities (K).

2 See the Appendix for a description of the variables and of the wage regressions.

3 Horrace and Oaxaca (2001) demonstrated that the gender wage gaps across industries estimated by Fields and Wolff (1995) were not invariant to the choice of the left-out reference group of the categorical variables in the wage equation.

## References

Abowd, J., Kramarz, F. and Margolis, D. (1999) 'High Wage Workers and High Wage Firms', *Econometrica*, 67, pp. 251–333.

Arai, M., Ballot, G. and Skalli A. (1996) 'Différentiels intersectoriels de salaire et caractéritiques des employeurs en France', *Economie et Statistique*, 299, pp. 37–58.

Bayard, K., Hellerstein, J., Neumark, D. and Troske, K. (2003) 'New Evidence on Sex Segregation and Sex Differences in Wages from Matched Employer–Employee Data', *Journal of Labor Economics*, 21, pp. 887–922.

Becker, G. (1957) *The Economics of Discrimination*. Chicago: University of Chicago Press.

Benito, A. (2000) 'Inter-Industry Wage Differentials in Great Britain', *Oxford Bulletin of Economics and Statistics*, 62, pp. 727–46.

Blau, F. and Kahn, L. (2000) 'Gender Differences in Pay', *Journal of Economic Perspectives*, 14, pp. 75–99.

Blinder, A. (1973) 'Wage Discrimination: Reduced Form and Structural Variables', *Journal of Human Resources*, 8, pp. 436–65.

Björklund, A., Bratsberg, B., Eriksson, T., Jäntti, M. and Raaum, O. (2004) 'Inter-Industry Wage Differentials and Unobserved Ability: Siblings Evidence from Five Countries', *IZA Discussion Paper* no. 1080.

Carrington, W. and Troske, K. (1998) 'Sex Segregation in U.S. Manufacturing', *Industrial and Labor Relations Reviews*, 51, pp. 445–64.

Edin, P.-A. and Zetterberg, J. (1992) 'Interindustry Wage Differentials: Evidence from Sweden and a Comparison with the USA', *American Economic Review*, 82, pp. 1341–9.

Fields, J. and Wolff, E. (1995) 'Interindustry Wage Differentials and the Gender Wage Gap', *Industrial and Labor Relations Review*, 49, pp. 105–20.

Gibbons, R. and Katz, L. (1992) 'Does Unmeasured Ability Explain Interindustry Wage Differentials?', *Review of Economic Studies*, 59, pp. 515–35.

Goux, D. and Maurin, E. (1999) 'Persistence of Inter-Industry Wage Differentials: A Reexamination using Matched Worker–Firm Panel Data', *Journal of Labor Economics*, 17, pp. 492–533.

Groshen, E. (1991) 'The Structure of the Female/Male Wage Differential: Is it Who You Are, What You Do, or Where You Work?', *Journal of Human Resources*, 26, pp. 457–72.

Haisken-DeNew, J. and Schmidt, C. (1997) 'Interindustry and Interregion Differentials: Mechanics and Interpretation', *Review of Economics and Statistics*, 79, pp. 516–21.
Hartog, J., Pereira, P. and Vieira, J. (2000) 'Inter-Industry Wage Dispersion in Portugal', *Empirica*, 27, pp. 353–64.
Hartog, J., Van Opstal, R. and Teulings, C. (1997) 'Inter-Industry Wage Differentials and Tenure Effects in the Netherlands and the U.S.', *De Economist*, 145, pp. 91–9.
Helwege, J. (1992) 'Sectoral Shifts and Interindustry Wage Differentials', *Journal of Labor Economics*, 10, pp. 55–84.
Horrace, W. and Oaxaca, R. (2001) 'Inter-Industry Wage Differentials and the Gender Wage Gap: An Identification Problem', *Industrial and Labor Relations Review*, 54, pp. 611–18.
Jepsen, M. (2001) 'Evaluation des differentiels salariaux en Belgique: homme-femme et temps partiel – temps plein', *Reflets et Perspectives de la vie economique*, 40, pp. 51–63.
Kahn, L. (1998) 'Collective Bargaining and Interindustry Wage Structure: International Evidence', *Economica*, 65, pp. 507–34.
Krueger, A. and Summers, L. (1988) 'Efficiency Wages and Inter-Industry Wage Structure', *Econometrica*, 56, pp. 259–93.
Lindbeck, A. and Snower, D. (1990) 'Interindustry Wage Structure and the Power of Incumbant Workers', in R. Brunette and C. Dell' Aringa (eds), *Labour Relations and Economic Performance*. London: Palgrave Macmillan, pp. 378–90.
Lucifora, C. (1993) 'Inter-Industry and Occupational Wage Differentials in Italy', *Applied Economics*, 25, pp. 1113–24.
MacPherson, D. and Hirsch, B. (1995) 'Wages and Gender Composition: Why Do Women's Jobs Pay Less?', *Journal of Labor Economics*, 13, pp. 426–71.
Oaxaca, R. (1973) 'Male–Female Wage Differentials in Urban Labour Markets', *International Economic Review*, 14, pp. 693–709.
Oaxaca, R. and Ransom, M. (1998) 'Calculation of Approximate Variance for the Wage Decomposition Differentials', *Journal of Economic and Social Measurement*, 24, pp. 55–61.
Plasman, A., Plasman, R., Rusinek, M. and Rycx, F. (2002) 'Indicators on Gender Pay Equality', *Brussels Economic Review*, 45, pp. 11–40.
Reilly, K. and Zanchi, L. (2003) 'Industry Wage Differentials: How Many, Big and Significant?', *International Journal of Manpower*, 24, pp. 367–98.
Rycx, F. (2002) 'Inter-Industry Wage Differentials: Evidence from Belgium in a Cross-National Perspective', *De Economist*, 150, pp. 555–68.
Rycx, F. (2003) 'Industry Wage Differentials and the Bargaining Regime in a Corporatist Country', *International Journal of Manpower*, 24, pp. 347–66.
Sissoko, S. (2004) 'Revisiting the Gender Wage Gap in an International Comparison', mimeo, Dulbea, Université Libre de Bruxelles.
Teulings, C. and Hartog, J. (1998) *Corporatism or Competition? Labour Contracts, Institutions and Wage Structures in International Comparison*. Cambridge: Cambridge University Press.
Thaler, R. (1989) 'Anomalities: Interindustry Wage Differentials', *Journal of Economic Perspectives*, 3, pp. 191–3.

Vainiomäki, J. Laaksonen, S. (1995) 'Interindustry Wage Differentials in Finland: Evidence from Longitudinal Census Data for 1975–85', *Labour Economics*, 2, pp. 161–73.
Walsh, F. (1999) 'A Multisector Model of Efficiency Wages', *Journal of Labor Economics*, 17, pp. 351–76.
White, H. (1980) 'A Heteroscedasticity-Consistent Covariance Matrix Estimator and a Direct Test for Heteroscedasticity', *Econometrica*, 48, pp. 817–30.
Zanchi, L. (1992) 'The Inter-Industry Wage Structure: Empirical Evidence for Germany and a Comparison with the U.S. and Sweden', *Working Papers in Economics*, 92/76, European University Institute, Florence.
Zweimuller, J. and Barth, E. (1994) 'Bargaining Structure, Wage Determination and Wage Dispersion in 6 OECD Countries', *Kyklos*, 47, pp. 81–93.

# 6
# Gender Wage Inequality and Rent-Sharing: Evidence from a German-Linked Employer–Employee Data-set

*Hermann Gartner**

## Motivation

In a perfectly competitive labour market wages are only determined by productivity characteristics; labour is remunerated with their marginal product. But in the real world we observe huge wage differences not attributable to productivity characteristics. We observe wage differences between industries (Krueger and Summers, 1988), between firms (Abowd, Kramarz and Margolis, 1999) and between gender (Blau and Kahn, 2000).

The main reasons for the wage differences between industries and firms discussed in literature are efficiency wages and wage-bargaining at firm or industrial level. Workers can try to extract rents by bargaining power to receive higher wages. They share rents with the employer, which leads to a correlation of profits with wages.

A reason for gender differences in wages is, as Groshen (1991) and Bayard *et al.* (1999) show, that women work in other industries, in other firms, and in other occupations than men with the same qualification.

* I thank the DFG (project Al 393/6–3 – Gender-Specific Wages and Organizations) for financial support. For valuable comments I thank an anonymous referee and the participants of the conference on the Econometrics of Labour Demand from the Applied Econometrics Association from 6 to 8 September 2004 in Mons (Belgium).

It may be that gender-specific sorting between and within firms leads to different opportunities for male and female employees to extract rents. The aim of this study is to investigate gender differences in rent-sharing for Germany by using a linked employer–employee data-set.

## Theoretical model

Theoretical models on rent-sharing are presented, for example, in Ashenfelter and Brown (1986) or Blanchflower, Oswald and Sanfey (1996). We can interpret this rent-sharing as the solution of a Nash bargaining process. A firm produces output with $L$ workers and receive a revenue for the products of $R(L)$. The firm pays for other goods and services an amount $pV$. The difference $R(L) - pV$ has to be shared between profit and wages. The negotiation problem is:

$$\max_{L,w}\{(1-\theta)\ln(R(L) - wL - pV) + \theta\ln((w - w_0)L)\}$$

The profit of the firm is the revenue $R(L)$ minus the sum of paid wages $wL$ minus the expenditure for other goods and services $pV$. The outside option for the firm is zero profit. $w_0$ represents the wage available to workers if bargaining is cancelled without an agreement; it depends on individual and sector-specific productivity characteristics. $\theta$ is the bargaining power of workers.

Maximization of the Nash product leads to the wage equation:

$$\ln(w) = \ln w_0 + \beta\ln\left(\frac{R(L) - wL - pV}{L}\right)$$

This equation can be estimated, but we have to cope with the endogeneity of profit. Some unobserved characteristics, such as the ability of employees, may affect both the wage and the efficiency of a firm's production and therefore the profit. Consequently, most studies on rent-sharing search for a proper instrument of profit. Blanchflower *et al.* (1996) use, for example, lagged profit and the energy share of costs. Kramarz (2003) use the export price of firms as an instrument for profit.

## Related studies

The development of linked employer–employee data-sets that contain information about firms' profits and information on wages of males and females, allows the empirical investigation of gender differences in rent-sharing. There are a number of new studies that discuss the empirical relationship between rent-sharing and gender inequality, but all studies have to deal with the endogeneity of profit.

Arai and Heyman (2001) use a data-set on Sweden for 1991 and 1995. They estimate a model with an interaction term of profit with gender and separate models for males and females. As instruments they use the lagged profit and the output elasticity. This is a measure for the degree of competition, which influences the profit exogenously. The estimated elasticity for males is 0.017 and for females 0.01. In a further study for Sweden, Nekby (2003) estimates the profit elasticity of wages and an interaction effect of profit with gender. She uses the lagged profit because of the endogeneity problem. Nekby finds an elasticity for males of 0.021 and for females of 0.015, but this difference explains less than 2 percentage points of the wage difference. For France, Fakhfakh and FritzRoy (2002) estimate a profit elasticity of 0.042 for males and 0.027 for females. They use lagged profit for gender-specific OLS estimations. Martins (2004) analyses rent-sharing in Portugal using interactions of exports share with exchange rate as an instrument for profit and finds a profit elasticity of wages of 0.261 for males and of 0.055 for females.

Rycx and Tojerow (2004) examine rent-sharing and gender inequality in Belgium. Profit is instrumented by the value-added and expenditures for goods and services, and they estimate an elasticity for males of 0.066 and for females of 0.056. An advantage of this study is the use of an Oaxaca–Blinder decomposition, which allows wage differences not only to be attributed to gender differences in the elasticity of wages, but also to attribute wage differences to gender-specific sorting between high and low-profit firms. They explain about 14 per cent of the wage gap through differences in the wage elasticity, and about 17 per cent through gender-specific sorting.

In all studies mentioned above, the elasticity of wages for females is lower than for males. The elasticity ranges form 0.01 to 0.26, as summarized by Table 6.1

## Data-set

This study uses the linked employer–employee data-set of the Institute of Employment Research (IAB), LIAB, which combines information on establishments in Germany and information on employees covered by the social security system in Germany. The LIAB data are described in Alda, Bender und Gartner (2005). The data on establishments come from the IAB-establishment panel, a yearly survey from 1993 until

*Table 6.1* Overview of studies investigating gender differences in rent-sharing

| *Author* | *Country* | *Method* | *Variables, instruments* | *Results, elasticity* |
|---|---|---|---|---|
| Nekby (2003) | Sweden | OLS, interaction of females and profit | Lagged profit | Males 0.021, females 0.015; explain 1.5% of wage gap |
| Arai and Heyman (2001) | Sweden | Interaction term and gender-specific estimation, OLS, IV | Lgged profit, output elasticity | Males 0.017, females 0.010 |
| Rycx and Tojerow (2004) | Belgium | Oaxaca–Blinder decomposition, OLS, IV | Value-added and expenditures for goods and services | Males 0.066, females 0.059; explain 14% of the wage gap |
| Fakhfakh and FritzRoy (2002) | France | OLS, gender-specific estimation | Lagged profit | Males 0.042, females 0.027 |
| Martins (2004) | Portugal | IV, gender-specific estimation | Interaction of share of exports with exchange rate | Males 0.261, females 0.055 |

present. The establishments are drawn according to the principle of optimal stratification, where the stratification cells are constructed by 10 classes of firm size and 16 classes of economic branches. Larger firms are overrepresented in the data-set. Therefore, the data represent about 1 per cent of all establishments and 7 per cent of all employees in Germany. The survey provides general information on the establishment, for example the amount of investment, revenues, the size and composition of workforce, the branch and firm size.

The second data source is the register of the employment statistics of the IAB. A documentation of the data-set can be found in Bender, Haas und Klose (2000). This data-set stems from the integrated notifying procedure for health insurance, statutory pension scheme and unemployment insurance in Germany. It covers information on sex, age, qualification, daily exact information on the beginning and the ending of occupation and wages of employees covered by the social security system in Germany. Because of legal sanctions on misreporting, the quality of the data is relatively high despite the fact that they are not produced for research but for administrative aims. The data cover about 80 per cent of all employed persons in Germany. Due to the regulations of the notifying procedure, civil servants, self-employed and unpaid family workers are not included in the data-set.

The analysis in this chapter is done for the year 2001. The establishment panel for 2001 contains about 14,000 establishments. For the combined data-set (LIAB) we merged information on all persons of the register data-set who have been employed in an establishment of the IAB establishment panel on 30 June 2001 (the reference date in the panel). The merging has been done using a firm identification number which is assigned to firms by the German labour office. The merged data-set of the LIAB contains information on about 2 million employees.

Because of the endogeneity of profit, the profit is calculated as the average profit of the previous years 1999 and 2000, and therefore we can only use 7,175 firms covered by the establishment panel from 1999 until 2001. The estimation is restricted to the private sector only. Because of the specific structure of the former planned economy in East Germany, only firms in West Germany are included in the data-set.

The working time of employees is only given by the categories fulltime or parttime. As we cannot calculate wages on an hourly base, we cannot compare fulltime and parttime workers. Therefore, parttime workers are excluded from the sample. We also drop apprentices and workers with implausibly low daily wages below 20 euros. Furthermore, we drop some observations with missing values. Due to these restrictions, the sample used for our analyses covers about 220,000 employees in 1,100 firms; 179,000 of the employees are males, 41,000 are females.

### Variables

The employee data are used to construct human-capital variables. The potential experience is constructed as *exp* = *age* − 6 − *years of schooling*. Six educational levels are distinguished. The average years of schooling are 10 years for lower or intermediate secondary school, 12.125 years for lower or intermediate secondary and vocational training, 13 years for academic secondary school (*Abitur*), 15.125 years for *Abitur* and vocational training, 15 years for college (*Fachhochschule*) and 18 years for university.

The firm-specific human capital is captured by the tenure, which is calculated as the sum of days the employees have worked in the firm. Interruptions of employment are not included in the tenure variable.

The dependent variable is the log of the daily wage. The daily wage is calculated as the mean gross wage paid during an employment spell with a maximum length of 12 months. The gross wage includes all bonus payments, as for example vacation payments.

Since the data come from the social security system, information on the wages are available only up to the contribution limit of the social security (right censoring). For employees with wages above the limit, only the limit is reported. To avoid biased estimations we impute the censored wages with estimated wages. The estimation is done with a Tobit model, where independent variables for the estimation are the qualification, region and branch. If we imputed the expected value for the censored wages, we would have two problems. First, the correlation of the imputed wages with the covariates would be higher than the correlation between the unobserved wages and the covariates. The standard errors of estimations with the imputed data-set would then be too low (a discussion on the problems of imputation of missing data is given in Little und Rubin, 1987, and Schafer, 1997). Second, for some observations the expected value is below the contribution limit of the social security, but we know the true value is above the limit. To solve both problems, the imputed wage is randomly drawn from a truncated normal distribution $N(x'\hat{\beta},\sigma^2)$.[1] In other words: we add to the expected wage an error term with the standard deviation $\sigma$. The standard deviation is estimated by the Tobit model. The drawn wages are truncated at the contribution limit, so that the imputed wage is above this value.[2]

## Econometric model

Most studies on gender wage differentials use the decomposition technique according to Oaxaca (1973); see also Blinder (1973). It allows decomposing the wage differential into two parts: a part explained by differences in observed characteristics and a part explained by differences in the estimated coefficients.

In the first step, wage equations are estimated for the subsamples of males and females:

$$\ln(w_{ij}) = \beta_{g0} + X_i\beta_g + Z_j\gamma_g + \varepsilon_i$$

where $g \in$ (males, females). $\ln(w_{ij})$ is the log of daily wage of employee $i$ in firm $j$. $X_i$ is a vector of human-capital variables of employee $i$. $Z_j$ is a vector of firm-specific variables for firm $j$. The vector includes the firm's profit per employee. There is unobserved firm heterogeneity which leads to errors correlated within firms, and therefore we calculate Huber–White standard errors for the coefficients, which allow for correlations of errors within clusters. Errors must be independent only across firms.

In the second step, mean log wages for males and females are calculated as:

$$\overline{\ln(w_{ij})} = \beta_{m0} + \overline{X}_i\beta_m + \overline{Z}_j\gamma_m \quad \text{and} \quad \overline{\ln(w_{ij})} = \beta_{f0} + \overline{X}_i\beta_f + \overline{Z}_j\gamma_f$$

After some manipulations, the log wage differential can be decomposed as:

$$\underbrace{\overline{\ln(w_m)} - \overline{\ln(w_f)}}_{D\,=\,\text{wage differential}} = \underbrace{(\beta_{m0} - \beta_{f0})}_{S\,=\,\text{shift effect}} + \underbrace{(\overline{X}_m - \overline{X}_f)\beta_m + (\overline{Z}_m - \overline{Z}_f)\gamma_m}_{E\,=\,\text{endowment effect}}$$

$$+ \underbrace{(\beta_m - \beta_f)\overline{X}_f + (\gamma_m - \gamma_f)\overline{Z}_f}_{P\,=\,\text{price effect}}$$

The first term on the right-hand side is the shift effect; it captures differences in the constant term. The second term has been named in the literature as the endowment effect, it captures the wage difference contributed to differences between males and females in the observed average endowment of individuals. The endowment effect of firm-specific variables can be interpreted as a gender-specific sorting between firms. For example: if males work more often in high-profit firms than females, and if the profit elasticity is above zero, then the endowment effect is positive and contributes to the gender wage gap. The third term is the price effect; it is attributed to differences of the estimated coefficients.

In the literature, the price effect is often interpreted as discrimination. But this interpretation assumes that all productivity characteristics are observed, which is not true in most cases. On the other hand, differences in the endowment can also be a result of discrimination, for example if differences in endowment of human capital or differences in firm-specific sorting is a result of discriminatory practice. Therefore, this decomposition technique can only distinguish between observed and unobserved reasons for the gender wage gap.

## Results

We estimate three model specifications. The first model includes only the log of profit per capita and the human-capital variables. The human-capital variables contain the formal level of education, the potential experience (linear, squared and cubic) and tenure. The estimated influence of potential experience has to be interpreted with caution; the potential experience overestimates the real experience of women more often than for males. If women decide to have children, they often reduce their labour supply because of family work. The difference between the coefficients of males and females is therefore partly attributed to measurement error.

The second model comprises, additionally, firm-specific variables: dummies for collective wage contracts and for workers' councils in the firm, 10 dummies for firm size, and 16 dummies for economic branches are included.

The third model deals with the problem of endogeneity of profit. Because of unobserved factors that influence both the wages and the profit of firms, the error term may be correlated with the profit. Therefore, we use instruments for profit and run a 2SLS (two-stage least squares) estimation. One instrument is the share of products sold in foreign countries; firms which produce for a greater market are faced with a higher amount of competition and receive a lower profit. Further instruments are the expenditures for goods and services per head in 1999.

The results of the first model are presented in Table 6.2. The first two columns present regression results; the column *endowment* shows the endowment effect for each variable; *price* shows the price effect. The price effect of the categorical variables is to be interpreted cautiously, because its value depends on the dropped-out category. The column *total* presents the sum of both, the part of the wage difference attributable to

*Table 6.2* Wage estimation: Oaxaca–Blinder decomposition, OLS 1

| | *Male* | | *Female* | | *Decomposition* | | |
|---|---|---|---|---|---|---|---|
| | *coefficient* | *P<\|t\|* | *coefficient* | *P<\|t\|* | *Endowment* | *Price* | *Total* |
| ln(profit) | 0.063 | 0.000 | 0.078 | 0.000 | 0.13 | −2.96 | −2.83 |
| vocat. training | 0.175 | 0.000 | 0.175 | 0.000 | 2.15 | 0.02 | 2.17 |
| second. school (*Abitur*) | 0.172 | 0.000 | 0.211 | 0.000 | −0.14 | −0.05 | −0.19 |
| *Abitur* + voc. training | 0.398 | 0.000 | 0.344 | 0.000 | −1.82 | 0.38 | −1.45 |
| College | 0.652 | 0.000 | 0.600 | 0.000 | 2.05 | 0.16 | 2.21 |
| University | 0.758 | 0.000 | 0.763 | 0.000 | 0.73 | −0.02 | 0.71 |
| experience | 0.044 | 0.000 | 0.037 | 0.000 | 8.06 | 14.34 | 22.39 |
| $experience^2/100$ | −0.152 | 0.000 | −0.146 | 0.000 | −8.59 | −2.97 | −11.56 |
| $experience^3/1000$ | 0.017 | 0.000 | 0.017 | 0.000 | 2.69 | 0.19 | 2.89 |
| tenure | 0.007 | 0.000 | 0.013 | 0.000 | 1.43 | −6.29 | −4.86 |
| const. | 3.850 | 0.000 | 3.705 | 0.000 | | | |
| $N$ | 178630 | | 40511 | sum | 6.69 | 2.79 | 9.48 |
| $R^2$ | 0.425 | | 0.260 | ln wage diff. 23.96 | | | |

*Notes*: Significance levels calculated from Huber–White standard errors; the dropped category is lower secondary school.

the price and endowment effect of the variable. The wage difference to be decomposed is 23.96 in logs multiplied by 100; this can be approximately interpreted as percentage points.

The estimated profit elasticity for male workers with 0.063 is lower than for female workers with 0.078. This leads to a price effect with negative sign, indicating an advantage of females. According to this result, gender differences in rent-sharing lowers the wage gap by 2.96 percentage points. A small part of 0.13 (endowment effect) can be attributed to gender-specific sorting between high and low-profit firms. The sum of all endowment effects of 6.69 stems almost entirely from differences in endowment with human capital. The price effects of human-capital variables explain 5.79 (2.79 + 2.96) percentage points of the gender wage gap.

The firm's profit may correlate with some other variables, not included in the first regression model, and in the second model we include firm-specific dummies. The results are presented in Table 6.3. The elasticity for males and females is lower than in the first model, indicating that rent-sharing explains a lower part of wage variation within industry than of overall wage variation. The elasticity for females is only slightly higher than for males, so that the price effect is minus 0.29 percentage points. In this specification we find no indication for substantial gender differences in rent-sharing.

The price effect of collective contracts and workers' councils together lowers the wage gap by about 10 percentage points. One reason for this may be that the distribution of wages is more compressed within these firms. This is advantageous for female employees, often working at the bottom of the wage distribution. Another reason may be that collective contracts and workers' councils reduce wage discrimination or unobserved productivity differences, or both. For an investigation of this question see Gartner and Stephan (2004).

Because profit is endogenous, the coefficients may be biased, and the third model uses instruments for profit. As in most studies (for example Abowd and Lemieux, 1993) the elasticity of wage rises if the profit is instrumented. The profit elasticity in this model (Table 6.4) is 0.126 for men and 0.101 for women. The higher elasticity for males compared with females leads to a price effect of 5.1 percentage points. But it must be noted that an *F*-test shows that the elasticities for men and women are not significantly different from each other. Again we observe a small endowment effect (0.3) indicating gender-specific sorting between firms. In total, 5.4 percentage points of the wage difference can be attributed to differences in rent-sharing. These are 21.3 per cent of the gender wage gap.

*Table 6.3* Wage estimation: Oaxaca–Blinder decomposition, OLS 2

| | *Male* | | *Female* | | *Decomposition* | | |
|---|---|---|---|---|---|---|---|
| | *coefficient* | *P<\|t\|* | *coefficient* | *P<\|t\|* | *Endowment* | *Price* | *Total* |
| ln(profit) | 0.053 | 0.000 | 0.055 | 0.000 | 0.11 | −0.29 | −0.18 |
| vocat. training | 0.178 | 0.000 | 0.200 | 0.000 | 2.18 | −1.23 | 0.95 |
| second. school (*Abitur*) | 0.184 | 0.000 | 0.215 | 0.000 | −0.14 | −0.04 | −0.19 |
| *Abitur* + voc. training | 0.407 | 0.000 | 0.341 | 0.000 | −1.87 | 0.46 | −1.41 |
| College | 0.640 | 0.000 | 0.578 | 0.000 | 2.01 | 0.19 | 2.20 |
| University | 0.751 | 0.000 | 0.723 | 0.000 | 0.72 | 0.13 | 0.85 |
| experience | 0.045 | 0.000 | 0.038 | 0.000 | 8.18 | 13.48 | 21.66 |
| $experience^2/100$ | −0.150 | 0.000 | −0.149 | 0.000 | −8.50 | −0.80 | −9.30 |
| $experience^3/1000$ | 0.017 | 0.000 | 0.018 | 0.000 | 2.63 | −1.51 | 1.12 |
| tenure | 0.005 | 0.000 | 0.010 | 0.000 | 1.13 | −4.63 | −3.50 |
| collective contract | 0.025 | 0.157 | 0.084 | 0.001 | 0.06 | −5.46 | −5.40 |
| workers' council | 0.070 | 0.002 | 0.120 | 0.001 | 0.19 | −4.69 | −4.50 |
| const. | 3.549 | 0.000 | 3.381 | 0.000 | | | |
| *N* | 178630 | | 40511 | sum | 8.23 | −1.03 | 7.2 |
| $R^2$ | 0.4555 | | 0.3425 | ln wage diff. 23.96 | | | |

*Notes*: Control variables: firm size and industries; significance levels calculated from Huber–White standard errors.

*Table 6.4* Wage estimation: Oaxaca–Blinder decomposition, 2SLS

| | *Male* | | *Female* | | *Decomposition* | | |
|---|---|---|---|---|---|---|---|
| | *coefficient* | $P<\|t\|$ | *coefficient* | $P<\|t\|$ | *Endowment* | *Price* | *Total* |
| ln(profit) | 0.126 | 0.000 | 0.101 | 0.000 | 0.3 | 5.1 | 5.4 |
| vocat. training | 0.174 | 0.000 | 0.196 | 0.000 | 2.0 | −1.2 | 0.8 |
| second. school (*Abitur*) | 0.121 | 0.008 | 0.138 | 0.007 | −0.1 | 0.0 | −0.1 |
| *Abitur* + voc. Training | 0.359 | 0.000 | 0.326 | 0.000 | −1.7 | 0.3 | −1.4 |
| College | 0.613 | 0.000 | 0.551 | 0.000 | 1.9 | 0.2 | 2.1 |
| University | 0.714 | 0.000 | 0.705 | 0.000 | 1.0 | 0.0 | 1.0 |
| experience | 0.046 | 0.000 | 0.038 | 0.000 | 8.4 | 16 | 24.4 |
| $experience^2/100$ | −0.151 | 0.000 | −0.142 | 0.000 | −8.8 | −4.4 | −13.2 |
| $experience^3/1000$ | 0.017 | 0.000 | 0.017 | 0.000 | 2.8 | 0.2 | 3.0 |
| Tenure | 0.005 | 0.000 | 0.010 | 0.000 | 1.0 | −5.4 | −4.4 |
| collective contract | 0.030 | 0.249 | 0.087 | 0.001 | 0.1 | −5.3 | −5.2 |
| workers' council | 0.084 | 0.001 | 0.125 | 0.001 | 0.2 | −3.8 | −3.6 |
| const. | 3.260 | 0.000 | 2.968 | 0.000 | | | |
| *N* | 177175 | | 40364 | sum | 8.4 | −14.3 | −6.0 |
| $R^2$ | 0.46 | | 0.37 | ln wage diff. 23.96 | | | |

*Notes*: Instruments: share of exports and expenditures for goods and services per capita; significance levels calculated from Huber–White standard errors.

To control the validity of the instruments I have applied an overidentification test according to Sargan (1958). The null hypothesis of this test, that excluded instruments are valid, can not be rejected at a level of 76 per cent. Thus the overidentification test gives no hint that the instruments are inappropriate.

## Conclusion

This study has investigated gender differences in rent-sharing. I have used the German linked employer–employee data of the Institute of Employment Research (IAB), LIAB, for 2001. The 2SLS procedure estimates a profit elasticity of wages of 0.126 for males and 0.101 for females, which are higher than estimates for other countries in similar studies. This may be because of a higher differentiated industry classification in other studies.

Differences in rent-sharing explain about 21 per cent (5.4 percentage points) of the gender wage gap; 0.3 percentage points are attributed to gender-specific sorting across high and low-profit firms; 5.1 percentage points are attributed to the difference in profit elasticity.

One possible reason for the differences in rent-sharing is a difference in the positions of male and female workers within the firm. Men are more frequently in higher positions in a firm and may therefore have more opportunities to extract rents. A question for future research concerns differences in rent-sharing across hierarchical positions, which may result in differences in wages across gender. The institutions of wage-bargaining are collective contracts and workers' councils, and a further topic for future research is the interaction of the wage bargaining institutions with rent-sharing.

### Notes

1 An assumption is that the wages follow a log-normal distribution, which empirically is a good approximation.

2 A detailed description of the method for imputation of censored wages in Gartner (2004) is available on request by the author.

### References

Abowd, J.M. and Lemieux, T. (1993) 'The Effects of Product Market Competition on Collective Bargaining Agreements: The Case of Foreign Competition in Canada', *Quarterly Journal of Economics*, 108, pp. 983–1014.

Abowd, J.M., Kramarz, F. and Margolis, D.N. (1999) 'High-Wage Workers and High-Wage Firms', *Econometrica*, 67, pp. 251–333.

Alda, H., Bender, S. and Gartner, H. (2005) 'The Linked Employer–Employee Data Set of the IAB (LIAB)', IAB Discussion Paper, Nurenberg.

Arai, M. and Heyman, F. (2001) 'Wages, Profits, and Individual Unemployment Risk: Evidence from Matched Worker–Firm Data', FIEF Working Paper series no. 172.

Ashenfelter, O. and Brown, J.N. (1986) 'Testing the Efficiency of Employment Contracts', *Journal of Political Economy*, XCIV, pp. 40–87.

Bayard, K., Hellerstein, J., Neumark, D. and Troske, K. (1999) 'New Evidence on Sex Differences in Wages from Matched Employee–Employer Data', NBER Working Paper no. 7003.

Bender, S., Haas, A. and Klose, C. (2000) 'IAB Employment Subsample 1975–1995. Opportunities for Analysis Provided by the Anonymised Subsample', IZA Discussion Paper no. 117 IZA, Bonn.

Blanchflower, D.G., Oswald, A.J. and Sanfey, P. (1996) 'Wages, Profits, and Rent-Sharing', *Quarterly Journal of Economics*, 111, pp. 227–251.

Blau, F.D. and Kahn, L.M. (2000) 'Gender Differences in Pay', *Journal of Economic Perspectives*, 14, pp. 75–99.

Blinder, A.S. (1973) 'Wage Discrimination: Reduced Form and Structural Estimates', *Journal of Human Resources*, 8, pp. 436–55.

Fakhfakh, F. and FritzRoy, F. (2002) 'Basic Wages and Firm Characteristics: Rent Sharing in French Manufacturing', CRIEFF Discussion Paper no. 0203, University of St Andrews.

Gartner, H. (2004) 'The Imputation of Wages above the Contribution Limit with the German IAB Employment Sample', IAB Technical Report, Nuremberg.

Gartner, H. and Stephen, G. (2004) 'How Collective Contracts and Works Councils Reduce the Gender Wage Gap', IAB Discussion Paper no. 8/04.

Groshen, E.L. (1991) 'The Structure of the Female/Male Wage Differential: Is it who you are, What you do, or Where you work?', *Journal of Human Resources*, 26, pp. 457–72.

Kramarz, F. (2003) 'Wages and International Trade', CEPR Discussion Papers 3936.

Krueger, A.B. and Summers, L.M. (1988) 'Efficiency Wages and the Interindustry Wage Structure', *Econometrica* 56, pp. 259–93.

Little, R.J.A. and Rubin, D.R. (1987) *Statistical Analysis with Missing Data*. New York: John Wiley.

Martins, P.S. (2004) 'Rent Sharing Before and After the Wage Bill', IZA Discussion Paper no. 1376.

Nekby, L. (2003) 'Gender Differences in Rent Sharing and Its Implications for the Gender Wage Gap, Evidence from Sweden', *Economic Letters*, 81, pp. 403–10.

Oaxaca, R. (1973) 'Male–female Wage Differentials in Urban Labor Markets', *International Economic Review*, 14, pp. 693–709.

Rycx, F. and Tojerow, I. (2004) 'Rent Sharing and the Gender Wage Gap in Belgium – Evidence from Matched Worker-Firm Data', *International Journal of Manpower*, 25, pp. 279–99.

Sargan, J.D. (1958) 'The Estimation of Economic Relationships using Instrumental Variables', *Econometrica*, 26, pp. 393–415.

Schafer, J.L. (1997) *Analysis of Incomplete Multivariate Data*. London: Chapman & Hall.

# Part IV

# Dynamics and Unobserved Heterogeneity

# 7

# Does Unobserved Heterogeneity Matter? A Panel-Data Analysis of the Gender Pay Gap

*Amynah Gangji, Kristian Orsini and Salimata Sissoko**

## Introduction

A large number of studies have documented a generalized tendency towards a reduction in the gross gender pay gap in the European countries during the 1970s. The following decades have nevertheless produced a more scattered pattern: while some countries have continued to witness a reduction in the gender wage inequalities, others have shown a stationary trend. The gender gap hence remains at an important level, although significant differences across countries may be observed.

Empirical research has pointed out several reasons that may lay behind the dynamic of the pay differential. The factors identified mainly concern labour-market mechanisms such as changes in human-capital endowments, overall wage structure, wage-setting arrangements, as well as legislation on equal opportunities (see for example Rosholm and Smith, 1996; Dolton, O'Neill and Sweetman, 1996; Blau and Kahn, 1997; Rice, 1999).

Most pay-gap analyses rely on the Oaxaca–Blinder (1973) technique. This method decomposes the gender pay gap into a part due to differences in productive characteristics (education, potential work experience,

---

* We thank Michele Cincera, Robert Plasman, Rodrigo Ruz-Torres, François Rycx, Jean-Luc Demeulemeester, and participants of the DULBEA-ETE internal seminar, SOLE (2004), EPUNet (2004) and AEA (2004) conferences for helpful comments and discussions on earlier drafts.

tenure, and so on), and a part shaped by non-productive characteristics (such as gender, race, and so on).

Earlier studies have shown that estimating wage equations by the ordinary least-squares (OLS) technique may produce biased results due to heterogeneity bias (see for example Hausman and Taylor, 1981). Heterogeneity bias arises because unobserved characteristics (such as motivation, ability) may be correlated with observed individual characteristics (for example work continuity education). In particular, if motivation is correlated with intermittent labour-force participation then estimates of the effects of intermittency might be picking up motivation and not earning-power losses caused by intermittency (Moon-Kak and Polachek, 1994). This issue is crucial for policy purposes, since the estimated rate of return on observed individual characteristics determines the extent of wage discrimination.

Fewer studies, however, have addressed the problem of endogeneity when estimating the gender pay gap. The only exceptions are Cornwell and Rupert (1988), Baltagi and Khanti-Akom (1990) and Moon-Kak and Polachek (1994).

Endogeneity occurs when one or more explicative variables are not exogenously assigned, but determined by some other characteristics of the individual. A typical example of endogeneity is education. If the latter is not exogenously assigned, but determined by the extent of own abilities and motivation, the estimated rate of return on education will be biased.

The aforementioned studies, however, do not provide an international comparison of the gender pay gap adjusted for unobserved heterogeneity and, more importantly, do not attempt to explain through which channels the inclusion of individual heterogeneity affects the gender pay gap in a particular country. The main purposes of this chapter are to estimate the adjusted gender pay gap over time for eight European countries, to analyse the effect of incorporating unobserved heterogeneity, and finally to evaluate the impact of changes in individual characteristics on the evolution of the pay differential.

We estimate the adjusted gender pay gap with the Oaxaca (1973) decomposition technique, and use the panel-data estimator proposed by Hausman and Taylor (1981). This estimator is preferred to the traditionally within-group fixed-effect estimators because it avoids a well-known drawback of the within estimators, namely that all time-invariant variables are eliminated by the data transformation – which implies that their coefficients cannot be estimated – and that the estimator is not fully efficient.

As far as we know, this study is the only one to use recent European panel data-sets to present a comparison of the (un)adjusted gender wage gap over time estimated with both cross-sectional and panel-data econometric techniques. Our results confirm the common findings of previous studies. Gender pay differentials are higher in more liberal economies and in economies providing lower supports for female employment (UK, Ireland, Germany and Spain). Although Italy and Spain are usually clustered together in the Mediterranean typology, these countries differ in the extent of their gender pay differential. Italy presents a smaller pay gap, probably owing to its concentrated wage structure and a high level of public supports for female employment (see Gornick *et al.*, 1997; Rice, 1999; Blau and Kahn, 1996).

Adjusting for individual heterogeneity, we find an increase in the rates of return of potential experience and education for both men and women. In addition, compared to the reference category, the wage differentials due to subordinate occupations, fixed-term contracts and relatively small enterprise size decreases. Furthermore, in accordance with the previous national studies, we observe a decrease of the adjusted wage differential. We observe that the decrease is related to the gender differences in our endogenous variables, that is to education and to a lesser extent to work experience. This fall ranges from 7 per cent in Belgium to 41 per cent and 54 per cent in the UK and Denmark respectively. Finally, our results suggest that the narrowing of pay differentials between men and women goes with a convergence of observed productive characteristics between men and women in all countries.

The remainder of the chapter is structured as follows. The next section describes our data, and subsequent sections present national studies on the gender wage gap, estimation methods and results, and a final section concludes.

## Data and descriptive statistics

The European Community Household Panel Study (ECHP) is a convenient data-set for estimating panel regressions. The data gathering was planned for nine years and started in 1994. In that year, the survey was conducted in 12 member states and collected information on a representative sample of 60,500 households, corresponding to 170,000 individuals. Since then, Austria (1995), Finland (1996) and Sweden (1997) have joined the survey.

Wage equations are estimated for eight European countries: Belgium, Denmark, Germany, Ireland, Italy, the Netherlands, Spain and the United Kingdom. This subset allows comparison of countries with welfare states of the conservative-corporatist model (Belgium, Germany, Italy, the Netherlands and Spain), the Scandinavian model (Denmark) and the liberal welfare model (Ireland and the UK). Finally, according to Gornick *et al.* (1997) these countries differ according to their level of public support to childcare arrangements, maternity and parental leave provision. High support is encountered in Denmark and Belgium, medium support in West Germany, Italy and the Netherlands and low support in Ireland, Spain and the United Kingdom.

The selected sub-sample consists of individuals aged between 20 and 60 years, who are employed in the private sector, are not self-employed and work more than 30 hours per week. The above restrictions lead to a sub-sample of 9,251 observations (1,905 individuals) in Belgium to 26,444 in Germany (5,430 individuals). The sample is unbalanced. In Belgium, about 36 per cent of individuals remained in the sub-sample the eight years. This rate falls to 33 per cent in Germany and about 30 per cent in the UK, Italy and Denmark.

The earning measure used in this analysis is the logarithm of the gross deflated hourly wage including bonus. The explanatory variables correspond to employees' working conditions and characteristics. We have included the level of education, the potential work experience[1] (in level, squared), the firm size (small, medium and large),[2] dummy variables for the occupations (1-digit) and the employment contract (fixed term or permanent contract).

The descriptive statistics (see Appendix 1) show that in general women in paid employment are better educated than men. On the other hand, female work experience is largely lower than that of men. This difference is partly explained by the average lower age of women relative to men, but also by different life-cycle employment strategies. Women are also more numerous in subordinate occupations, as clerk or service workers, in small and medium-sized firms and are also more likely to be employed with fixed-term employment contracts.

In 1994, the unadjusted gender pay differential was highest in the UK (31.9%), in Ireland (27.6%) and in the Netherlands (26.0%), and smallest in Denmark (14.4%), Italy (15.9%) and Belgium (16.2%)

*Table 7.1* Average gender wage gap in European countries, 1994 and 2001 (euros)

| | *1994* | | | *2001* | | |
|---|---|---|---|---|---|---|
| | *Male* | *Female* | *Gap* | *Male* | *Female* | *Gap* |
| Belgium | 11.96 | 10.03 | 16.2% | 14.09 | 12.08 | 14.3% |
| Denmark | 17.16 | 14.69 | 14.4% | 20.35 | 17.15 | 15.7% |
| Germany | 12.36 | 9.48 | 23.3% | 13.75 | 10.65 | 22.5% |
| Ireland | 9.33 | 6.75 | 27.6% | 11.71 | 9.49 | 18.9% |
| Italy | 7.39 | 6.21 | 15.9% | 7.66 | 6.46 | 15.6% |
| The Netherlands | 15.58 | 11.52 | 26.0% | 16.18 | 12.67 | 21.7% |
| Spain | 6.20 | 4.77 | 23.0% | 7.02 | 5.38 | 23.3% |
| United-Kingdom | 12.25 | 8.34 | 31.9% | 14.77 | 10.90 | 26.2% |

*Note*: Wage gap $\bar{w}^m - \bar{w}^f / \bar{w}^m$, where $\bar{w}^m$ and $\bar{w}^f$ are the male and female deflated average hourly wages.

*Source*: European Community Household Panel (ECHP).

(see Table 7.1). In 2001, the UK still showed the most important gender pay differentials (26.2%), while Spain (23.3%) and Germany (22.5%) stagnated at a level close to that of the beginning of the period. The smallest gender pay gap (14.3%) in 2001 is found in Belgium. Noteworthy is the case of Denmark, which shows a slight increase in the gender pay differential. The largest reduction is observed in Ireland (−32%) and in the UK and Netherlands (−18% and −17% respectively). This ranking is in accordance with most studies using the ECHP in the literature and analysing gender pay gaps in the EU (Rice, 1999; Beblo *et al.*, 2003; Rubery *et al.*, 2003; Plasman *et al.*, 2004).

## An overview of the gender wage gap in Europe

According to Naur and Smith (1996), after a period of decrease (1960–70), the Danish gender wage gap has been slightly increased since the mid-1980s (also see Rosholm and Smith, 1996). An important explanation is the decentralization of the wage formation process and the increased wage dispersion. Datta Gupta, Oaxaca and Smith (2001) show that female gains in human capital were wiped out by the idiosyncratic increase in observed skill prices, which hurt women relative to men.

In Germany the gender pay gap has decreased over last 20 years, while female employment has progressively increased. Nevertheless, this country is characterized by a dominant 'single male breadwinner' model: family and tax policies discourage the labour-force participation of married women by imposing high implicit marginal tax rates on labour income (Rice, 1999). According to Beblo and Wolf (2000), the typical female employment record (maternity break followed by part-time employment) results in a substantial lower wage rate. Kunze (2002) has showed the importance of the gender-biased effect of work interruptions is in disfavour of women.

The study by Harkness (1996) finds that the reduction of discrimination played a stronger role than the progressive convergence of human capital (see also Blackaby *et al.*, 1997) in the evolution of the British gender pay gap. On the other hand, a study by Joshi and Paci (1998) demonstrates that more than the equal opportunity legislation, the main reason for the reduction of the British gap since the mid-1970s is women catching up with men in measures of human capital (see also Dolton *et al.*, 1996). Finally, the high level of wage inequalities in the UK explains an important part of the pay gap (Blau and Kahn, 1996).

According to Barrett and Callan (2000) the Irish adjusted pay gap narrowed significantly between 1987 and 1997. The shift in the wage structure towards greater vertical inequality partly explains why this fall off in the 'discrimination' component was not paralleled to a similar reduction of the unadjusted gender pay gap. Further, a significant part of the pay gap seems to be attributable to gender differences in length of work experience and absences from the labour market (Russell *et al.*, 2002).

According to Villa (2002), the Italian gender pay gap decreased between 1985–96. Wage inequalities decreased between the late 1970s and 1980s and remained quite constant in the rest of the decade (Brandolini *et al.*, 2001). The Spanish gender pay gap narrowed during the 1980s and 1990s. A substantial part of this differential is due to differences in returns to observable characteristics (Ugidos, 1997; Molto, 2002), and further, according to Molto (2002), the gender gap is also particularly influenced by the over-representation of women on the lower earnings steps.

In the Netherlands, overall wage inequality rose both in the 1980s and the 1990s due to the increasing return to skills. At the same time the wage differential between men and women remained fairly constant (Plantenga *et al.*, 2002).

Finally, the study by Plasman and Sissoko (2002) indicates that Belgium experienced a decrease in its gender pay differential during the 1980s and 1990s and nowadays presents a relatively narrowed pay gap. This is mainly due to its wage structure: the traditionally high levels of guaranteed minimum income and guaranteed minimum wage (introduced in 1974 and 1975 respectively) and a centralized wage-bargaining system produce a relatively concentrated wage dispersion.

## Estimation method

### Wage equations

The wage equations have been estimated taking into account both labour supply characteristics (chiefly human-capital variables such as level of education or potential prior work experience) and labour demand characteristics (namely occupations, size of establishments, contract type). We have estimated wage equations with ordinary least-squares (OLS) on cross-section samples (1994 and 2001), and with the Hausman and Taylor (1981) estimation method on the pooled sample.

We assume that wages are determined according to the following equation:

$$\ln W_{it} = \beta_0 + \beta_1 X_{it} + \beta_2 Z_i + \alpha_i + \varepsilon_{it} \tag{7.1}$$

where $i = 1,\ldots,N$ indexes individuals and $t = 1,\ldots,T$ indexes time periods; $\ln W_{it}$ (the logarithm of hourly wage) is the dependant variable; $X_{it}$ represents the time-varying regressors; $Z_i$ is the matrix of the time-invariant regressors; and $\alpha_i$ is the unobserved heterogeneity term. It is supposed time-invariant and individual-specific; in fact, it measures the effects of unobserved characteristics such as ability, motivation, ambition or efforts on wages, which may vary between individuals but remain constant in time. It is assumed to have zero mean and constant variance $\sigma_\alpha^2$ conditional on $X$ and $Z$. Failure to take into account this heterogeneity term will lead to correlation between the error terms of same individuals. Following Hausman Taylor we may divide $X_{it}$ and $Z_{it}$: $X_{it} = (X_{1it}, X_{2it})$ and $Z_{it} = (Z_{1it}, Z_{2it})$, with $X_{2it}$ and $Z_{2it}$ being correlated with the unobserved heterogeneity term. $\varepsilon_{it}$ is the error term measuring the effects of unobserved variables that vary both across individuals and over time; it is supposed to be not correlated with $X$, $Z$ and $\alpha_i$, and distributed with mean zero and constant variance ($\sigma^2\varepsilon$).

As far as the pooled sample estimations are concerned, we know that if $\alpha_i$ is correlated with $X$ and $Z$, ordinary least-squares (OLS) and generalized least-squares (GLS) estimation methods would yield biased and inconsistent estimates of the parameters. The fixed effects (within-group fixed effect, FE) model overcomes this problem by eliminating the individual effect in the sample and transforming the data with either a first-difference or a mean-deviation operator. Resulting estimators are unbiased, but important information concerning time-invariant characteristics (for example education, sex) is lost, provoking a loss of efficiency. The IV(Instrumental Variables)/GLS estimation technique applied in this study yields unbiased estimators that are more efficient than those obtained with fixed effects.

Following Rosholm and Smith (1996), the estimation procedure is as follows. First a fixed effects model is applied:

$$\ln W_{it} - \ln W_{i.} = \beta_1 (X_{it} - X_{i.}) + (\varepsilon_{it} - \varepsilon_{i.}) \tag{7.2}$$

where $W_i = (1/T_i)\sum_{t=1}^{T_i} W_{it}$, $X_{i.} = (1/T_i)\sum_{t=1}^{T_i} X_{it}$, $\varepsilon_i = (1/T_i)\sum_{t=1}^{T_i} \varepsilon_{it}$.

In a second step, the mean individual residuals are computed using the estimators obtained in the fixed-effects equation:

$$\hat{d}_{i.} = \ln W_{i.} - X_{i.}\hat{\beta} \tag{7.3}$$

These residuals are then regressed on time-invariant characteristics (*'between effect model'*):

$$\hat{d}_{i.} = Z_i\gamma + (\alpha_i + \varepsilon_{i.}) \tag{7.4}$$

If the $Z_i$ variables are correlated with the unobserved error term, the estimation method suggested by Hausman and Taylor involving instrumental variables must be employed.[3]

In the third step, the estimates of the variances obtained in the preceding regressions will be used in order to calculate the weights for the final GLS estimation:

$$\theta_i = 1 - \frac{\sigma_\varepsilon}{\sqrt{\sigma_\varepsilon^2 + T_i\sigma_\alpha^2}} \tag{7.5}$$

where $\hat{\sigma}_\alpha^2 = \hat{\sigma}_{be}^2 + (1/N)\sum_{i=1}^{N} (1/T_i)\hat{\sigma}_\varepsilon^2$.

Finally, after having computed the individual weights, it is possible to estimate the following GLS equation:

$$Y_{it} - \theta_i Y_{i\cdot} = (X_{it} - \theta_i)\beta + (1 - \theta_i)Z_i\gamma + (\varepsilon_{it} - \theta_i \varepsilon_i X_{i.}) \tag{7.6}$$

**Cross-section and panel-data decompositions**

We use the standard Oaxaca (1973) decomposition technique to differentiating the gender gap into a market component (explained by differences in labour supply and demand characteristics) and a residual component. Different specifications are presented: we use the OLS estimators of 1994 or 2001 with the corresponding average observed characteristics of men and women and the GLS estimators with instrumentation with the average observed characteristics of men and women of 1994 or 2001. To perform the first decomposition for 2001 for example, we estimate semi-log wage regressions for men and women separately:

$$\ln \overline{w}^m_{2001} = \alpha^m_{\mathrm{OLS}} + \beta^m_{\mathrm{OLS}} \overline{x}^m_{2001} \tag{7.7}$$

$$\ln \overline{w}^f_{2001} = \alpha^f_{\mathrm{OLS}} + \beta^f_{\mathrm{OLS}} \overline{x}^f_{2001} \tag{7.8}$$

The $m$ and $f$ superscripts refer to men and women respectively, $\overline{w}^m_{2001}/\overline{w}^f_{2001}$ denotes the average wage of men/women in the sample of 2001, $\beta^m_{\mathrm{OLS}}/\beta^f_{\mathrm{OLS}}$ are the OLS estimators of the separated wage equations of men/women, $\alpha^m_{\mathrm{OLS}}/\alpha^f_{\mathrm{OLS}}$ are the intercepts, and $\overline{x}^m_{2001}/\overline{x}^f_{2001}$ the average observed characteristics of men/women in the sample of 2001.

The gender wage gap then has the following specification:

$$\begin{aligned} \ln \overline{w}^m_{2001} - \ln \overline{w}^f_{2001} = {} & \beta^m_{\mathrm{OLS}}(\overline{x}^m_{2001} - \overline{x}^f_{2001}) \\ & + (\alpha^m_{\mathrm{OLS}} - \alpha^f_{\mathrm{OLS}}) + \overline{x}^f_{2001}(\beta^m_{\mathrm{OLS}} - \beta^f_{\mathrm{OLS}}) \end{aligned} \tag{7.9}$$

In the latter equation, the first term represents the explained part: the differences between men and women in individual characteristics, $x$; the second term gives the residual part. This last term regroups the unobserved characteristic differences and the differentials in return for equal characteristics between men and women.

As far as the analysis of the impact of changes in productive characteristics between men and women is concerned, following Rosholm and Smith (1996) we compare the explained part of the year 1994 with that of 2001:

$$\text{Explained part (1994): } \beta^{m}_{IV/GLS}(\overline{x}^{m}_{1994} - \overline{x}^{f}_{1994}) \tag{7.10}$$

$$\text{Explained part (2001): } \beta^{m}_{IV/GLS}(\overline{x}^{m}_{2001} - \overline{x}^{f}_{2001}) \tag{7.11}$$

where $\beta^{m}_{IV/GLS}$ are the GLS estimators with instrumentation of the wage equation of men on the pooled sample, and $\overline{x}^{m}/\overline{x}^{f}$ the average observed characteristics of men/women in the sample of 1994 or 2001.

Following Oaxaca and Ransom (1998), we have also tested the significance of the components of the wage decomposition using a Wald test for testing non-linear restrictions as well as the delta method. Since it is difficult to find the finite sample distribution of the elements of the decomposition, we use the delta method to find its asymptotic distribution, based on maximum likelihood principles.

Suppose $H_0$: $c(b) = 0$, where $c(b)$ is the non-linear function of the estimated coefficients of the semi-log wage equation given by the elements of the decomposition. Let the estimated coefficient vector be $\beta$ and the estimated variance–covariance matrix be $V(c(b))$. Let $Rb = c(b) = r$ denote the set of $q$ linear hypotheses to be tested jointly. The asymptotic variance of $c(\beta)$ is approximated by:

$$V(c(b)) = \left(\frac{\partial c(\beta)}{\partial \beta}\right)' V(\beta)\left(\frac{\partial c(\beta)}{\partial \beta}\right)$$

where $(\partial c(\beta)/\partial \beta)$ is a vector of partial derivatives of the constraint with respect to each of its arguments; that is $(\partial c(\beta_1)/\partial \beta_1 \; \partial c(\beta_2)/\partial \beta_2 \; \ldots \; \partial c(\beta_k)/\partial \beta_k)$(this is known as the delta method).

The test statistic is:

$$W = (c(b) - r)'[RV(c(b))R']^{-1}(c(b) - r) \sim \chi^2_q$$

and $F = (1/q)\, W$

## Results

### The wage equations

We obtain wage equations for the whole sample as well as separated equations by gender estimated by OLS, GLS, FE, IV/GLS on the pooled sample, and wage equations estimated by OLS on the samples of 1994 and 2001 (see Appendix 2 for wage equations).[4] Adjusting for individual heterogeneity and applying a variance component model (IV/GLS), reduces the standard errors compared with those obtained with fixed-effect (FE).

Our separated wage equations by gender for 1994 and 2001 are in accordance with previous studies using ECHP data (Rice, 1999; Rückert, 1997; Plasman *et al.*, 2002). Estimated coefficients of education variables confirm the strong positive effect of education upon wage; whatever the level, men are better remunerated than women for their level of education. The wage equations also confirm the positive influence of experience upon wages. In agreement with the literature, we observe a concave relation between wages and experience. Our results from the pooled sample indicate that an additional year of experience leads to about 1.5 per cent higher wages in Belgium, Denmark, Italy and Spain, and to 2.1–2.6 per cent in Germany, Ireland, the Netherlands and the UK. For all countries, except Spain, the return of experience is larger for men. The variables relative to the size of the company and type of contract show a positive relation between wage and the size of firm or the permanent nature of an employment contract.

As with OLS, GLS estimates assume no correlation between explanatory variables and the latent $\alpha_{i.}$. Although GLS estimators differ from OLS estimates, results remain globally the same. Let us note the decrease of the male–female differential and the increase of the rates of return of experience, education as well as the reduction of penalty due to low skilled and subordinate occupations,[5] fixed employment contract and relatively small enterprise size.

The within-groups estimates eliminate the latent variable ($\alpha_i$) as well as our time-invariant variables (level of education and sex in pooled male–female samples). Estimators are unbiased. Comparing fixed-effect estimates with GLS, we see the continuous increase of the return of experience and fall of penalty relative to subordinate occupations, fixed-term contracts, and so on. Finally, using the Hausman and Taylor test (1981) for heterogeneity, we find a correlation between explanatory variables and the latent $\alpha_i$. This is solved by instrumentation of the variables potentially correlated with the heterogeneity term.

We have first chosen to take the level of education as the only endogenous variable (see Appendix 2 for the wage equations).[6] The Hausman test[7] indicates that we cannot reject the null hypothesis of no correlation with the heterogeneity term, with this specification. We have checked the sensitivity of our results to an alternative choice of the exogenous variable ($X_1$). Appendix 2 also presents the wage equations for education and experience (level and squared) as the endogenous variables.[8] Once again, the Hausman test does not reject the null hypothesis and the test statistics are even lower than with the first specification. Furthermore, globally, IV/GLS estimates treating both education and experience as endogenous are very similar to within-groups estimates.

## Cross-section decomposition over time

We analyse the evolution of the gender pay gap over time using OLS estimates of the wage equations of 1994 and 2004 (see Table 7.2). As mentioned above, a standard Oaxaca decomposition identifies an explained and a residual part of the wage differential. The former represents the gender differences in observed characteristics and the latter is constituted by the gender differences in observed characteristic prices and by the difference in the constant between men and women. The explained and residual components are significant at the 1% level for all countries under study.

In 1994, the unadjusted gender pay gap was higher than 35 per cent in the UK, between 20–30 per cent in the Netherlands, Spain, Germany and Ireland, and below 20 per cent in Denmark, Belgium and Italy. In 2001, the UK still recorded the highest gender differential with around 30 per cent and the Netherlands, Spain and Germany a gap between 20–30 per cent. Ireland feel below the 20 per cent level and Belgium, Italy and Denmark remained below 20 per cent.

These results confirm that the gender pay differential is higher in more liberal economies and in economies providing lower supports of female employment (UK, Ireland, Germany and Spain). We note that although Italy and Spain are both Mediterranean welfare models, Italy has a higher level of public support of female employment than Spain and records a lower gender pay differential.

*Table 7.2* Cross-section decomposition, Oaxaca (1973), 1994 and 2001

| | *1994* | | | *2001* | | |
|---|---|---|---|---|---|---|
| | *Gap* | *Explained*[a] | *Residual*[b] | *Gap* | *Explained*[a] | *Residual*[b] |
| Belgium | 0.158 | 0.015** | 0.143*** | 0.134 | 0.014** | 0.12*** |
| | | 9.7% | 90.3% | | 10.7% | 89.3% |
| Denmark | 0.137 | 0.047*** | 0.090*** | 0.157 | 0.047*** | 0.110*** |
| | | 34.1% | 65.9% | | 29.7% | 70.3% |
| Germany | 0.269 | 0.053*** | 0.216*** | 0.248 | 0.052*** | 0.196*** |
| | | 19.8% | 80.2% | | 20.9% | 79.1% |
| Ireland | 0.276 | 0.107*** | 0.169*** | 0.193 | 0.075*** | 0.118*** |
| | | 38.7% | 61.3% | | 39.0% | 61.0% |
| Italy | 0.168 | 0.037*** | 0.131*** | 0.151 | 0.020*** | 0.131*** |
| | | 22.2% | 77.8% | | 13.2% | 86.8% |
| The Netherlands | 0.239 | 0.067*** | 0.173*** | 0.213 | 0.091*** | 0.122*** |
| | | 27.9% | 72.1% | | 42.6% | 57.4% |
| Spain | 0.258 | 0.064*** | 0.194*** | 0.253 | 0.035*** | 0.218*** |
| | | 24.9% | 75.1% | | 13.8% | 86.2% |
| UK | 0.365 | 0.171*** | 0.194*** | 0.298 | 0.101*** | 0.197*** |
| | | 46.8% | 53.2% | | 33.8% | 66.2% |

*Notes*: ***Statistically significant at 1% level, tested with the delta method. [a] The 3rd and 6th columns give the explained part: $\beta^m_{OLS}(\bar{x}^m - \bar{x}^f)$. [b] The 4th and 7th columns give the residual the part: $(\alpha^m_{OLS} - \alpha^f_{OLS}) + \bar{x}^f(\beta^m_{OLS} - \beta^f_{OLS})$.

*Source*: European Community Household Panel (ECHP).

Moreover, the results indicate that the unadjusted gender pay gap has slightly decreased in all countries with the exception of Denmark, and that the explained part has diminished in all countries except in Denmark and the Netherlands.

We have analysed the effect of changes in observed individual characteristics on the evolution of the pay gap over the period 1994–2001. Comparing the results of the Oaxaca decomposition obtained by using the IV/GLS estimators[9] with the individual characteristics of the years 1994 or 2001, we see that the convergence of the gender pay gap goes with a decrease of gender differences in productivity characteristics in all countries. This also indicates that the increase in the Danish pay gap is not due to a deterioration of female characteristics (see also Rosholm and Smith, 1996). The effect of the improvement for Irish women is noteworthy (see also Barrett *et al.*, 2000) (Table 7.3).

*Table 7.3* Panel-data decomposition, Oaxaca (1973), 1994 and 2001

| | *1994* | | *2001* | |
|---|---|---|---|---|
| | *Gap* | *Explained*[a] | *Gap* | *Explained*[a] |
| Belgium | 0.158 | 0.043*** | 0.134 | 0.023*** |
| Denmark | 0.137 | 0.087*** | 0.157 | 0.080*** |
| Germany | 0.269 | 0.104*** | 0.248 | 0.083*** |
| Ireland | 0.276 | 0.134*** | 0.193 | −0.016*** |
| Italy | 0.168 | 0.064*** | 0.151 | 0.027*** |
| The Netherlands | 0.239 | 0.106*** | 0.213 | 0.101*** |
| Spain | 0.258 | 0.097*** | 0.253 | 0.052*** |
| UK | 0.365 | 0.191*** | 0.298 | 0.171*** |

*Notes*: ***Statistically significant at 1% level, tested with the delta method.
[a] The 3rd /5th columns give the explained part: $\beta_{IV/GLS}(\bar{x}^m - \bar{x}^f)$ with characteristics of 1994 and 2001 respectively.

*Source*: European Community Household Panel (ECHP).

## The effects of accounting for individual heterogeneity on the adjusted gender pay gap

We now turn to the impact of individual heterogeneity on the adjusted gender pay gap. Let us compare the results of the adjusted gender pay gap obtained with OLS, GLS and IV/GLS estimations on the pooled sample (Table 7.4).

These estimators of the adjusted gender wage gap are significant at the 1 per cent level in all models[10] and indicate that, for example, according to OLS estimations on the male–female pooled sample, Belgian women earn, *ceteris paribus*, 14.2 per cent less than Belgian men. The estimated adjusted gender pay gap by OLS is higher in the UK, Germany, Spain and Ireland and lower in Denmark, Belgium and the Netherlands. Our results for the GLS estimators show a decrease of the male–female wage differential for all countries except Ireland, the Netherlands and the UK. Finally, by adjusting for heterogeneity, that is using either education or education and experience as endogenous variables, the gender difference decreases in all countries in comparison with the OLS and GLS estimations. For instance, taking education and experience as endogenous produces a reduction of 7 per cent in Belgium, of 14 per cent in Ireland, between about 20–30 per cent Germany, Italy, the Netherlands and Spain and of 41.2 per cent in the UK and 54.1 per cent in

*Table 7.4* Adjusted gender pay differentials, gender coefficients (std. error in parentheses)

| | *OLS*[a] | *GLS* | *IV/GLS*[b] | *IV/GLS*[c] |
|---|---|---|---|---|
| Belgium | −0.142 | −0.136 | −0.139 | −0.132 |
| | (0.007)*** | (0.012)*** | (0.019)*** | (0.018)*** |
| Denmark | −0.111 | −0.103 | −0.044 | −0.051 |
| | (0.006)*** | (0.012)*** | (0.022)** | (0.022)** |
| Germany | −0.208 | −0.2 | −0.153 | −0.164 |
| | (0.006)*** | (0.011)*** | (0.015)*** | (0.015)*** |
| Ireland | −0.198 | −0.203 | −0.166 | −0.169 |
| | (0.009)*** | (0.015)*** | (0.030)*** | (0.028)*** |
| Italy | −0.151 | −0.144 | −0.131 | −0.123 |
| | (0.005)*** | (0.008)*** | (0.011)*** | (0.011)*** |
| The Netherlands | −0.148 | −0.158 | −0.111 | −0.114 |
| | (0.006)*** | (0.010)*** | (0.041)*** | −0.116 |
| Spain | −0.199 | −0.191 | −0.173 | −0.148 |
| | (0.006)*** | (0.010)*** | (0.016)*** | (0.016)*** |
| UK | −0.204 | −0.237 | −0.034 | −0.12 |
| | (0.006)*** | (0.012)*** | −0.032 | (0.027)*** |

*Notes*: [a] Standard errors of the OLS regressions are inconsistent since they do not account for variance components. [b] $X_1$ = (experience (level, squared), dummy variables for the occupation, the firm size and the employment contract). [c] $X_1$ = (dummy variables for occupation, the firm size and the employment contract). ***/**/*: statistically significant at 1%/ 5%/ 1%, tested with the delta method.

*Source*: European Community Household Panel (ECHP).

Denmark. Therefore, we first observe that even when we control for unobserved heterogeneity the gender pay gap remains in all countries. Furthermore, individual heterogeneity seems to play a significant role in shaping the gap, and taking this element into account produces a different ranking of countries: Denmark, the Netherlands and the UK are now the three countries with the lowest gender pay gap; Belgium loses its second place and gets the fifth; and finally Ireland – and not the UK – records the highest pay differential.

What can explain this shift? We see that the results are influenced by the choice of the endogenous variables. In this chapter we have chosen to take the number of years of schooling as well as that of experience as endogenous variables. Controlling for unobserved heterogeneity with the Hausman–Taylor (1981) procedure avoids the endogeneity bias, and in particular the returns on education and

*Table 7.5* Reduction of the adjusted gender pay gap and gender differences in education and experience

| | *% decrease of the adjusted pay gap*[a] | *Rank* | *Diff. in years of schooling* | *Rank* | *Diff. in years of experience* | *Rank* |
|---|---|---|---|---|---|---|
| Belgium | 7.0% | 8 | −0.664 | 8 | 3.191 | 3 |
| Denmark | 54.1% | 1 | 0.068 | 2 | 1.153 | 6 |
| Germany | 21.2% | 5 | 0.298 | 6 | 0.460 | 7 |
| Ireland | 14.6% | 7 | −0.263 | 5 | 1.984 | 5 |
| Italy | 18.5% | 6 | −0.198 | 4 | 3.135 | 4 |
| The Netherlands | 23.0% | 4 | −0.080 | 3 | 3.419 | 2 |
| Spain | 25.6% | 3 | −0.635 | 7 | 5.057 | 1 |
| UK | 41.2% | 2 | 0.961 | 1 | −0.412 | 8 |

*Note*: [a] $X_1$ = (dummy variables for occupation, the firm size and the employment contract).
*Source*: European Community Household Panel (ECHP).

experience increase for both men and women with respect to the OLS estimators.

We note that the extent of the reduction of the adjusted pay gap is close to the ranking of countries according to their gender differences in years of schooling and to a lesser extent to their gender differences in years of experience.

Table 7.5 shows that the impact on the adjusted gender pay gap of taking education and experience as endogenous variable increases with the level of differences in education between men and women for all countries, except for Spain where gender differences in experience seem to play a more important role than the differences in education. This suggests that the fewer women are relatively endowed for these characteristics (or the more they are endowed) the more (the fewer) unobserved characteristics play a negative role on the gender pay gap.

## Conclusion

Using the European Community Household Panel (ECHP) we have analysed the evolution of the gender pay gap of eight European countries between 1994 and 2001. Wage equations, (un)adjusted gender pay differentials have been estimated by cross-section and panel-data techniques.

Our results regarding the analysis over time indicate that the general trend of the explained and residual part is a reduction, with some exceptions. We have analysed the impact of changes in individual characteristics between men and women on the evolution of the pay gap, and have chosen to use the panel-data dimension of the database in order to control for both observed and unobserved (constant over time) heterogeneity. Using these estimations, we have compared the explained parts between 1994 and 2001 taking estimators as constant. The results confirm that a part of the reduction of the unadjusted pay gap is due to improvements in female characteristics over time for all countries.

Finally, we have estimated the impact of controlling for individual heterogeneity on the gender pay gap. As with the other national studies, our results indicate that taking this element into account reduces the adjusted pay gap significantly compared to OLS estimations on pooled samples: from 7 per cent in Belgium to 41 per cent and 54 per cent in the UK and Denmark respectively. Therefore, the original ranking of the countries is modified. Moreover, adjusting for individual heterogeneity produces an increase of the rates of return of experience and education as well as a reduction of penalties due to low-skilled occupations, fixed employment contracts and relatively small enterprise size for both men and women. These results suggest that unobserved heterogeneity (as motivation, ability, and so on) are in disfavour of women. Therefore, controlling for this element reduces the residual part of the pay gap. Furthermore, we observe a link between the level of reduction of the adjusted pay gap and the ranking of countries according to their gender differences in education and experience. These observed characteristics are actually correlated with the unobserved heterogeneity, which biases the OLS estimates.

Finally, our results show that the gender pay gap remains, even after controlling for productive individual characteristics and unobserved individual effects. A direct policy recommendation would be to tackle gender differences in productive characteristics. This would reduce the gap due to differences in observed characteristics as well as that relative to the unobserved effect as far as both effects are correlated.

## Appendix 1: descriptive statistics

*Table 7A.1* Descriptive statistics, wave 1

| | | *Belgium* | *Denmark* | *Germany* | *Ireland* | *Italy* | *The Netherlands* | *Spain* | *United Kingdom* |
|---|---|---|---|---|---|---|---|---|---|
| Hourly wage | Total | 11.193 | 16.287 | 11.340 | 8.315 | 7.004 | 14.219 | 5.776 | 10.473 |
| | Male | 11.964 | 17.158 | 12.360 | 9.330 | 7.393 | 15.582 | 6.199 | 12.246 |
| | Female | 10.031 | 14.688 | 9.481 | 6.754 | 6.214 | 11.523 | 4.773 | 8.341 |
| Male | Total | 0.601 | 0.647 | 0.646 | 0.606 | 0.670 | 0.664 | 0.704 | 0.546 |
| | Male | 1.000 | 1.000 | 1.000 | 1.000 | 1.000 | 1.000 | 0.000 | 1.000 |
| | Female | 0.000 | 0.000 | 0.000 | 0.000 | 0.000 | 0.000 | 1.000 | 0.000 |
| Female | Total | 0.399 | 0.353 | 0.354 | 0.394 | 0.330 | 0.336 | 0.296 | 0.454 |
| | Male | 0.000 | 0.000 | 0.000 | 0.000 | 0.000 | 0.000 | 0.000 | 0.000 |
| | Female | 1.000 | 1.000 | 1.000 | 1.000 | 1.000 | 1.000 | 1.000 | 1.000 |
| Experience | Total | 16.701 | 20.295 | 19.867 | 15.965 | 17.299 | 18.560 | 19.138 | 18.694 |
| | Male | 17.895 | 19.320 | 20.086 | 17.109 | 18.545 | 19.623 | 20.477 | 18.279 |
| | Female | 14.902 | 20.826 | 19.466 | 14.207 | 14.770 | 16.459 | 15.959 | 19.194 |
| Occupation 1 | Total | 0.048 | 0.070 | 0.038 | 0.071 | 0.026 | 0.126 | 0.027 | 0.161 |
| | Male | 0.064 | 0.092 | 0.044 | 0.097 | 0.036 | 0.167 | 0.036 | 0.196 |
| | Female | 0.024 | 0.031 | 0.027 | 0.030 | 0.005 | 0.046 | 0.005 | 0.120 |
| Occupation 2 | Total | 0.131 | 0.109 | 0.063 | 0.076 | 0.021 | 0.109 | 0.054 | 0.103 |
| | Male | 0.116 | 0.127 | 0.074 | 0.083 | 0.022 | 0.123 | 0.043 | 0.142 |
| | Female | 0.154 | 0.077 | 0.043 | 0.065 | 0.021 | 0.080 | 0.079 | 0.057 |
| Occupation 3 | Total | 0.117 | 0.182 | 0.157 | 0.099 | 0.075 | 0.220 | 0.105 | 0.107 |
| | Male | 0.105 | 0.154 | 0.125 | 0.092 | 0.083 | 0.192 | 0.104 | 0.105 |
| | Female | 0.136 | 0.233 | 0.215 | 0.108 | 0.057 | 0.274 | 0.107 | 0.110 |
| Occupation 4 | Total | 0.255 | 0.150 | 0.129 | 0.150 | 0.243 | 0.161 | 0.125 | 0.197 |
| | Male | 0.185 | 0.050 | 0.066 | 0.072 | 0.180 | 0.094 | 0.091 | 0.082 |
| | Female | 0.362 | 0.333 | 0.242 | 0.271 | 0.371 | 0.294 | 0.206 | 0.335 |

| | | | | | | | | | |
|---|---|---|---|---|---|---|---|---|---|
| Occupation 5 | Total | 0.079 | 0.073 | 0.101 | 0.150 | 0.080 | 0.101 | 0.138 | 0.126 |
| | Male | 0.042 | 0.043 | 0.036 | 0.083 | 0.064 | 0.051 | 0.099 | 0.053 |
| | Female | 0.134 | 0.127 | 0.219 | 0.254 | 0.112 | 0.201 | 0.231 | 0.214 |
| Occupation 7 | Total | 0.107 | 0.202 | 0.298 | 0.175 | 0.307 | 0.145 | 0.266 | 0.134 |
| | Male | 0.159 | 0.296 | 0.416 | 0.268 | 0.357 | 0.208 | 0.340 | 0.227 |
| | Female | 0.028 | 0.031 | 0.084 | 0.032 | 0.206 | 0.020 | 0.090 | 0.022 |
| Occupation 8 | Total | 0.101 | 0.126 | 0.138 | 0.160 | 0.069 | 0.090 | 0.112 | 0.110 |
| | Male | 0.147 | 0.149 | 0.168 | 0.172 | 0.092 | 0.116 | 0.141 | 0.137 |
| | Female | 0.032 | 0.083 | 0.084 | 0.142 | 0.022 | 0.039 | 0.044 | 0.078 |
| Occupation 9 | Total | 0.161 | 0.088 | 0.076 | 0.120 | 0.179 | 0.047 | 0.173 | 0.060 |
| | Male | 0.182 | 0.089 | 0.071 | 0.099 | 0.166 | 0.048 | 0.146 | 0.058 |
| | Female | 0.130 | 0.085 | 0.086 | 0.133 | 0.205 | 0.046 | 0.237 | 0.063 |
| Fixed contract | Total | 0.024 | 0.013 | 0.027 | 0.015 | 0.030 | 0.009 | 0.142 | 0.006 |
| | Male | 0.017 | 0.015 | 0.027 | 0.015 | 0.025 | 0.006 | 0.141 | 0.009 |
| | Female | 0.034 | 0.010 | 0.026 | 0.017 | 0.042 | 0.015 | 0.144 | 0.002 |
| Medium-size enterprise | Total | 0.209 | 0.213 | 0.192 | 0.210 | 0.160 | 0.241 | 0.129 | 0.122 |
| | Male | 0.198 | 0.219 | 0.217 | 0.205 | 0.172 | 0.244 | 0.131 | 0.126 |
| | Female | 0.226 | 0.204 | 0.146 | 0.218 | 0.136 | 0.234 | 0.124 | 0.117 |
| Large-size enterprise | Total | 0.513 | 0.463 | 0.549 | 0.412 | 0.372 | 0.558 | 0.417 | 0.562 |
| | Male | 0.574 | 0.480 | 0.558 | 0.428 | 0.380 | 0.582 | 0.432 | 0.608 |
| | Female | 0.422 | 0.432 | 0.532 | 0.386 | 0.357 | 0.510 | 0.384 | 0.506 |
| Years of schooling | Total | 12.140 | 11.985 | 11.886 | 11.374 | 10.406 | 9.635 | 10.672 | 11.762 |
| | Male | 11.911 | 11.978 | 12.017 | 11.339 | 10.361 | 9.559 | 10.542 | 12.311 |
| | Female | 12.486 | 11.996 | 11.648 | 11.429 | 10.498 | 9.786 | 10.981 | 11.101 |
| Married | Total | 0.725 | 0.547 | 0.694 | 0.538 | 0.642 | 0.668 | 0.635 | 0.609 |
| | Male | 0.741 | 0.561 | 0.733 | 0.572 | 0.678 | 0.730 | 0.693 | 0.619 |
| | Female | 0.702 | 0.522 | 0.623 | 0.485 | 0.568 | 0.543 | 0.497 | 0.598 |

*Notes*: Legislators and senior officials (isco 1), professionals (isco 2), technicians and associate professionals (isco 3), clerks (isco 4), service workers and shop and market sales workers (isco 5), craft and related workers (isco 7), plant and machine operators and assemblers (isco 8), elementary occupation (isco 9).

*Table 7A.2* Descriptive statistics, wave 8

| | | *Belgium* | *Denmark* | *Germany* | *Ireland* | *Italy* | *The Netherlands* | *Spain* | *United Kingdom* |
|---|---|---|---|---|---|---|---|---|---|
| Hourly wage | Total | 13.266 | 19.25235 | 12.58062 | 10.76393 | 7.260693 | 14.95621 | 6.473675 | 13.14111 |
| | Male | 14.09 | 20.34956 | 13.74723 | 11.71091 | 7.659459 | 16.17508 | 7.023735 | 14.77496 |
| | Female | 12.077 | 17.1457 | 10.65236 | 9.492358 | 6.461286 | 12.66908 | 5.384327 | 10.90408 |
| Male | Total | 0.589 | 0.6575342 | 0.6230508 | 0.573156 | 0.6671883 | 0.6523472 | 0.6644764 | 0.5779136 |
| | Male | 1 | 1 | 1 | 1 | 1 | 1 | 1 | 1 |
| | Female | 0 | 0 | 0 | 0 | 0 | 0 | 0 | 0 |
| Female | Total | 0.411 | 0.3424658 | 0.3769492 | 0.426844 | 0.3328117 | 0.3476528 | 0.3355236 | 0.4220864 |
| | Male | 0 | 0 | 0 | 0 | 0 | 0 | 0 | 0 |
| | Female | 1 | 1 | 1 | 1 | 1 | 1 | 1 | 1 |
| Experience | Total | 18.89533 | 22.43053 | 21.22441 | 18.29383 | 17.80856 | 20.76971 | 18.41807 | 20.05412 |
| | Male | 20.26552 | 22.80506 | 21.23939 | 18.62025 | 18.77248 | 22.15682 | 20.11681 | 20.03021 |
| | Female | 16.92822 | 21.71143 | 21.19964 | 17.85552 | 15.87618 | 18.16688 | 15.05386 | 20.08687 |
| Occupation 1 | Total | 0.0863821 | 0.0831703 | 0.0464407 | 0.1039903 | 0.0182577 | 0.1527901 | 0.0291581 | 0.1959843 |
| | Male | 0.1155172 | 0.1011905 | 0.0484222 | 0.1139241 | 0.0265833 | 0.1860149 | 0.0370828 | 0.2107251 |
| | Female | 0.0445545 | 0.0485714 | 0.0431655 | 0.0906516 | 0.0015674 | 0.0904459 | 0.0134639 | 0.1758014 |
| Occupation 2 | Total | 0.1300813 | 0.148728 | 0.0966102 | 0.0725514 | 0.0292123 | 0.1452613 | 0.0640657 | 0.1104321 |
| | Male | 0.112069 | 0.1800595 | 0.1196953 | 0.07173 | 0.0273651 | 0.1588595 | 0.0519159 | 0.1314199 |
| | Female | 0.1559406 | 0.0885714 | 0.0584532 | 0.0736544 | 0.0329154 | 0.1197452 | 0.0881273 | 0.081696 |
| Occupation 3 | Total | 0.1493902 | 0.2103718 | 0.1786441 | 0.1064087 | 0.1043297 | 0.2280779 | 0.1523614 | 0.11567 |
| | Male | 0.1310345 | 0.1770833 | 0.1305767 | 0.092827 | 0.1164973 | 0.2050238 | 0.1341162 | 0.108006 |
| | Female | 0.1757426 | 0.2742857 | 0.2580935 | 0.1246459 | 0.0799373 | 0.2713376 | 0.1884945 | 0.1261634 |
| Occupation 4 | Total | 0.2408537 | 0.146771 | 0.1376271 | 0.1451028 | 0.2217006 | 0.1474756 | 0.0850103 | 0.1846355 |
| | Male | 0.1724138 | 0.0654762 | 0.0707291 | 0.0548523 | 0.1485536 | 0.0855397 | 0.0512979 | 0.0861027 |
| | Female | 0.3391089 | 0.3028571 | 0.2482014 | 0.266289 | 0.3683386 | 0.2636943 | 0.1517748 | 0.319545 |
| Occupation 5 | Total | 0.0945122 | 0.053816 | 0.0867797 | 0.1499395 | 0.1225874 | 0.0890168 | 0.1470226 | 0.1025753 |
| | Male | 0.0482759 | 0.03125 | 0.0272035 | 0.0632911 | 0.0914777 | 0.0529532 | 0.0945612 | 0.0468278 |
| | Female | 0.1608911 | 0.0971429 | 0.1852518 | 0.266289 | 0.184953 | 0.1566879 | 0.250918 | 0.1789038 |

| | | | | | | | | | |
|---|---|---|---|---|---|---|---|---|---|
| Occupation 7 | Total | 0.1189024 | 0.1771037 | 0.2620339 | 0.1765417 | 0.295253 | 0.108946 | 0.250924 | 0.1383675 |
| | Male | 0.187931 | 0.2544643 | 0.3770403 | 0.2890295 | 0.3580923 | 0.155465 | 0.3362176 | 0.2228097 |
| | Female | 0.019802 | 0.0285714 | 0.0719424 | 0.0254958 | 0.169279 | 0.0216561 | 0.0820073 | 0.0227508 |
| Occupation 8 | Total | 0.0873984 | 0.1076321 | 0.1240678 | 0.171705 | 0.124674 | 0.085031 | 0.1281314 | 0.1030118 |
| | Male | 0.1310345 | 0.1205357 | 0.1594124 | 0.2088608 | 0.1540266 | 0.1133741 | 0.1668727 | 0.1397281 |
| | Female | 0.0247525 | 0.0828571 | 0.0656475 | 0.121813 | 0.0658307 | 0.0318471 | 0.0514076 | 0.0527404 |
| Occupation 9 | Total | 0.0924797 | 0.072407 | 0.0677966 | 0.0737606 | 0.0839854 | 0.0434012 | 0.1433265 | 0.0493234 |
| | Male | 0.1017241 | 0.0699405 | 0.0669206 | 0.1054852 | 0.0774042 | 0.0427699 | 0.1279357 | 0.0543807 |
| | Female | 0.0792079 | 0.0771429 | 0.0692446 | 0.0311615 | 0.0971787 | 0.044586 | 0.1738066 | 0.0423992 |
| Fixed contract | Total | 0.0447154 | 0.0234834 | 0.0477966 | 0.0241838 | 0.0636411 | 0.0115146 | 0.2525667 | 0.0279354 |
| | Male | 0.0327586 | 0.0238095 | 0.0462459 | 0.0189873 | 0.0586396 | 0.0101833 | 0.2620519 | 0.0287009 |
| | Female | 0.0618812 | 0.0228571 | 0.0503597 | 0.0311615 | 0.0736677 | 0.0140127 | 0.2337821 | 0.0268873 |
| Medium-size enterprise | Total | 0.2154472 | 0.2152642 | 0.2033898 | 0.1970979 | 0.124674 | 0.2360496 | 0.1531828 | 0.1065037 |
| | Male | 0.2206897 | 0.2261905 | 0.2208923 | 0.1919831 | 0.1282252 | 0.2410048 | 0.1526576 | 0.1110272 |
| | Female | 0.2079208 | 0.1942857 | 0.1744604 | 0.203966 | 0.1175549 | 0.2267516 | 0.1542228 | 0.1003102 |
| Large-size enterprise | Total | 0.5315041 | 0.4481409 | 0.5349153 | 0.4232164 | 0.3495044 | 0.5606732 | 0.3560575 | 0.5608904 |
| | Male | 0.5706897 | 0.4553571 | 0.5565832 | 0.443038 | 0.370602 | 0.5756959 | 0.3831891 | 0.5129266 |
| | Female | 0.4752475 | 0.4342857 | 0.4991007 | 0.3966006 | 0.30721 | 0.5324841 | 0.3023256 | 0.5959215 |
| Years of schooling | Total | 12.65142 | 11.7407 | 11.78949 | 11.13301 | 10.64424 | 9.039415 | 10.97084 | 11.90223 |
| | Male | 12.31897 | 11.79911 | 11.87758 | 10.89241 | 10.54965 | 9.039375 | 10.68789 | 12.28701 |
| | Female | 13.12871 | 11.62857 | 11.64388 | 11.45609 | 10.83386 | 9.03949 | 11.53121 | 11.37539 |
| Married | Total | 0.675813 | 0.6183953 | 0.6583051 | 0.5356711 | 0.6442358 | 0.6532329 | 0.6049281 | 0.5918813 |
| | Male | 0.7034483 | 0.6205357 | 0.6974973 | 0.5654008 | 0.6778733 | 0.7053632 | 0.6532756 | 0.6193353 |
| | Female | 0.6361386 | 0.6142857 | 0.5935252 | 0.4957507 | 0.5768025 | 0.555414 | 0.5091799 | 0.5542916 |

*Notes*: Legislators and senior officials (isco 1), professionals (isco 2), technicians and associate professionals (isco 3), clerks (isco 4), service workers and shop and market sales workers (isco 5), craft and related workers (isco 7), plant and machine operators and assemblers (isco 8), elementary occupation (isco 9).

## Appendix 2: wage equations

*Table 7A.3* Wage equation OLS (male–female pooled sample)

| | *Belgium* | *Denmark* | *Germany* | *Ireland* | *Italy* | *The Netherlands* | *Spain* | *United Kingdom* |
|---|---|---|---|---|---|---|---|---|
| Potential experience | 0.023 | 0.033 | 0.029 | 0.025 | 0.023 | 0.025 | 0.023 | 0.023 |
| | (0.001)*** | (0.001)*** | (0.001)*** | (0.001)*** | (0.001)*** | (0.001)*** | (0.001)*** | (0.001)*** |
| Potential squared | −0.034 | −0.059 | −0.052 | −0.041 | −0.038 | −0.042 | −0.033 | −0.047 |
| experience /100 | (0.003)*** | (0.002)*** | (0.002)*** | (0.003)*** | (0.002)*** | (0.002)*** | (0.002)*** | (0.002)*** |
| Occupation 1 | 0.258 | 0.289 | 0.205 | 0.245 | 0.357 | 0.205 | 0.476 | 0.312 |
| | (0.014)*** | (0.013)*** | (0.014)*** | (0.018)*** | (0.015)*** | (0.010)*** | (0.017)*** | (0.009)*** |
| Occupation 2 | 0.182 | 0.285 | 0.239 | 0.252 | 0.063 | 0.273 | 0.284 | 0.339 |
| | (0.011)*** | (0.011)*** | (0.012)*** | (0.018)*** | (0.014)*** | (0.010)*** | (0.013)*** | (0.011)*** |
| Occupation 3 | 0.064 | 0.118 | 0.034 | 0.179 | −0.021 | 0.105 | 0.061 | 0.201 |
| | (0.010)*** | (0.009)*** | (0.009)*** | (0.016)*** | (0.008)*** | (0.009)*** | (0.010)*** | (0.010)*** |
| Occupation 5 | −0.162 | −0.103 | −0.221 | −0.24 | −0.165 | −0.149 | −0.227 | −0.305 |
| | (0.012)*** | (0.013)*** | (0.011)*** | (0.014)*** | (0.008)*** | (0.011)*** | (0.010)*** | (0.010)*** |
| Occupation 7 | −0.14 | −0.058 | −0.113 | −0.025 | −0.196 | −0.134 | −0.176 | −0.014 |
| | (0.012)*** | (0.010)*** | (0.009)*** | (0.015)* | (0.006)*** | (0.010)*** | (0.009)*** | −0.011 |
| Occupation 8 | −0.115 | −0.12 | −0.11 | −0.093 | −0.146 | −0.129 | −0.179 | −0.141 |
| | (0.013)*** | (0.011)*** | (0.010)*** | (0.015)*** | (0.008)*** | (0.012)*** | (0.011)*** | (0.011)*** |
| Occupation 9 | −0.192 | −0.098 | −0.192 | −0.263 | −0.248 | −0.205 | −0.321 | −0.262 |
| | (0.012)*** | (0.012)*** | (0.012)*** | (0.016)*** | (0.008)*** | (0.014)*** | (0.010)*** | (0.013)*** |
| Fixed contract | −0.071 | −0.163 | −0.139 | −0.03 | −0.062 | −0.195 | −0.128 | −0.006 |
| | (0.014)*** | (0.016)*** | (0.011)*** | −0.021 | (0.009)*** | (0.017)*** | (0.006)*** | −0.018 |

| | | | | | | | | |
|---|---|---|---|---|---|---|---|---|
| Medium-size enterprise | 0.131 | 0.102 | 0.376 | 0.294 | 0.136 | 0.086 | 0.264 | 0.159 |
| | (0.009)*** | (0.007)*** | (0.007)*** | (0.011)*** | (0.006)*** | (0.008)*** | (0.008)*** | (0.009)*** |
| Large-size enterprise | 0.137 | 0.076 | 0.181 | 0.219 | 0.112 | 0.097 | 0.209 | 0.172 |
| | (0.007)*** | (0.006)*** | (0.006)*** | (0.009)*** | (0.005)*** | (0.007)*** | (0.005)*** | (0.006)*** |
| Married | 0.021 | 0.032 | 0.063 | 0.112 | 0.048 | 0.097 | 0.059 | 0.058 |
| | (0.007)*** | (0.006)*** | (0.006)*** | (0.010)*** | (0.005)*** | (0.006)*** | (0.006)*** | (0.006)*** |
| Female | −0.142 | −0.111 | −0.208 | −0.198 | −0.151 | −0.148 | −0.199 | −0.204 |
| | (0.007)*** | (0.006)*** | (0.006)*** | (0.009)*** | (0.005)*** | (0.006)*** | (0.006)*** | (0.006)*** |
| Years of schooling | 0.033 | 0.023 | 0.018 | 0.034 | 0.034 | 0.012 | 0.032 | 0.028 |
| | (0.001)*** | (0.001)*** | (0.001)*** | (0.002)*** | (0.001)*** | (0.003)*** | (0.001)*** | (0.001)*** |
| Constant | 1.71 | 2.107 | 1.77 | 1.356 | 1.373 | 2.057 | 1.12 | 1.656 |
| | (0.024)*** | (0.021)*** | (0.020)*** | (0.031)*** | (0.019)*** | (0.027)*** | (0.019)*** | (0.016)*** |
| Number of observations | 9251 | 9819 | 26444 | 9896 | 19106 | 20216 | 20801 | 19593 |
| Number of individuals | 1905 | 2035 | 5430 | 2465 | 4220 | 4225 | 4915 | 3900 |
| *R*-squared | 0.42 | 0.44 | 0.33 | 0.43 | 0.39 | 0.29 | 0.49 | 0.44 |

*Notes*: * significant at 10%, ** significant at 5% and *** significant at1%; legislators and senior officials (isco 1), professionals (isco 2), technicians and associate professionals (isco 3), clerks (isco 4 – not in table), service workers and shop and market sales workers (isco 5), craft and related workers (isco 7), plant and machine operators and assemblers (isco 8), elementary occupation (isco 9).

*Table 7A.4* Wage equation IV/GLS[a] (male–female pooled sample)

| | *Belgium* | *Denmark* | *Germany* | *Ireland* | *Italy* | *The Netherlands* | *Spain* | *United Kingdom* |
|---|---|---|---|---|---|---|---|---|
| Potential experience | 0.036 | 0.06 | 0.05 | 0.08 | 0.033 | 0.05 | 0.05 | 0.07 |
| | (0.002)*** | (0.002)*** | (0.001)*** | (0.002)*** | (0.001)*** | (0.002)*** | (0.001)*** | (0.002)*** |
| Potential squared | −0.04 | −0.10 | −0.08 | −0.11 | −0.048 | −0.071 | −0.061 | −0.083 |
| experience/100 | (0.004)*** | (0.004)*** | (0.003)*** | (0.006)*** | (0.003)*** | (0.004)*** | (0.003)*** | (0.003)*** |
| Occupation 1 | 0.028 | 0.14 | 0.07 | 0.05 | 0.066 | 0.014 | 0.114 | 0.062 |
| | (0.014)** | (0.018)*** | (0.013)*** | (0.017)*** | (0.017)*** | −0.011 | (0.016)*** | (0.009)*** |
| Occupation 2 | −0.015 | 0.13 | 0.05 | 0.06 | −0.011 | 0.023 | 0.077 | 0.054 |
| | −0.012 | (0.017)*** | (0.013)*** | (0.020)*** | −0.014 | (0.012)* | (0.014)*** | (0.011)*** |
| Occupation 3 | 0.003 | 0.10 | 0.02 | 0.06 | 0.01 | 0 | 0.021 | 0.038 |
| | −0.01 | (0.014)*** | (0.009)** | (0.014)*** | −0.009 | −0.009 | (0.009)** | (0.009)*** |
| Occupation 5 | −0.015 | 0.02 | −0.10 | −0.09 | −0.013 | −0.041 | −0.013 | −0.103 |
| | −0.012 | −0.02 | (0.012)*** | (0.016)*** | −0.01 | (0.013)*** | −0.012 | (0.011)*** |
| Occupation 7 | 0.04 | 0.06 | 0.02 | 0.04 | −0.003 | −0.027 | 0.03 | 0.037 |
| | (0.014)*** | (0.017)*** | −0.01 | (0.018)** | −0.01 | (0.015)* | (0.012)*** | (0.012)*** |
| Occupation 8 | 0.071 | 0.08 | 0.04 | 0.03 | 0.008 | −0.066 | 0.034 | 0.017 |
| | (0.015)*** | (0.017)*** | (0.012)*** | −0.02 | −0.011 | (0.015)*** | (0.012)*** | −0.012 |
| Occupation 9 | 0.055 | 0.09 | −0.02 | −0.04 | −0.009 | −0.026 | −0.015 | −0.007 |
| | (0.014)*** | (0.017)*** | −0.01 | (0.017)** | −0.011 | −0.016 | −0.012 | −0.013 |
| Fixed contract | 0 | −0.08 | −0.02 | −0.03 | −0.003 | −0.039 | −0.027 | −0.031 |
| | −0.011 | (0.012)*** | (0.008)*** | (0.017)** | −0.007 | (0.015)*** | (0.005)*** | (0.013)** |

| | | | | | | | | |
|---|---|---|---|---|---|---|---|---|
| Medium-size enterprise | 0.051 | 0.05 | 0.15 | 0.13 | 0.074 | 0.03 | 0.082 | 0.048 |
| | (0.011)*** | (0.010)*** | (0.008)*** | (0.011)*** | (0.007)*** | (0.009)*** | (0.008)*** | (0.008)*** |
| Large-size enterprise | 0.04 | 0.06 | 0.09 | 0.09 | 0.044 | 0.032 | 0.065 | 0.052 |
| | (0.009)*** | (0.008)*** | (0.006)*** | (0.009)*** | (0.005)*** | (0.008)*** | (0.005)*** | (0.006)*** |
| Married | 0.001 | 0.01 | 0.01 | −0.02 | 0.032 | 0.063 | 0.023 | −0.007 |
| | −0.011 | −0.01 | (0.007)** | −0.02 | (0.007)*** | (0.010)*** | (0.009)*** | −0.008 |
| Female | −0.139 | −0.04 | −0.15 | −0.17 | −0.131 | −0.111 | −0.173 | −0.034 |
| | (0.019)*** | (0.022)** | (0.015)*** | (0.030)*** | (0.011)*** | (0.041)*** | (0.016)*** | −0.032 |
| Years of schooling | 0.134 | 0.14 | 0.10 | 0.21 | 0.133 | 0.075 | 0.161 | 0.258 |
| | (0.005)*** | (0.010)*** | (0.006)*** | (0.010)*** | (0.005)*** | −0.071 | (0.005)*** | (0.011)*** |
| Constant | 0.278 | 0.27 | 0.54 | −1.21 | 0.095 | 1.205 | −0.726 | −1.701 |
| | (0.072)*** | (0.124)** | (0.074)*** | (0.129)*** | −0.061 | (0.670)* | (0.060)*** | (0.136)*** |
| Number of observations | 9251 | 9819 | 26444 | 9896 | 19106 | 20216 | 20801 | 19593 |
| Number of individuals | 1905 | 2035 | 5430 | 2465 | 4220 | 4225 | 4915 | 3900 |
| Hausman test: $\chi^2_{28}$ | 1.55 | 6.60 | 24.40 | 16.98 | 3.99 | 1.91 | 15.50 | 16.39 |
| Critical value 95 per cent 28 degrees of freedom | 41.33 | | | | | | | |

*Notes*: [a] $X_1$ = (experience (level, squared), dummy variables for the occupation, the firm size and the employment contract); * significant at 10%, ** significant at 5% and *** significant at 1%. Legislators and senior officials (isco 1), professionals (isco 2), technicians and associate professionals (isco 3), clerks (isco 4 – not in table), service workers and shop and market sales workers (isco 5), craft and related workers (isco 7), plant and machine operators and assemblers (isco 8), elementary occupation (isco 9).

*Table 7A.5* Wage equation IV/GLS[a] (male–female pooled sample)

| | *Belgium* | *Denmark* | *Germany* | *Ireland* | *Italy* | *The Netherlands* | *Spain* | *United Kingdom* |
|---|---|---|---|---|---|---|---|---|
| Potential experience | 0.039 | 0.07 | 0.06 | 0.088 | 0.034 | 0.053 | 0.057 | 0.074 |
| | (0.002)*** | (0.002)*** | (0.002)*** | (0.003)*** | (0.001)*** | (0.002)*** | (0.002)*** | (0.002)*** |
| Potential squared | −0.038 | −0.095 | −0.084 | −0.105 | −0.042 | −0.071 | −0.058 | −0.08 |
| experience/100 | (0.005)*** | (0.004)*** | (0.003)*** | (0.006)*** | (0.003)*** | (0.004)*** | (0.004)*** | (0.004)*** |
| Occupation 1 | 0.028 | 0.122 | 0.056 | 0.041 | 0.066 | 0.007 | 0.109 | 0.058 |
| | (0.014)** | (0.018)*** | (0.013)*** | (0.017)** | (0.017)*** | −0.011 | (0.016)*** | (0.009)*** |
| Occupation 2 | −0.01 | 0.125 | 0.036 | 0.068 | −0.008 | 0.013 | 0.078 | 0.054 |
| | −0.012 | (0.018)*** | (0.013)*** | (0.020)*** | −0.014 | −0.012 | (0.014)*** | (0.011)*** |
| Occupation 3 | 0.004 | 0.086 | 0.009 | 0.057 | 0.01 | −0.005 | 0.014 | 0.036 |
| | −0.01 | (0.014)*** | −0.009 | (0.015)*** | −0.009 | −0.009 | −0.009 | (0.009)*** |
| Occupation 5 | −0.019 | 0.02 | −0.097 | −0.099 | −0.016 | −0.038 | −0.024 | −0.111 |
| | −0.012 | −0.018 | (0.012)*** | (0.016)*** | −0.01 | (0.013)*** | (0.012)** | (0.011)*** |
| Occupation 7 | 0.03 | 0.054 | 0.014 | 0.026 | −0.008 | −0.019 | 0.011 | 0.029 |
| | (0.014)** | (0.017)*** | −0.011 | −0.018 | −0.01 | −0.015 | −0.012 | (0.012)** |
| Occupation 8 | 0.063 | 0.07 | 0.034 | 0.012 | 0.001 | −0.059 | 0.012 | 0.007 |
| | (0.015)*** | (0.018)*** | (0.012)*** | −0.016 | −0.011 | (0.015)*** | −0.012 | −0.012 |
| Occupation 9 | 0.047 | 0.082 | −0.019 | −0.047 | −0.014 | −0.018 | −0.032 | −0.016 |
| | (0.014)*** | (0.017)*** | −0.012 | (0.017)*** | −0.011 | −0.016 | (0.012)*** | −0.013 |
| Fixed contract | 0.002 | −0.072 | −0.017 | −0.028 | −0.002 | −0.036 | −0.021 | −0.032 |
| | −0.011 | (0.013)*** | (0.008)** | (0.017)* | −0.007 | (0.015)** | (0.005)*** | (0.013)** |

| | | | | | | | | |
|---|---|---|---|---|---|---|---|---|
| Medium-size enterprise | 0.05 | 0.053 | 0.142 | 0.128 | 0.075 | 0.027 | 0.081 | 0.05 |
| | (0.011)*** | (0.010)*** | (0.008)*** | (0.011)*** | (0.007)*** | (0.009)*** | (0.008)*** | (0.008)*** |
| Large-size enterprise | 0.039 | 0.059 | 0.086 | 0.089 | 0.045 | 0.029 | 0.066 | 0.053 |
| | (0.009)*** | (0.008)*** | (0.006)*** | (0.009)*** | (0.005)*** | (0.008)*** | (0.005)*** | (0.006)*** |
| Married | −0.007 | −0.019 | −0.013 | −0.085 | 0.018 | 0.061 | −0.017 | −0.025 |
| | −0.011 | (0.008)** | (0.007)* | (0.016)*** | (0.008)** | (0.010)*** | (0.009)* | (0.008)*** |
| Female | −0.132 | −0.051 | −0.164 | −0.169 | −0.123 | −0.114 | −0.148 | −0.12 |
| | (0.018)*** | (0.022)** | (0.015)*** | (0.028)*** | (0.011)*** | −0.116 | (0.016)*** | (0.027)*** |
| Years of schooling | 0.127 | 0.136 | 0.112 | 0.176 | 0.129 | −0.003 | 0.149 | 0.194 |
| | (0.005)*** | (0.010)*** | (0.006)*** | (0.010)*** | (0.005)*** | −0.218 | (0.005)*** | (0.009)*** |
| Constant | 0.325 | 0.204 | 0.245 | −0.901 | 0.113 | 1.9 | −0.698 | −0.97 |
| | (0.071)*** | (0.122)* | (0.078)*** | (0.123)*** | (0.061)* | −2.05 | (0.059)*** | (0.120)*** |
| Number of observations | 9251 | 9819 | 26444 | 9896 | 19106 | 20216 | 20801 | 19593 |
| Number of individuals | 1905 | 2035 | 5430 | 2465 | 4220 | 4225 | 4915 | 3900 |
| Hausman test: $\chi^2_{26}$ | 0.96 | 2.26 | 9.67 | 10.14 | 3.21 | 0.01 | 7.60 | 7.84 |
| Critical value 95 per cent 26 degrees of freedom | 38.89 | | | | | | | |

*Notes*: [a] $X_1$ = (dummy variables for occupation, the firm size and the employment contract); * significant at 10%, ** significant at 5% and *** significant at 1%. Legislators and senior officials (isco 1), professionals (isco 2), technicians and associate professionals (isco 3), clerks (isco 4 – not in table), service workers and shop and market sales workers (isco 5), craft and related workers (isco 7), plant and machine operators and assemblers (isco 8), elementary occupation (isco 9).

## Notes

1 Work experience is computed as follows: age minus age when the individual has started his/her working life.

2 Small firms have less than 20 employees, medium firms have between 20–100 employees and large firms more than 100 employees.

3 The instrumental variables must be strongly correlated with $Z_i$ and not correlated with $\alpha_i$. A procedure commonly found in the economic literature is to employ the $X_{1i.}$, the mean deviations $(X_{it} - X_{i.})$ and $Z_{1i.}$ uncorrelated with $\alpha_i$ as instruments.

4 Due to the large number of wage equations produced and the number of countries, only the wage equations estimated by OLS and IV/GLS on the pooled samples are presented in Appendix 2. The other wage equations are available from the authors upon request.

5 Low and subordinate occupations include clerks (isco 4), service workers and shop and market sales workers (isco 5), craft and related workers (isco 7), plant and machine operators and assemblers (isco 8) and elementary occupation (isco 9). High-skilled occupations are the following: legislators and senior officials (isco 1), professionals (isco 2) and technicians and associate professionals (isco 3).

6 $X_1$ = (experience (level, square), dummy variables for occupation, the firm size and the employment contract).

7 Hausman test: $\tilde{W} = \sigma_\varepsilon^2(\hat{\beta}_w - \hat{\beta}_{\text{GLS}})'(\hat{\Omega}(\hat{\beta}_w) - \hat{\Omega}(\hat{\beta}_{\text{GLS}}))^{-1}(\hat{\beta}_w - \hat{\beta}_{\text{GLS}})$, which is distributed as chi-squared where the degree of freedom corresponds to the number of instruments used minus the number of time-invariant regressors instrumented.

8 $X_1$ = (dummy variables for occupation, the firm size and the employment contract).

9 The endogenous time-invariant variable is the level of education, the endogenous time-variant variable is the experience (level and square) and the instruments are the individual means over time of the time-varying regressors $(X_{i.})$ and the deviation from the mean transformation of these time-varying regressors $(X_{it} - X.)$

10 Exceptions are coefficients of UK (IV/GLS$^b$) and of NLD (IV/GLS$^c$)

## References

Amemiya, T. and McCurdy, T.E. (1986) 'Instrumental-Variable Estimation of Error-Components Model', *Econometrica*, 54 (4), pp. 869–80.

Baltagi, B.H. and Khanti-Akom, S. (1990) 'On Efficient Estimation with Panel Data: An Empirical Comparison of Instrumental Variables Estimators', *Journal of Applied Econometrics*, 5 (4), pp. 401–6.

Barrett, A. and Callan, T. (2000) *How Unequal – Men and Women in the Irish Labour Market*. Dublin: Economic and Social Research Institute.

Beblo, M. and Wolf, E. (2000) 'How Much does a Year Off Cost? Estimating the Wage Effects of Employment Breaks and Part-Time Periods', ZEW Mannheim Discussion Paper no. 00–69.

Beblo, M., Beninger, D., Heinze, A. and Laisney, F. (2003) 'Measuring Selectivity-Corrected Gender Wage Gap in EU', ZEW Mannheim Discussion Paper no. 03–74.

Blackaby, D., Clark, K., Leslie, D.G. and Murphy, P.D. (1997) 'The Distribution of Male and Female Earnings 1973–91: Evidence for Britain', *Oxford Economic Papers*, (49) 2, pp. 256–72.

Blau, F.D. and Kahn, L.M. (1992) 'The Gender Earnings Gap: Learning from International Comparisons', *American Economic Review*, 8, Papers and Proceedings of the 104th Annual Meeting of the American Economic Association, pp. 533–8.

Blau, F.D. and Kahn, L.M. (1996) 'Wage Structure and Gender Earnings Differentials: An International Comparison', *Economica*, 63, pp. S29–S62.

Brandolini, A., Cipollone, P. and Sestito, P. (2001) 'Earnings Dispersion, Low Pay and Household Poverty in Italy, 1977–1998', Temi di discussione del Servizio Studi. Rome: Banca d'Italia.

Breusch, T.S., Mizon, G.E. and Schmidt, P. (1989) 'Efficient Estimation Using Panel Data', *Econometrica*, 57(3), pp. 695–700.

Cornwell, C. and Rupert, P. (1988) 'Efficient Estimation With Panel Data: An Empirical Comparison of Instrumental Variables Estimators', *Journal of Applied Econometrics*, 3(2), pp. 149–55.

Datta Gupta, N., Oaxaca, R.L. and Smith, N. (2001) 'Swimming Upstream, Floating Downstream: trends in the U.S and Danish Gender Wage' *CLS* Working Paper 01–06, Aarhus.

Dolton P., O'Neill, D. and Sweetman, O. (1996) 'Gender Differences in the Changing Labour Market: The Role of Legislation and Inequality in Changing Wage Gap for Qualified Workers in the United Kingdom' *Journal of Human Resources*, 31 (3), pp. 549–65.

Gornick, J.C., Meyers, M.K. and Ross, K.E. (1997) 'Supporting the Employment of Mothers: Public Variation Across Fourteen Welfare States', *Journal of European Social Policy*, 7 (1), pp. 45–70.

Hansen, J. and Wahlberg, R. (1997) 'The Return to Education and the Gender Wage Gap: Results from Swedish Panel Data'. Cahier de Recherche 2297 Université de Montreal, Développement Economique.

Harkness, S. (1996) 'The Gender Earnings Gap: Evidence from the UK', *Fiscal Studies*, 17 (2), pp. 1–36.

Hausman, J.A. and Taylor W.E. (1981) 'Panel Data and Unobservable Individual Effects', *Econometrica*, 49(6), pp. 1377–98.

Jenkins, S.P. (1994) 'Earnings Discrimination Measurement: A Distributional Approach', *Journal of Econometrics*, 61, pp. 81–102.

Joshi, H. and Paci, P. (1998) 'Unequal Pay for Women and Men'. London, Cambridge: The MIT Press.

Juhn, C., Murphy, K.M. and Pierce, B. (1993) 'Wage Inequality and the Rise in Returns to Skill', *Journal of Political Economy*, 101, pp. 410–42.

Kunze A. (2002) 'Gender Differences in Entry Wages and Early Career Wages', *IZA Discussion Paper* No. 626.

Molto, M.L. (2002) *National Reports on the Unadjusted and Adjusted Gender Pay Gap in Spain*. European Expert Group on Gender and Employment Report to the Equal Opportunities Unit, DG Employment.

Moon-Kak, K. and Polachek, S.W. (1994) 'Panel Estimates of Male–Female Earnings Functions', *Journal of Human Resources*, 29(2), pp. 406–28.

Naur, M. and Smith, N. (1996) 'Cohort Effects on the Gender wage Gap in Denmark'. *CLS* Working Paper 96–05, Aarhus.

Oaxaca, R.L. and Ransom, M. (1998) 'Calculation of Approximate Variance for Wage Decomposition Differentials', *Journal of Economic and Social Measurement,* 24, pp. 55–61.

Oaxaca, R. (1973) 'Male–Female Wage Differentials in Urban Labour Markets', *International Economic Review,* 14, pp. 693–709.

Pedersen, L. and Dedinger, M. (2000) 'Lønforskelle mellem Kvinder', Socialforskningsinstitutet, 00:4, Copenhagen.

Plantenga, J. and Sjoerd-Wiemer, S. (2002) *National Reports on the Unadjusted and Adjusted Gender Pay Gap in Netherlands.* European Expert Group on Gender and Employment Report to the Equal Opportunities Unit, DG Employment.

Plasman, A., Plasman, R. and Rusinek, M. (2002) 'L'Evolution de l'Ecart Salarial De Genre Dans L'Union Européenne', *Cahiers Economiques De Bruxelles,* Special Issue, 'Gender Wage Gaps: A European Perspective', Guest Editors: R. Plasman, D. Meulders, F. Rycx.

Plasman, R. and Sissoko, S. (2002) *National Reports on the Unadjusted and Adjusted Gender Pay Gap in Belgium.* European Expert Group on Gender and Employment Report to the Equal Opportunities Unit, DG Employment.

Rice, P. (1999) 'Gender Earnings Differentials: The European Experience, Policy Research Report on Gender and Development'. Working Paper Series 8. The World Bank.

Rosholm, M. and Smith, N. (1996) 'The Danish Gender Wage Gap in the 1980s: A Panel Data Study', *Oxford Economic Papers,* New Series, 48 (2), pp. 254–79.

Rubery, J., Grimshaw, D. and Figueiredo, H. (2003) 'How to Close the Gender Pay Gap in Europe: Towards the Gender Mainstreaming of Pay Policy'. Expert Group Gender and Employment, DG Employment and Social Affairs, October.

Rückert E. (1997). 'Bootstrapping the European Gender Wage Gap'. *IRISS* Working Paper Series no. 2003–10.

Russell, H. and Gannon, B. (2002) *Equal Opportunities between Men and Women in Impact Evaluation of European Employment Strategy in Ireland.* Department of Enterprise, Trade and Employment: Dublin.

Ugidos, A. (1997) 'Gender wage discrimination in the Spanish Labour market', *Revista Española de Economía,* 14 (1), pp. 3–21.

Villa, P. (2002) *National Reports on the Unadjusted and Adjusted Gender Pay Gap in Italy.* European Expert Group on Gender and Employment Report to the Equal Opportunities Unit, DG Employment.

Wooldridge, J.M. (2002) *Econometrics Analysis of Cross-section and Panel Data.* Massachusetts: The MIT Press.

# 8

# The Gender Wage Ratio in New Zealand, 1997–2003

*W. Robert J. Alexander, Murat Genç and Mohammad Jaforullah**

## Introduction

New Zealand, a small and geographically isolated developed nation, provides an interesting context for the study of gender differences in the labour market. New Zealand was the first nation state in the world to grant women the right to vote in parliamentary elections, was an early adopter of equal-pay legislation and is currently notable for having women filling the positions of Prime Minister, Governor General (Head of State), Chief Justice and Attorney General. Yet simple descriptive statistics indicate that there remains a significant wage gap between males and females.

The human-capital models of Mincer and Polachek (1974) and Polachek (1981) provide an economic explanation for gender wage gaps. Gender differences are explained as a result of different levels of acquired skills that lead to differences in productivity and hence in wages. The statistical discrimination literature deals with whether these

* The authors would like to express their thanks for the assistance of staff of Statistics New Zealand, especially Kimberley Cullen, Frances Krsinich, Janelle Langstraat, Sandra McDonald, John McGuigan, Peter O'Brien, Richard Penny, John Scott and John Upfold. The results presented in this study are the work of the authors, not Statistics New Zealand. Access to the data used in this study was provided by Statistics New Zealand in a secure environment in its Wellington offices designed to give effect to the confidentiality provisions of the Statistics Act. For this reason, access to the original unit record data cannot be provided by the authors of this chapter. Financial support for this study came from a University of Otago Research Grant and the Department of Economics, University of Otago.

gaps are fully accounted for by human-capital variables such as age, experience and educational attainment. The usual approach is to estimate an earnings function either by extending the standard form developed by Mincer (1974) by including gender dummy variables, or by estimating it separately for males and females and applying the Blinder–Oaxaca wage decomposition method to wage differentials. However, either approach may suffer from sample selection bias (Heckman, 1979) because wages are only observed for individuals who are employed. The resulting truncated sample of wages might lead to biased inferences, since the decision to work may be systematically correlated to potential wage. Heckman (1979) was the first to develop a procedure to correct the sample selection bias inherent in ordinary least-squares (OLS). Here, we use both Heckman's two-step approach, known as Heckit, and the maximum likelihood estimation (MLE) method to estimate wage and participation equations simultaneously, to correct for sample selection bias. We refrain from applying wage decompositions, since Heckit selectivity correction introduces some fundamental ambiguities (Neuman and Oaxaca, 2004).

We use unit record data from the Income Survey (IS) of Statistics New Zealand, which since 1997 has been conducted as an annual supplement to the quarterly Household Labour-Force Survey (HLFS) in each June quarter. We have access to data from both the first survey in 1997 and the latest available data from 2003.

We find statistically and economically significant evidence of a gender wage differential in favour of males. We also examine the data for evidence of discrimination on an ethnic basis and find the picture there much less clear-cut.

The outline of the remainder of this chapter is as follows. In the next section we give some background information on New Zealand society that is needed to place our results in context. Subsequent sections briefly examine previous empirical evidence, followed by the methodology and the data used. The results are then presented, and a final section concludes.

## New Zealand society

In 1893, New Zealand was the first nation state in the world to grant the franchise to women. Nevertheless, the role of women in New Zealand society remained very much the traditional one prior to 'the second wave of active feminism' in the 1970s (MacDonald, 1993, p. 161). As in other developed nations at that time, the Women's Liberation movement centred on the issues of equal pay, the effects of gender stereotyping and the exploitation of female sexuality for commercial gain. The New Zealand Parliament enacted a number of pieces of legislation designed to address these issues, including the Equal Pay Act (1972), the Matrimonial Property Act (1976) and the Human Rights Commission Act (1977).

Thirty years on from this period of major legislative activity, there is no doubt that the role of women in New Zealand society has changed markedly. This is particularly noticeable in political and public life. New Zealand ranks fourteenth equal in the world for the proportion of women in Parliament, with 28 per cent of Members of Parliament at the 2002 election, with eight out of 26 Ministers of the Crown women, and women holding all four key constitutional positions (Ministry of Women's Affairs, 2002, p. 48). Despite this apparent progress, there remain fairly evident gender differences in the labour market. Female labour-force participation, while increasing, remains lower than male labour-force participation, and female average earnings are about 84 per cent of men's (Ministry of Women's Affairs, 2002, pp. 73–6).

Apart from by gender, the other obvious way in which groups in the New Zealand labour market may be observationally distinct is by ethnicity. People of predominantly European, in fact British, extraction form the majority group, but there are other sizeable minorities. Therefore, in the context of the New Zealand labour market it is important to consider gender and ethnicity simultaneously.

There is archaeological evidence to indicate that the indigenous population (Maori) had settled the country by the thirteenth century AD, but, in the absence of written history from this period, estimates of the timing of human settlement vary widely. Belich (1996, p. 36) suggests the eleventh century as a reasonable estimate, while Sinclair (2000, p. 14) prefers the eighth. Whatever the details of the timing, prior to the arrival of Europeans the indigenous inhabitants had no concept of ethnicity or race. The word Maori simply means ordinary people to distinguish them from the new arrivals, whom they dubbed Pakeha.

The British explorer James Cook took possession of the country for the British Crown in 1769, and in 1839 William Hobson established British rule as a dependency of the colony of New South Wales. British sovereignty was proclaimed and the Treaty of Waitangi signed between the British Crown and a number of Maori Chiefs on 6 February 1840 (Sinclair, 2000, p. 72). This treaty ceded sovereignty to the British Crown, while affording Maori the protection of the Crown and 'the unqualified exercise of their chieftainship over their lands, villages and all their treasures' (State Services Commission, 2003).

During the first half of the twentieth century Maori and Pakeha populations remained largely geographically separated (King, 1997, p. 69) but from the Second World War onwards, Maori increasingly migrated to the cities, attracted by well-paid unskilled work, particularly in the economic boom times of the 1950s and 1960s. King (1997, p. 88) notes that in 1936 only about 11 per cent of the Maori population was urbanized, but in the 1980s this proportion had risen to nearly 80 per cent. This process left Maori vulnerable in times of economic downturn.

The last 30 years has been characterized by a renaissance of interest in Maori culture and language. In 1975 the Treaty of Waitangi Act established the Waitangi Tribunal to investigate Treaty grievances by Maori against the Crown. The Ministry of Maori Development (Te Puni Kokiri) was set up in 1992 with the specific aims 'to improve outcomes for Maori and ensure the quality of government services delivered to Maori' (Te Puni Kokiri, 2004a). This agency, in conjunction with Statistics New Zealand, maintains evidence highlighting the position of Maori relative to the rest of the population. These statistics tend to show Maori overrepresented amongst the unemployed, the imprisoned and those on welfare, and Maori youth faring less well in the education system (Te Puni Kokiri, 2004b).

The position of Pacific Peoples in New Zealand to some extent mirrors the Maori migration to the cities, although the large-scale migrations of Pacific people to New Zealand started somewhat later, in the 1960s. In 2001, people claiming Pacific ethnicity made up 6.5 per cent of New Zealand's population, with 58 per cent of them born in New Zealand (Ministry of Pacific Island Affairs, 2002, p. 17). Treating this group as a whole hides considerable ethnic diversity. There are six major ethnic groups making up the New Zealand resident Pacific population (Samoan, Cook Islands, Tongan, Niuean, Tokelauan and Fijian) with a number of other smaller groups. However, to ensure reasonable sample sizes for many statistical purposes, Pacific Peoples are treated as one group. As such, they share with Maori an apparently economically disadvantaged position. For example, their median hourly earnings are about 85 per cent of the national median and they are overrepresented in the lower annual income bands (Ministry of Pacific Island Affairs, 2002, p. 108).

The other major ethnic classification reported by Statistics New Zealand (2003a) is 'Other', a classification which hides a great deal of ethnic diversity. In our analysis we use the category 'Other' to refer to all those not identifying as European, Maori or Pacific. This classification is dominated by Asian people. Migration of sizeable numbers of Asian people to New Zealand occurred in the 1990s. In particular, the highest rate of growth of any ethnic group between 1991 and 1996 was 71 per cent amongst Asians (Statistics New Zealand, 2003a). It is difficult to generalize about people from such diverse backgrounds, but some individuals, even amongst the highly qualified, have faced difficulties of access to the labour market.

## Previous evidence on discrimination in the New Zealand labour market

There is so much worldwide literature on discrimination in the labour market that we only focus on empirical evidence specific to New Zealand.[1] Recent econometric evidence on labour-market discrimination specific to New Zealand includes work by Winkelmann and Winkelmann (1997), Winkelmann (1999), Kirkwood and Wigbout (1999), and Dixon (1996a, 1996b, 1998, 2000).

Winkelmann (1999) draws random samples of only the male working-age population from the censuses of 1986, 1991 and 1996. Each individual is classified as in full-time employment, part-time employment, unemployed or not in the labour force. Multinomial logit models are estimated using this unit-record data, controlling for changes in socio-economic and demographic factors. Winkelmann identifies two potential contributors for the declining labour-market outcomes of Maori men from 1986 to 1996; namely an increase in the return to skill and changes in the sectoral composition of the workforce.

Winkelmann adopts the usual Statistics New Zealand hierarchical definition of ethnicity whereby any person giving Maori as one of the responses to the question about ethnicity is classified as Maori. Chapple and Rea (1998, p. 129) point out that if Statistics New Zealand's 'rule was the equally arbitrary criteria (*sic*) that anyone who reported any non-Maori ethnic group was non-Maori, a stroke of the statistical pen would currently convert a quarter of the Maori ethnic group in the HLFS into non-Maori.' This issue is taken up again when we consider our use of the data.

Winkelmann and Winkelmann (1997) also use the multinomial logit model, finding that the observed individual characteristics to be insufficient to explain all differences in labour-force status, except in some years of their study for women.

Kirkwood and Wigbout (1999) set out to explore the gender income gap. They use data from the HLFS supplemented by the IS to apply 'tree analysis' to identify sub-groups of the sample each with their own unique characteristics which explain the differing levels of average weekly earnings. At each branch of the tree analysis, the algorithm used

(Ghosh and Phillips, 1998) finds the variable and the associated threshold point of that variable which best discriminates between high and low earners. As it turns out, the most significant factors are occupation, hours worked, age and highest qualification, with gender a distant fifth in importance and ethnicity not rating at all in the tree analysis.

Dixon (1998), in an update of her earlier work (Dixon, 1996a, 1996b), uses Household Economic Survey (HES) data to estimate by OLS the log of real hourly earnings as a function of gender, age, education and ethnicity. Dixon finds a significant gender differential but no significant difference between Maori and non-Maori, but does raise the issues of the small sample size of the HES and the possibility of systematic measurement bias in the survey, for which she presents some evidence related to the idea that low-earners tend to underreport hours worked and high-earners overreport. Dixon (2000, p. 129) mentions the issue of sample selection bias in an appendix but fails 'to estimate significant and stable selection parameters' and so presents only separate OLS wage regressions for women and men in order to implement a Blinder–Oaxaca decomposition of the wage gap.

## Methodology and data

Following the convention in the applied literature, we intend to estimate an earnings function of the form:

$$w_i = \mathbf{x}'_{i1}\beta + u_{i1} \tag{8.1}$$

where $\mathbf{x}'_{i1}$ is the vector of exogenous characteristics described in Tables 8.1 and 8.2 below, $w_i$ is the natural logarithm of person $i$'s wage, and $u_{i1}$ is a zero mean random error term. The coefficients of the dummy variables in $\mathbf{x}'_{i1}$ reflect the unexplained gap – the difference in wages after controlling for human-capital variables – in wages, and can be interpreted as evidence of discrimination.

It is well-known that OLS estimation of equation (8.1) is subject to what is known as the sample selection problem (Heckman, 1979). We can only observe wages for working people, and therefore the sample at hand is a truncated sample. This is, however, not a case of straightforward truncation; truncation is based on the outcome of another variable since people self-select employment. Whether or not we observe a wage depends on the individual's decision to work. Because this decision may be systematically correlated to (potential) wage, the sample may have effectively been selected in a non-random fashion, which might lead to a so-called sample selection bias in the OLS estimator. The OLS estimation can yield biased and inconsistent estimators in the presence of such non-random sample selection.

The usual approach to account for sample selection bias is to model wages jointly with the decision to work and add an explicit selection equation, which is of the binary choice type. Letting $s_i^*$ be the latent variable that denotes whether the individual is employed or not, and $\mathbf{x}_{2i}$ be the vector of exogenous variables that affect this decision, the selection equation can be expressed as:

$$s_i^* = \mathbf{x}_{2i}'\gamma + u_{2i}, \quad s_i = 1 \ \text{ if } s_i^* > 0, \quad s_i = 0 \text{ otherwise} \tag{8.2}$$

so that the wage is observed only when the indicator $s_i$ equals 1.

The most common way of estimating the resulting sample selectivity model, equations (8.1) and (8.2), is the easy-to-implement two-step procedure proposed by Heckman (1979), known as Heckit. His method is based on the assumption that the error terms $(u_{1i}, u_{2i})$ follow a bivariate normal distribution, and first estimates a probit model for the selection equation (8.2). The coefficient estimates $\hat{\gamma}$ are used to construct the inverse Mills ratio $f(\mathbf{x}_{2i}\hat{\gamma})/F(\mathbf{x}_{2i}\hat{\gamma})$ which is then included in the wage equation to obtain:

$$w_i = \mathbf{x}_{1i}'\beta + \rho\sigma_1 \frac{f(\mathbf{x}_{2i}\hat{\gamma})}{F(\mathbf{x}_{2i}\hat{\gamma})} + \eta_i \tag{8.3}$$

Equation (8.3) is then estimated by OLS for the selected sample of employed people. This results in consistent and asymptotically normal estimators of the parameters of the wage regression equation. The parameter $\rho$ denotes the correlation between the error terms $u_1$ and $u_2$. $\sigma_1$ is the standard error of $u_1$ which is normalized to 1, and $f$ and $F$ are the standard normal probability density and cumulative density functions. Because a zero correlation implies no selection bias, it is easy to test the null hypothesis of no sample selection bias.

This two-step procedure is, in general, not efficient. An alternative method is to estimate equations (8.1) and (8.2) simultaneously by full information maximum likelihood estimation (MLE), which produces consistent and asymptotically efficient estimators that have an asymptotic normal distribution. A direct estimate of the correlation coefficient, $\rho$, between the two error terms is also obtained, which can be used to test for sample selection bias.

Vella (1998) and Puhani (2000) summarize the potential problems in using these methods. Most of the criticism of the maximum likelihood method is about the sensitivity of it to the assumed parametric distribution of the error terms, which is valid for any parametric estimation method. A critical issue with Heckit is the case when $\mathbf{x}_1$ and $\mathbf{x}_2$ are identical. Although the inverse Mills ratio in equation (8.2) may be highly correlated to the remaining regressors in this case, the equation may still be identified through the nonlinearity of the inverse Mills ratio. Such weak identification may cause inflated standard errors in the second step of the Heckit method, making the coefficient estimates unreliable. It is therefore important to apply exclusion restrictions so that there is at least one variable in the selection equation that does not enter the earnings function.

Taking these criticisms into consideration we estimate earning functions by both methods as well as OLS. We use unit-record data from the New Zealand Household Labour Force Survey (HLFS) and its supplement of Income Survey (IS) for the years 1997 and 2003. An important difference in our data-sets compared to those used by other researchers is that we asked SNZ to classify separately those respondents who ticked only Maori and those who ticked both Maori and some other ethnic group in answering the ethnicity question. Accordingly, we were able to separately identify those individuals who identify solely with the Maori ethnic group and those (whom we call 'Mixed') who identify themselves as Maori as well as at least one other classification. This enables us to address the criticism made by Chapple and Rea (1998) and to avoid conclusions that are driven by a changing proportion of the sample identifying as Maori over time. In order for economic discrimination to operate, there must be observationally distinct groups. We have no information on the degree to which ethnic identification and observational distinctness coincide, but it seems reasonable to assume a lower degree of observational distinctiveness amongst the group describing themselves by multiple rather than single ethnicities.

We have 28,292 observations for 1997 and 28,982 for 2003. Of these, 17,571 in 1997 and 18,364 in 2003 are in the labour force. We exclude the individuals with inconsistent observations – employed but working zero hours and earning zero wages – from our sample. We then estimate earnings functions by using the remaining 17,081 observations in 1997 and 18,236 in 2003. There are also 2,839 individuals in 1997 and 3,254 in 2003 who earn less than 75 per cent of the relevant – youth or adult – minimum wage. We include these observations in estimating the probit equation but exclude them in estimating the wage equation when we use Heckit. MLE and OLS naturally require them to be excluded altogether.

Table 8.1 above defines the variables used in the probit analysis, all of which are also potentially available for use in the wage regressions. The motivation for each of these variables is now discussed in turn.

*Table 8.1* Independent variables in the probit analysis

| *Variable* | *Definition* |
|---|---|
| *Age variables* | |
| AGE | Age in years |
| AGESQ | Square of AGE |
| *Household-type variables* | |
| CWCH | 1 if a couple with dependent children, 0 otherwise |
| SWCH | 1 if a single parent with dependent children, 0 otherwise |
| SOLO | 1 if a single parent with no dependent children, 0 otherwise |
| ONEP | 1 if a sole person household, 0 otherwise |
| OTHRHH | 1 if another household type (except couple with no dependent children), 0 otherwise |
| *Marital-status variables* | |
| MARR | 1 if living as married, 0 otherwise |
| SEP | 1 if separated, divorced or widowed, 0 otherwise |
| *Qualification variables* | |
| UNIQ | 1 if highest qualification a first degree or higher degree, 0 otherwise |
| PSCQ | 1 if highest qualification post-school but not university, 0 otherwise |
| SCHQ | 1 if highest qualification is school level, 0 otherwise |
| NSQAL | 1 if highest qualification is not specified (but not none), 0 otherwise |
| *Regional variable* | |
| MCNT | 1 if resident in Auckland, Wellington or Canterbury regions, 0 otherwise |
| *Gender variable* | 1 if female, 0 if male |
| GNDR | |
| *Ethnicity variables* | |
| MAOR | 1 if Maori, 0 otherwise |
| MIXD | 1 if Maori and other ethnic group, 0 otherwise |
| PACI | 1 if Pacific Islander, 0 otherwise |
| OTHRETH | 1 if other ethnic group (except European), 0 otherwise |

Age and its square are entered in the regressions as proxies for experience. This does fail to account for the details of individuals' differing labour-market experiences; for example, females will often take leave from the work force for child rearing purposes. Unfortunately, we simply do not have access to detailed labour market profiles on the people in our samples. The effect of age on wage is likely to be positive but diminishing, hence the use of the squared term.

Household-type dummies, with a couple with no dependent children as the reference class, are included to account for the possibly differing opportunities and incentives facing those with and without children, as well as those living alone. Marital status dummies are included for much the same reason, with a greater expectation of finding a significant effect for those 'living as married' than those who are 'widowed, separated or divorced', the reference class being 'never married'.

A set of qualification dummies, ranging from a person's highest qualification being at secondary-school level to university level, is used to capture the positive effect of increasing educational qualifications. The reference class is 'no qualifications' and one of the qualification groups (containing relatively few observations) is 'unspecified' to allow for completeness in treating the sample.

A regional dummy, taking the value 1 for survey participants who reside in one of the three main urban centres, is used to account for relatively lower wages in the provincial areas. A more complete set of regional dummies, based on 13 regional council areas (using the principal urban area, Auckland, as reference class) was also tried. These results, which we do not present here, indicate that our findings are very robust to this change in specification. Although the regions that show up as negative vary from sample to sample, none of the other estimates differs much.

Ethnicity and gender dummies are included, not for any supposed productivity effect, but to test for labour-market discrimination.

The wage regressions do not include all of the variables from the original probits. The variables chosen for exclusion here are the household-type variables and the marital-status variables, which do arguably affect an individual's participation decision, most especially in the case of females, but not the wage offer (Puhani, 2000). We experiment with excluding just household-type variables, just marital-status variables and then both sets of variables to check the robustness of our findings to these exclusion restrictions.

*Table 8.2* Additional variables used in the wage regression

| *Variable* | *Definition* |
|---|---|
| *Occupational variables* | |
| OCCT | 1 if in top two occupational groups, 0 otherwise |
| OCCM | 1 if in middle three occupational groups, 0 otherwise |
| *Part-time status* | |
| PT | 1 if part-time, 0 if full-time |
| *Variable to correct for sample selection bias (Heckit method)* | |
| MILLS | Inverse Mills ratio |
| RHO ($\rho$) | Correlation between error terms in MLE (maximum likelihood estimation) |

The wage regressions also include occupational class and part-time dummies as defined in Table 8.2. These variables cannot, of course, be defined for individuals who are not observed to be in employment. Occupational class dummies allow for the obviously different wage structure of professional against skilled, semi-skilled and unskilled occupations. Part-time work in the survey is defined as fewer than 30 hours per week and this dummy is included to allow for the possibility that part-time and full-time work are differently rewarded. Given both the secondary nature of the market for part-time labour and the fact that the official definition of 'part-time' varies from working as little as 1 to as many as 29 hours per week, we also explore the effect on our findings of estimating the regressions separately for full-time and part-time workers.

The dependent variable in the wage regressions presented here is the natural logarithm of the actual hourly rate (LNACHRLY).[2] Similar results were found using reported 'usual' in place of actual hourly rates.

## Results

Table 8.3 presents descriptive wage data from our samples broken down by gender and ethnicity. It is clear from Table 8.3a, which is based on the full samples, that the raw data indicate that males earn more per hour than females, while Pakeha (Europeans) earn more than any other ethnic group. The position of women relative to men and all ethnic groups except 'Other' relative to Pakeha appears to have worsened over this period. Table 8.3b shows the data from each year broken down into

*Table 8.3* Average actual hourly earnings (wages and salaries) ($NZ) in primary job
(a) Full sample

| | *1997* | | *2003* | |
|---|---|---|---|---|
| Male | 15.70 | % of male | 19.70 | % of male |
| Female | 13.43 | 85.54 | 16.50 | 83.76 |
| Pakeha | 15.01 | % of Pakeha | 18.82 | % of Pakeha |
| Sole Maori | 12.69 | 84.54 | 15.30 | 81.30 |
| Mixed Maori | 12.72 | 85.74 | 15.74 | 83.63 |
| Pacific Islander | 11.30 | 75.28 | 13.87 | 73.70 |
| Other | 14.26 | 95.00 | 18.32 | 97.34 |
| Overall | 14.53 | | 18.09 | |
| Number of observations | 12,955 | | 14,131 | |

(b) Sample split into full-time and part-time workers

| | *1997* | | | | *2003* | | | |
|---|---|---|---|---|---|---|---|---|
| | *Full-time* | | *Part-time* | | *Full-time* | | *Part-time* | |
| Male | 16.29 | % of male | 10.66 | % of male | 20.41 | % of male | 14.03 | % of male |
| Female | 13.81 | 84.48 | 12.46 | 116.89 | 17.89 | 87.65 | 14.10 | 100.50 |
| Pakeha | 15.83 | % of Pakeha | 12.34 | % of Pakeha | 20.23 | % of Pakeha | 14.50 | |
| Sole Maori | 13.20 | 83.39 | 10.61 | 85.98 | 16.02 | 79.19 | 12.65 | 87.24 |
| Mixed Maori | 13.33 | 84.21 | 10.99 | 89.06 | 16.69 | 82.50 | 12.78 | 88.14 |
| Pacific Islander | 11.51 | 72.71 | 10.24 | 82.98 | 14.30 | 70.69 | 11.63 | 80.21 |
| Other | 15.37 | 97.09 | 11.10 | 89.95 | 20.16 | 99.65 | 13.00 | 89.66 |
| Overall | 15.28 | | 12.04 | | 19.35 | | 14.08 | |
| Number of observations | 9980 | | 2975 | | 10750 | | 3381 | |

*Note*: Individuals who were employed but reported zero hours worked or zero wages earned, and individuals who earned below 75 per cent of the relevant minimum wage were omitted from these calculations.

full-time and part-time workers.[3] There are striking differences between the two types of workers. Most notably, part-time female workers actually earn a higher hourly rate than part-time males. Amongst part-timers the position of all minority groups except 'Other' is better relative to the majority group than amongst full-timers.

We present the results from estimating wage regressions by OLS, Heckit and MLE methods in Tables 8.4 to 8.7 inclusive.[4] Tables 8.4 and 8.5 present estimates for the coefficients on the control variables, with the estimates concerning gender and ethnicity reserved to Tables 8.6 and 8.7.

*Table 8.4* Estimated coefficients from wage regressions, 1997

| *Exclusion restrictions* | | *None* | *Martial status* | *Household type* | *Both* |
|---|---|---|---|---|---|
| INTERCEPT | OLS | 1.50 | 1.43 | 1.50 | 1.41 |
| | Heckit | 1.44 | 1.61[1] | 1.49 | 1.57 |
| | MLE | 1.35 | 1.27 | 1.34 | 1.45 |
| AGE | OLS | 0.0390 | 0.0465 | 0.0404 | 0.0469 |
| | Heckit | 0.0407 | 0.0409[1] | 0.0407 | 0.0424 |
| | MLE | 0.0433 | 0.0519 | 0.0439 | 0.0460 |
| AGESQ | OLS | −0.000419 | −0.000494 | −0.000432 | −0.000499 |
| | Heckit | −0.000435 | −0.000439[1] | −0.000435 | −0.000456 |
| | MLE | −0.000464 | −0.000553 | −0.000467 | −0.000490 |
| UNIQ | OLS | 0.344 | 0.344 | 0.348 | 0.345 |
| | Heckit | 0.356 | 0.314[1] | 0.351 | 0.322 |
| | MLE | 0.378 | 0.379 | 0.383 | 0.340 |
| PSCQ | OLS | 0.182 | 0.186 | 0.185 | 0.186 |
| | Heckit | 0.194 | 0.156[1] | 0.187 | 0.164 |
| | MLE | 0.211 | 0.215 | 0.214 | 0.181 |
| SCHQ | OLS | 0.123 | 0.123 | 0.124 | 0.124 |
| | Heckit | 0.136 | 0.091[1] | 0.127 | 0.099 |
| | MLE | 0.153 | 0.153 | 0.155 | 0.118 |
| NSQAL | OLS | −0.057 | −0.080 | −0.047 | −0.087 |
| | | (0.611) | (0.474) | (0.676) | (0.437) |
| | Heckit | −0.054 | −0.081[1] | −0.046 | −0.078 |
| | | (0.631) | (0.496) | (0.683) | (0.501) |
| | MLE | −0.053 | −0.079 | −0.040 | −0.085 |
| | | (0.655) | (0.508) | (0.731) | (0.408) |
| MCNT | OLS | 0.0682 | 0.0655 | 0.0686 | 0.0651 |
| | Heckit | 0.0704 | 0.061[1] | 0.0691 | 0.0620 |
| | MLE | 0.0737 | 0.0706 | 0.0731 | 0.0644 |
| OCCT | OLS | 0.232 | 0.234 | 0.232 | 0.236 |
| | Heckit | 0.232 | 0.235[1] | 0.232 | 0.235 |
| | MLE | 0.209 | 0.211 | 0.209 | 0.236 |
| OCCM | OLS | 0.086 | 0.087 | 0.086 | 0.088 |
| | Heckit | 0.086 | 0.088[1] | 0.086 | 0.087 |
| | MLE | 0.076 | 0.077 | 0.076 | 0.088 |
| PT | OLS | −0.130 | −0.133 | −0.135 | −0.133 |
| | Heckit | −0.130 | −0.132[1] | −0.135 | −0.130 |
| | MLE | −0.125 | −0.129 | −0.133 | −0.133 |
| Mills ratio in Heckit | | 0.162 | −0.400[1] | −0.035 | −0.300 |
| | | (0.172) | | (0.633) | |
| $\rho$ in MLE | | 0.860 | 0.860 | 0.858 | −0.168 |
| | | | | | (0.054) |
| Log likelihood in MLE | | −8530 | −8588 | −8551 | −8800 |

*Notes*: Dependent variable: ln(actual hourly rate); $p$-value only shown if $p > 0.01$.
[1] The estimated correlation is outside the range (−1,1), $\rho$ set to 1.

*Table 8.5* Estimated coefficients from wage regressions, 2003

| *Exclusion restrictions* | | *None* | *Marital status* | *Household type* | *Both* |
|---|---|---|---|---|---|
| INTERCEPT | OLS | 1.73 | 1.72 | 1.72 | 1.69 |
| | Heckit | 1.58[1] | 1.64 | 1.64 | 1.80 |
| | MLE | 1.64 | 1.59 | 1.63 | 1.71 |
| AGE | OLS | 0.0371 | 0.0399 | 0.0383 | 0.0412 |
| | Heckit | 0.0408[1] | 0.0427 | 0.0388 | 0.0377 |
| | MLE | 0.0394 | 0.0454 | 0.0396 | 0.0406 |
| AGESQ | OLS | −0.000384 | −0.000415 | −0.000398 | −0.000430 |
| | Heckit | −0.000426[1] | −0.000444 | −0.000404 | −0.000395 |
| | MLE | −0.000417 | −0.000476 | −0.000416 | −0.000423 |
| UNIQ | OLS | 0.347 | 0.348 | 0.347 | 0.348 |
| | Heckit | 0.377[1] | 0.361 | 0.365 | 0.331 |
| | MLE | 0.390 | 0.391 | 0.392 | 0.345 |
| PSCQ | OLS | 0.159 | 0.160 | 0.159 | 0.162 |
| | Heckit | 0.181[1] | 0.170 | 0.172 | 0.149 |
| | MLE | 0.184 | 0.186 | 0.185 | 0.159 |
| SCHQ | OLS | 0.094 | 0.093 | 0.094 | 0.096 |
| | Heckit | 0.121[1] | 0.104 | 0.110 | 0.080 |
| | MLE | 0.119 | 0.117 | 0.120 | 0.093 |
| NSQAL | OLS | 0.156 | 0.156 | 0.172 | 0.152 |
| | Heckit | 0.169[1] | 0.161 | 0.183 | 0.150 |
| | MLE | 0.173 | 0.172 | 0.192 | 0.152 |
| MCNT | OLS | 0.0907 | 0.0893 | 0.0896 | 0.0876 |
| | Heckit | 0.0950[1] | 0.0908 | 0.0929 | 0.0861 |
| | MLE | 0.0946 | 0.0927 | 0.0943 | 0.0874 |
| OCCT | OLS | 0.278 | 0.281 | 0.278 | 0.283 |
| | Heckit | 0.275[1] | 0.280 | 0.275 | 0.283 |
| | MLE | 0.220 | 0.223 | 0.220 | 0.283 |
| OCCM | OLS | 0.060 | 0.060 | 0.059 | 0.061 |
| | Heckit | 0.058[1] | 0.060 | 0.059 | 0.060 |
| | MLE | 0.036 | 0.037 | 0.036 | 0.061 |
| PT | OLS | −0.133 | −0.135 | −0.132 | −0.132 |
| | Heckit | −0.134[1] | −0.135 | −0.135 | −0.130 |
| | MLE | −0.127 | −0.129 | −0.129 | −0.132 |
| Mills ratio in Heckit | | 0.506[1] | 0.221 (0.148) | 0.295 | −0.268 |
| $\rho$ in MLE | | | 0.946 | 0.946 | −0.114 (0.313) |
| Log likelihood in MLE | | −8693 | −8734 | −8703 | −9257 |

*Notes*: Dependent variable: ln(actual hourly rate); *p*-value only shown if $p > 0.01$.
[1] The estimated correlation is outside the range $(-1,1)$, $\rho$ set to 1.

*Table 8.6* Estimated coefficients on gender and ethnicity, 1997

| *Exclusion restrictions* | | *None* | *Marital status* | *Household type* | *Both* |
|---|---|---|---|---|---|
| GENDER | OLS | −0.132 | −0.130 | −0.131 | −0.133 |
| | Heckit | −0.130 | −0.136[1] | −0.131 | −0.135 |
| | MLE | −0.121 | −0.119 | −0.121 | −0.134 |
| MAORI | OLS | −0.044 | −0.040 | −0.044 | −0.044 |
| | Heckit | −0.069 | 0.022[1] | −0.050 | 0.008 |
| | | | (0.276) | | (0.620) |
| | MLE | −0.097 | −0.092 | −0.103 | −0.034 |
| | | | | | (0.014) |
| MIXED | OLS | −0.032 | −0.030 | −0.033 | −0.033 |
| | | (0.078) | (0.100) | (0.068) | (0.065) |
| | Heckit | −0.047 | 0.009[1] | −0.036 | −0.0002 |
| | | (0.028) | (0.686) | (0.063) | (0.992) |
| | MLE | −0.065 | −0.062 | −0.071 | −0.026 |
| | | | | | (0.185) |
| PACI | OLS | −0.133 | −0.129 | −0.133 | −0.128 |
| | Heckit | −0.157 | −0.071[1] | −0.139 | −0.084 |
| | MLE | −0.178 | −0.173 | −0.182 | −0.120 |
| OTHER | OLS | −0.092 | −0.087 | −0.092 | −0.086 |
| | Heckit | −0.116 | −0.027[1] | −0.097 | −0.042 |
| | | | (0.236) | | (0.024) |
| | MLE | −0.154 | −0.147 | −0.155 | −0.076 |

*Notes*: Dependent variable: ln(actual hourly rate); *p*-value only shown if $p \geq 0.01$.
[1] The estimated correlation is outside the range (−1,1), $\rho$ set to 1.

*Table 8.7* Estimated coefficients on gender and ethnicity 2003

| *Exclusion restrictions* | | *None* | *Marital status* | *Household type* | *Both* |
|---|---|---|---|---|---|
| GENDER | OLS | −0.120 | −0.122 | −0.121 | −0.126 |
| | Heckit | −0.122[1] | −0.122 | −0.124 | −0.124 |
| | MLE | −0.115 | −0.114 | −0.117 | −0.126 |
| MAORI | OLS | −0.047 | −0.044 | −0.046 | −0.047 |
| | Heckit | −0.096[1] | −0.065 | −0.078 | −0.019 |
| | | | | | (0.183) |
| | MLE | −0.086 | −0.082 | −0.090 | −0.043 |
| MIXED | OLS | −0.023 | −0.022 | −0.023 | −0.023 |
| | | (0.184) | (0.201) | (0.182) | (0.186) |
| | Heckit | −0.070[1] | −0.043 | −0.052 | 0.003 |
| | | | (0.058) | | (0.858) |
| | MLE | −0.062 | −0.062 | −0.065 | −0.019 |
| | | | | | (0.337) |

*continued*

*Table 8.7 continued*

| *Exclusion restrictions* | | *None* | *Marital status* | *Household type* | *Both* |
|---|---|---|---|---|---|
| PACI | OLS | −0.144 | −0.139 | −0.144 | −0.140 |
| | Heckit | −0.174[1] | −0.152 | −0.164 | −0.123 |
| | MLE | −0.164 | −0.160 | −0.168 | −0.137 |
| OTHER | OLS | −0.112 | −0.109 | −0.112 | −0.107 |
| | Heckit | −0.164[1] | −0.131 | −0.143 | −0.086 |
| | MLE | −0.161 | −0.157 | −0.161 | −0.102 |

*Notes*: Dependent variable: ln(actual hourly rate); *p*-value only shown if $p \geq 0.01$.
[1] The estimated correlation is outside the range $(-1,1)$, $\rho$ set to 1.

The purpose of Tables 8.4 and 8.5 is to examine the robustness of the results both as to estimating technique and to model specification, in particular the issue of exclusion restrictions as discussed above. The first column of estimates in each table presents the results of running the models including the marital status and household-type variables as defined in Table 8.1. The second column excludes the marital-status variables, the third excludes the household-type variables and the fourth excludes both marital-status and household-type variables.

In general, we note that the estimated coefficients are quite robust across the three models and four specifications. In addition, with few exceptions the estimates are highly statistically significant as well as economically meaningful. We have reported *p*-values only if they are larger than 0.01 and we discuss the economic importance of the results below.

The reported coefficients on dummy variables are not immediately economically interpretable, but are easily transformed to find the percentage effects of the variables of interest by taking the exponential function of each coefficient and subtracting 1. For example, in the case of the qualification variable UNIQ in 1997 this results in effects over all 12 estimates in the range of 41 per cent to 47 per cent. Given that this represents higher wages for holders of university qualifications *ceteris paribus*, in particular holding constant age, location and occupational grouping, it is of an appropriately plausible magnitude. Similarly plausible results hold for other qualification groupings in 1997: a 21 per cent to 24 per cent wage premium for holders of post-school qualifications and 13 per cent to 17 per cent for holders of school qualifications. The exception is the catch-all class of NSQAL, which is defined as qualifications that are unspecified. Given the uncertainty of how such diverse qualifications might relate to the other qualification groupings, this is to be expected.

The coefficients on MCNT, OCCT and OCCM suggest 7–8 per cent, 23–26 per cent and 8–9 per cent premiums for main centre residence, top and middle occupational classes, respectively in 1997. The estimated coefficients on PT in 1997 suggest that, *ceteris paribus*, part-time workers earn 88 per cent of the hourly rate of full-timers.

The age variable enters the regressions in a quadratic form that permits calculation of a turning point, representing the age at which the effect of an extra year becomes negative. The turning point can be computed as the negative of the coefficient on AGE divided by twice the coefficient on AGESQ. The 1997 estimates of these turning points range only from 46 years to 48 years across the 12 reported estimates. Thus, the estimate of the effect of age on earnings is robust and economically plausible.

The results from 2003 are presented in Table 8.5 and are very similar to those from 1997. The only noteworthy difference is that the unspecified class of qualifications becomes statistically significant and gives holders of such qualifications a 16 per cent to 21 per cent wage premium over the unqualified. We can only speculate that the 2003 sample happened to include only qualifications that truly gave their holders a labour-market advantage.

Also reported in Tables 8.4 and 8.5 are estimates for MILLS (Heckit models) or RHO (MLE models). These, if significant, indicate the existence of sample selection bias. More often than not, there is evidence of significant sample selection bias. When there is such bias, the use of OLS is not appropriate, although we note that the OLS estimates discussed so far (those on the control variables as opposed to the gender and ethnicity coefficients) are pretty much the same as those found by Heckit or MLE.

Tables 8.6 and 8.7 report the remaining coefficients from the wage regressions, being those on gender and ethnicity. The economic importance of the estimated effects is calculated in the same way as described above for the qualification and occupational class variables.

In the case of gender, the estimated coefficients, which are always statistically significant at a very high level, imply that females, even after controlling for a range of other productivity characteristics, earn between 88 per cent and 89 per cent of male earnings. This finding is similar in 1997 and 2003 so that there is little evidence of a change in women's relative earnings over this period. Some of the difference is often attributed to females having fewer years of labour-market experience as a result of time devoted to child rearing, and to the clustering of females in certain traditional occupations. While no doubt it is possible to explain part of the differential in these ways, the estimate of an 11 per cent to 12 per cent wage disadvantage does reflect society's continued undervaluation of child rearing relative to labour-market experience and lower pay in traditionally female-dominated occupations, regardless of the skill demands of that work relative to male-dominated occupations.

Of the different non-European ethnic groups, the most clear-cut finding relates to Pacific Peoples. This group earns between 85 per cent to 89 per cent of the European wage. In the case of the ethnic group 'Other', dominated by Asians, although there are a couple of non-significant estimates in 1997, the MLE estimates indicate this group earns about 93 per cent of European wages in 1997 and about 90 per cent in 2003. For the group who identify simultaneously as Maori and European ('Mixed') most estimates are not statistically significant and are very sensitive to the exclusion restrictions imposed. For the indigenous people, Maori, the results are least clear-cut. OLS estimates very consistently suggest they earn about 96 per cent of European wages. However, there is quite a lot of evidence of sample selection bias. There is also a high degree of sensitivity to exclusion restrictions, with the ethnic wage gap as measured by the Heckit technique even turning in favour of the minority group in two cases. MLE is also sensitive to the choice of exclusion restrictions, but most often the results suggest a Maori–European wage ratio of 91 per cent to 92 per cent after correcting for sample selection bias.

Given the questions raised earlier concerning the definition of part-time employment, we estimated the models separately for full-time and part-time workers. The use of the MLE is not feasible when restricting the sample to full-time workers because MLE simultaneously estimates the probability of being in employment and the wage equation. At the probit estimation stage no distinction can be made between those in part-time and those in full-time employment. Therefore, we present results only for OLS and Heckit models.

In the case of part-time workers we found no significant gender or ethnic differentials, suggesting that the part-time market does not reward these observationally distinct characteristics differentially. This may be because part-time work is predominantly in the secondary labour market where many jobs are paid at or near minimum wage.

*Table 8.8* Estimated coefficients on gender and ethnicity, full-time employees only

| *Exclusion restrictions* | | | *None* | *Marital status* | *Household type* | *Both* |
|---|---|---|---|---|---|---|
| GENDER | OLS | 1997 | −0.153 | −0.152 | −0.151 | −0.154 |
| | | 2003 | −0.133 | −0.135 | −0.134 | −0.140 |
| | Heckit | 1997 | −0.149 | −0.157 | −0.149 | −0.155 |
| | | 2003 | −0.135[1] | −0.135[1] | −0.137 | −0.138 |
| MAORI | OLS | 1997 | −0.055 | −0.051 | −0.056 | −0.054 |
| | | 2003 | −0.039 | −0.036 | −0.040 | −0.039 |
| | Heckit | 1997 | −0.094 | −0.001 | −0.070 | −0.008 |
| | | | | (0.9632) | | (0.620) |
| | | 2003 | −0.118[1] | −0.083[1] | −0.074 | −0.010 |
| | | | | | | (0.516) |
| MIXED | OLS | 1997 | −0.035 | −0.035 | −0.038 | −0.037 |
| | | | (0.092) | (0.089) | (0.068) | (0.071) |
| | | 2003 | −0.030 | −0.030 | −0.030 | −0.030 |
| | | | (0.139) | (0.134) | (0.132) | (0.140) |
| | Heckit | 1997 | −0.059 | −0.003 | −0.047 | −0.008 |
| | | | (0.017) | (0.883) | (0.039) | (0.717) |
| | | 2003 | −0.104[1] | −0.075[1] | −0.060 | −0.004 |
| | | | | | | (0.860) |
| PACI | OLS | 1997 | −0.154 | −0.151 | −0.158 | −0.153 |
| | | 2003 | −0.164 | −0.161 | −0.166 | −0.160 |
| | Heckit | 1997 | −0.192 | −0.103 | −0.172 | −0.112 |
| | | 2003 | −0.210[1] | −0.188[1] | −0.186 | −0.144 |
| OTHER | OLS | 1997 | −0.100 | −0.094 | −0.100 | −0.094 |
| | | 2003 | −0.110 | −0.107 | −0.111 | −0.104 |
| | Heckit | 1997 | −0.137 | −0.048 | −0.113 | −0.056 |
| | | 2003 | −0.189[1] | −0.153[1] | −0.142 | −0.080 |
| Mills ratio in Heckit | | 1997 | 0.259 | −0.336 | 0.091 | −0.285 |
| | | | (0.063) | | (0.325) | |
| | | 2003 | 0.844[1] | 0.502[1] | 0.331 | −0.285 |
| | | | | (0.011) | | |

*Notes*: Dependent variable: ln(actual hourly rate); *p*-value only shown if $p \geq 0.01$.
[1] The estimated correlation is outside the range $(-1,1)$, $\rho$ set to 1.

Table 8.8 presents the estimated coefficients on gender and ethnicity when we restricted our sample to full-time workers only. Again, for gender, there is a consistent picture of females earning less than males and amongst full-time employees the female–male wage ratio is slightly lower, at 86 per cent to 87 per cent, than in the full sample. Pacific Peoples in full-time employment, on correction for sample selection bias, earn 83 per cent to 87 per cent of the European wage, less than in the full sample. The lower figure (83%) is for 2003, suggesting a worsening of the labour market position of Pacific Peoples. The 'Other'–European wage ratio also appears to have dropped from around 92 per cent in 1997 to 87 per cent in 2003. The group of 'Mixed' identity more often than not shows no significant difference from the reference (European) group. According to the OLS results, Maori are slightly better-off in 2003 than in 1997, with the Maori–European wage ratio increasing from 95 per cent to 96 per cent, but there is some evidence of sample selection bias and, again unfortunately, the results from Heckit are quite sensitive to the exclusion restrictions. On balance, they give less cause to suggest an improvement in the relative position of full-time Maori employees over the period under consideration.

## Conclusion

In this chapter we have made use of data from the inaugural New Zealand Income Survey of 1997 and the latest available survey of 2003 to estimate wage regressions by OLS and two other methods, Heckit and MLE, which take into account the possibility of sample selection bias. In addition, we examined the robustness of the estimates to various sets of exclusion restrictions. It turned out that all three estimation techniques gave very similar results for a set of control variables typically used in wage regressions with the vast majority of the estimates being statistically significant and of economically plausible and significant magnitudes. This gives us confidence in our key result regarding the gender wage ratio. In the full sample, the female–male wage ratio is about 88 per cent in 1997 and 88 per cent to 89 per cent in 2003, depending on estimation technique and exclusion restrictions. Amongst full-time workers, the corresponding ratios are 86 per cent and 87 per cent. These results are not strikingly different from the raw figures, unadjusted for any worker characteristics. It seems that women actually are rewarded less favourably than comparable males. Of New Zealand's three main ethnic classifications, apart from the majority European group, Pacific Peoples suffer the greatest wage disadvantage relative to the majority, with the Pacific–European wage ratio of a similar magnitude to the female–male ratio.

Apart from using the Income Survey to continue to monitor changes over time, we consider the most promising extension of the present work would involve the use of more detailed information on individuals in explaining their labour-market participation decision. In the case of females, in particular, the number of dependent children, especially those of pre-school age, is likely to be a crucial factor. This sort of information has just recently been part of a trial release of a confidentialized unit record file (CURF) by Statistics New Zealand based only on the 2003 Income Survey. From 2005 such CURF data may become more regularly available to researchers.

## Notes

1 Cain (1986) and Altonji and Blank (1999) summarize numerous studies. Recently, there has been a resurgence of interest in reevaluating labour-market outcomes for both women and minority groups. Cawley, Heckman and Vytlacil (2001) confirm that wage payment still does vary by gender and race in the USA. Bell and Ritchie (1998), Christofides, Li, Liu and Min (2003), Kidd and Ferko (2001) and Albrecht, Björklund and Vroman (2003) document the continuing gender differentials in the UK, Canada, Austalia and Sweden, respectively. All of these authors explicitly recognize the issue of sample selection bias. Blau and Kahn (2003) offer comparative international evidence on the gender pay gap across 22 countries. Garcia, Hernández and López-Nicolás (2001) is a recent example of applying quantile regression to investigate wage gaps.

2 The actual hourly rate is calculated as the reported total weekly income from working divided by the number of hours worked in that week.

3 Full-time is defined in the standard way as working 30 or more hours per week.

4 Although a probit model is estimated as part of each of the two sample selection methods, we do not report the probit results themselves here, as we are primarily interested in the wage equation. They are available on request.

## References


Albrecht, J., Björklund, A. and Vroman, S. (2003) 'Is there a Glass Ceiling in Sweden?', *Journal of Labour Economics*, 21(1), pp. 145–77.

Altonji, J.G. and Blank, R.M. (1999) 'Race and Gender in the Labor Market', in O. Ashenfelter and D. Card (eds), *Handbook of Labor Economics, Volume 3*. Elsevier Science Publishers: Amsterdam.

Belich, J. (1996) *Making Peoples. A History of the New Zealanders: From Polynesian Settlement to the End of the Nineteenth Century*. Auckland: Penguin Books.

Bell, D. and Ritchie, F. (1998) 'Female Earnings and Gender Differentials in Great Britain 1977–1994', *Labour Economics*, 5, pp. 331–57.

Blau, F.D. and Kahn, L.M. (2003) 'Understanding International Differences in the Gender Pay Gap', *Journal of Labour Economics*, 21(1), pp. 106–44.

Cain, G.G. (1986) 'The Economic Analysis of Labor Market Discrimination: A Survey', in O. Ashenfelter and R. Layard (eds), *Handbook of Labour Economics, Volume I*. Elsevier Science Publishers: Amsterdam.

Cawley, J., Heckman, J. and Vytlacil, E. (2001) 'Three Observations on Wages and Measured Cognitive Ability', *Labour Economics*, 8, pp. 419–42.

Chapple, S. and Rea, D. (1998) 'Time Series Analysis of Disparity between Maori and non-Maori Labour Market Outcomes in the Household Labour Force Survey', *Labour Market Bulletin*, 1&2, pp. 127–44.

Christofides, L.N., Li, Q., Liu, Z. and Min, I. (2003) 'Recent Two-Stage Sample Selection Procedures with an Application to the Gender Wage Gap', *Journal of Business and Economic Statistics*, 21(3), pp. 396–405.

Dixon, S. (1996a) 'The Distribution of Earnings in New Zealand: 1984–94', *Labour Market Bulletin*, 1, pp. 45–100.

Dixon, S. (1996b) 'The Distribution of Eearnings in New Zealand: 1984–95', in *Proceedings of the Seventh Labour, Employment and Work Conference, 28–29 November*1996, Wellington, Victoria University of Wellington, 1997, pp. 31–42.

Dixon, S. (1998) 'Growth in the Dispersion of Earnings: 1984–97', *Labour Market Bulletin*, 1&2, pp. 71–107.

Dixon, S. (2000) 'Pay Inequality between Men and Women in New Zealand', Occasional Paper 2000/1, Labour Market Policy Group, Department of Labour, Wellington.

Garcia, J., Hernández, P.J. and López-Nicolás, N. (2001) 'How Wide is the Gap? An Investigation of Gender Wage Differences using Quantile Regression', *Empirical Economics*, 26, pp. 149–67.

Ghosh and Phillips (1998) 'Warning: Inflation may be harmful to your growth', *IMF Staff Papers*, 45, pp. 672–710.

Heckman, James J. (1979) 'Sample selection as a specification error', *Econometrica*, 47, pp. 153–61.

Kidd, M. and Ferko, I. (2001) 'The Employment Effects of Gender Discrimination in Australia 1994–95', *The Economic Record*, 77(236), pp. 71–88.

King, M. (1997) *Nga Iwi O Te Motu: One Thousand Years of Maori History*. Auckland:Reed Books.

Kirkwood, H. and Wigbout, M. (1999) *Exploring the gap. An exploration of the difference in income received from wages and salaries by women and men in full-time employment*, Statistics New Zealand, Wellington.

MacDonald, C. (1993) *The Vote, the Pill and the Demon Drink: A History of Feminist Writing in New Zealand 1869–1993*. Wellington: Bridget Williams Books.

Mincer, J. (1974) *Schooling, Experience and Earnings*, Columbia University Press for the National Bureau of Economic Research, New York.

Mincer, J. and Polachek, S.W. (1974) 'Family Investments in Human Capital: Earnings of Women', *Journal of Political Economy*, 82, pp. S76–S108.

Ministry of Pacific Island Affairs (2002) *Pacific Progress*. Wellington: Ministry of Pacific Island Affairs.

Ministry of Women's Affairs (2002) *The Status of Women in New Zealand 2002*. Wellington: Ministry of Women's Affairs.

Neuman, S. and Oaxaca, R.L. (2004) 'Wage Decompositions with Selectivity-corrected Wage Equations: A Methodological Note', *Journal of Economic Inequality*, 2, pp. 3–10.

Polachek, S.W. (1981) 'Occupational Self-selection: A Human Capital Approach to Sex Differences in Occupational Structure', *Review of Economics and Statistics*, 63, pp. 60–9.

Puhani, P.A. (2000) 'The Heckman Correction for sample Selection and its Critique', *Journal of Economic Surveys*, 14(1), pp. 53–67.

Sinclair, K. (2000) *A History of New Zealand*. Auckland: Penguin Books.

State Services Commission (2003), *govt.nz*, accessed on 27 January 2004 at http://www.govt.nz/en/aboutnz/?id = 77737fd3275e394a8ed9d416a72591d0
Statistics New Zealand (2003a), 2001 *Census: Ethnic groups*, http://www.stats.govt.nz/domino/external/pasfull/pasfull.nsf/7cf46ae26dcb6800cc256a62000a2248/4c2567ef00247c6acc256bf9000ef7ff?OpenDocument, accessed on 4 September 2003.
Te Puni Kokiri (2004a) http://www.tpk.govt.nz/about/role/default.asp, accessed on 27 January 2004.
Te Puni Kokiri (2004b) http://www.tpk.govt.nz/publications/factsheets/default.asp, accessed on 27 January 2004.
Vella, F. (1998) 'Estimating Models with Sample Selection Bias: A Survey,' *Journal of Human Resources*, 33, pp. 127–69.
Winkelmann, R. (1999) 'The economic progress of Maori men 1986–1996', paper presented at the tenth Labour, Employment and Work conference, Victoria University of Wellington.
Winkelmann, R. and Winkelmann, L. (1997) 'Determining the Relative Labour Force Status of Maori and non-Maori using a Multinomial Logit Model', *Labour Market Bulletin*, 1, pp. 24–62.

# Index

*Notes*: b = box; f = figure; n = note; t = table; **bold** = extended discussion or heading emphasized in main text